COOPERATION: AN AMERICAN WAY

Also by John Daniels

IN FREEDOM'S BIRTHPLACE

AMERICA VIA THE NEIGHBORHOOD

COOPERATION:

AN AMERICAN WAY

by John Daniels

NEW YORK · COVICI · FRIEDE · PUBLISHERS

DESIGNED BY ROBERT JOSEPHY
PRINTED IN THE UNITED STATES OF AMERICA
BY J. J. LITTLE AND IVES COMPANY, NEW YORK

To Carol

Whitman, Lincoln and Jack

this book is lovingly dedicated

IN APPRECIATION

I am heartily grateful to David Lloyd for friendly help and counsel; to R. H. Elsworth for generous aid in arranging contacts at the nation's Capital and providing invaluable information and statistics; to Victor N. Valgren for highly illuminating facts and figures regarding the farmers' cooperative fire insurance groups which have achieved more than a century's success; to Joseph G. Knapp for broad-visioned interpretation of farmers' cooperative purchasing in relation to the American cooperative movement as a whole; and to Florence E. Parker for important data and assistance with respect to urban cooperation especially.

So numerous are the cooperators who have given liberally of their time, thought and experience, in conversations and correspondence, that their names would make a long array. Many citations appear in the text. In general token I wish to express to the President of the Cooperative League of the U. S. A., James Peter Warbasse, my warm appreciation of this collective help, and of his own personal interest and encouragement.

More detailed acknowledgments and references will be found on page 391.

CONTENTS

ix

COOPERATION: AN AMERICAN WAY

1 . EVOLUTION IN PROCESS

WHEN a man writes a book he owes it to possible readers, I think, to tell them something about his approach to the subject and the point of view from which he intends to present it.

My acquaintance with cooperatives began in 1919, when I was making a survey for the Carnegie Corporation of New York which had to do with social and economic conditions affecting neighborhood life. I found that in our present-day hurly-burly and hurry-scurry the neighborhood was a lost unit, at any rate in the cities. Tenancy and transiency made for detachment. People living next door to each other or in the same apartment house did not know or care to know one another. They were absorbed in the problem of making a living. Their occupational interests differed and took them thither and yon. Their recreation of sorts was taken catch-as-catch-can wherever they happened to find it. There was no local body politic that lived and breathed. Few indeed were the citizens who had any clear idea about the candidates or office-holders of their own home districts, and local posts went by default to petty politicians who knew what they wanted. Neighborhood disintegration left a void in people's lives. The warm feeling of belonging somewhere in close relation with one's fellows gave way to a lonely sense of wandering in the wilderness.

So I began to look for something which was capable of replacing the unit that was lost. Propinquity in itself was no longer sufficient to the need. Many philanthropic and civic agencies were doing what they could. But things which are done *for* people by outsiders are not equivalent to things done *by* the people themselves. Labor unions were vital but followed craft lines not identified with the neighborhood. Local political clubs were sometimes stimulating but always partisan. The old-fashioned town-meeting still maintained its vigor in New England villages but was not adaptable to the complexities of city conditions and municipal government. What then was available as a means of restoring to people the local participation and sense of responsibility which in simpler days they got from neighborhood activities?

With that question in mind I came upon consumers' cooperative units. They were practical in their objects, local in membership and control, and virtually neighborhoods in themselves. A cooperative grocery store, for example, always represented and served a group of people who lived in the area immediately surrounding it. It was established by those people on their own motion after they had first come together and formed a cooperative association. The opening of the store was preceded by a period of preparation, during which the members held a series of meetings to study cooperative principles and consider practical details.

These meetings unified the group before it undertook the concrete project. After the store was opened, the members were identified with it in a double way: first as shareholders and part-owners, with equal voting power in controlling the enterprise; and also as patrons who bought their groceries at this store and periodically got back savings-returns in proportion to their patronage. Besides electing a board of directors, which made provision for competent day-to-day management, the members served on auxiliary committees and held general meetings to hear and discuss reports, determine major policies and thrash out problems. All this served to weave a fabric of mutuality. As membership grew, the real cooperative neighborhood thus created gradually expanded over the local area, and brought unity and constructive purpose to what had previously been an inert aggregation of people.

That was what first impressed me with regard to the cooperative unit. It looked like a rebirth of the old township and town-meeting in a new form to meet new conditions. Although the cooperative association had no political character and no direct function in local government, its responsible activity centering about a store, an apartment house, a health clinic, or including all these things and others in an integrated whole, with the accompaniment of constant education could hardly fail to make more intelligent and active citizens and voters of its members. For them, and especially for their sons and daughters who were enlisted in youth groups, cooperation was a first-rate training school in the principles and practice of American democracy.

As I continued my exploration of this field and saw how the local units were linked together in regional federations and a national league, and what a wide variety and growing volume of cooperative activity was going forward in America, I became more and more interested in the economic and social potentialities of the movement. So I have kept in close touch with its progress ever since my first contact with it nineteen years ago. During this period the American movement has had its greatest growth, and has now reached proportions far beyond any notion of its stature which has thus far found lodgment in the public mind, notwithstanding the fact that magazines and newspapers have recently printed a good deal about it. Cooperation's upward surge in the last five years, during the very time that capitalistic business has been wallowing in the mire of depression, has been so striking, indeed amazing, that I was impelled to make a current survey in the field.

Early last year I started to work my way through a lot of piecemeal material about cooperative activities in many sections of the country, with a view to selecting what was most distinctive and mapping out my route accordingly. During the summer I traveled some five thousand miles in the East, the Upper South, and the Middle West as far as Minnesota, Iowa and Kansas. My advance notes were the skeletons, which I did not lock in the closet but took along with me. As I visited each cooperative enterprise, talked with its officers and members, sensed its tone and color, the dry bones were vivified with flesh and blood and cooperative individualities stood forth. Back of those composite individualities were the human beings, the men, women and rising generation of boys and girls, who in legions of hundreds of thousands are blazing cooperative trails throughout the country. As I saw them pressing forward with their Co-op banners flying, I was reminded of these lines from a stirring poem by America's prophetic bard, Walt Whitman:

We to-day's procession heading, we the route for travel clearing,
> *Pioneers! O Pioneers!*

My purpose was not to cover everything nor to make a catalog, but rather to observe the principal types of consumers' cooperative activity and see the most distinctive enterprises of each type in operation. So I tried to utilize my time to the best advantage in that regard, and availed myself of the advice of well-informed people as I went along. To have visited all the important cooperative organizations in every part of the country would have been interesting but duplicative. If my main object had been to study cooperative marketing I would certainly have included California and the Lower South, where some of the largest and most successful marketing associations have their seats. But cooperative marketing is another story, as I shall presently point out, and is essentially different in character from cooperative purchasing or *consumers'* cooperation broadly defined, with which I was chiefly concerned.

My journey took me to the headquarters of most of the leading purchasing associations and to a representative assortment of their local units. I saw the coordinated sequence of cooperative retailing, wholesaling and production, went through the principal productive plants, and came into contact with cooperative undertakings of many kinds, sizes and stages of development. All along the way I talked with rank and file members and outstanding leaders, with impartial observers on the side lines, and with outspoken opponents in the field of profit-business. At the beginning and end of my trip I conferred with federal officials at Washington who are charged with collecting statistics and other information about cooperatives or with administering laws and regulations which affect them. And of course I have supplemented my own first-hand observations by reading all the reports and other printed matter I could gather up.

Here in the large are my net impressions, which have shaped the contents, order and emphasis of my account of the consumers' cooperative movement in the United States:

The distinctively American character of this movement in its origin and beginnings, its growth, and its present form and spirit. It has grown from native American roots—in fact from the grass roots. American farmers have been its chief creators. But what they have created does not pertain to them alone. They have builded even better than they knew, not for the country's farms and rural districts only but also for its towns and cities. Their gift is to the nation as a whole;

The present total size, resources and energy of the American movement, which prefigure for it a momentous future;

The inherent soundness of consumers' cooperation as a system of social economy which aims to eliminate the waste of competition for profit and serve the greatest good of the greatest number;

The cooperative vision of building on an economic base "more stately mansions" where the mind and heart and spirit of man will find high satisfactions—satisfactions not for the privileged few only or for others as recipients of largesse, but for everyone in his own right because "a man's a man for a' that."

The conviction, which has grown in my mind from year to year and been confirmed and strengthened by my recent journey, is that in the growth of the cooperative movement in America we are witnessing a process of social-economic evolution. Consumers' cooperation has sometimes been called a mutation of capitalism. That strikes me as just the right term to convey its present significance.

In the sphere of biological evolution a *mutation*—to my layman's comprehension and begging kindly indulgence of the savants—is a pronounced variation which appears within some plant or animal species.

Whether it comes in response to some outer demand of the environment or as an expression of some inner creative urge is a question about which biologists and philosophers could argue interminably, for the reason that thus far no one knows. The mutation may apply only to a slight segment of the species—even a few individuals—but is transmissible through heredity. Sometimes nothing comes of it; the mutated individuals die off and the species continues as before. But at other times the mutation proves to be so useful in overcoming environmental problems that the mutated individuals get on better than their fellows and transmit this mutation to their descendants—with the eventual result that a new species is evolved. The species from which the mutation sprang may either survive as a less efficient biological form, or disappear.

Some exponents of evolution say there is good reason to believe that away back in the age of reptiles when giant dinosaurs were overrunning the earth, there was an inconspicuous little animal in the offing which was so hard put to save itself from being crushed underfoot or eaten at a gulp, that it developed more agility and wit than the dinosaurs with their ponderous bodies and inadequate brains. This little animal may have come into being as a mutation of some lesser breed of dinosaurs. Another advantage which it had besides intelligence or what you will, was warm-bloodedness. That fitted it better than the cold-blooded reptiles to combat the chill which came over the earth in the ice age. Well, that little animal turned out to be the progenitor of the mammals, up to *Homo sapiens* himself. And the dinosaurs completely disappeared, leaving behind them only a few huge footprints and fossils.

Consumers' cooperation is now I believe evolving in the United States as a mutation of capitalism and a new species of social-economic organization. This is the viewpoint from which the American cooperative movement may be viewed most clearly and adequately, and from which I have accordingly written my account. The chapter on American democracy suggests the spiritual soil from which this movement has sprung, and the next one deals with the problem of social economy to which it is directed. The working plan and principles of consumers' cooperation are then outlined. Subsequent chapters tell the story of this evolution which is still unfolding before our eyes, and describe the cooperative activities which are now going forward in America. Those chapters which portray what American farmers have achieved bear no less importantly on urban than on rural cooperation. Only by noting the direction in which the farmers' organizations are moving and the ways in which they are beginning to take urban cooperatives into partnership, can the observer survey the scene aright.

The picture which I shall try to project will not be replete with detail. Much is omitted. But I hope that it will show the American cooperative movement in its nativeness and wholeness.

2 . AMERICA FOUNDED
ON COOPERATION

CONSUMERS' cooperation, with which this book will deal, is a specific application of the principle of all cooperation. So the simplest and most natural way to approach and understand consumers' cooperation is to give some consideration first to the underlying meaning of the word "cooperation."

Cooperation in the broad and general sense is any human activity in which a group of two or more individuals voluntarily take part to attain a common object, for the benefit or satisfaction not only of one or some but of *all* the members of the group.

An individual completely isolated could not possibly cooperate, because cooperation implies common action. Any individual who is in contact with others (unless he subjugates them or is subjugated by them) cooperates with them somewhat, if only from motives of self-preservation. Manifestly, cooperation is as old as human society, and has been a leading factor in the slow evolution of society from families to clans, from clans to tribes, and from tribes to peoples and nations.

A nation's life and activities, though forming an organic whole, may be viewed in three main aspects; political, economic and cultural.

The American nation, as a political entity, is founded

on cooperation, and takes its democratic being and character from the principle and practice of cooperation. Our forefathers laid the spiritual foundation for cooperation in America in the Declaration of Independence, when they proclaimed that "all men are created equal" and are "endowed by their Creator with certain unalienable rights."

When the nation had successfully asserted these rights and won its liberty, however, it did not (as we have now almost forgotten) become forthwith a Union in which cooperation had free scope. For seven perilous years it was a loose Confederation with an almost impotent Congress as its only central body. The individual States were jealous and distrustful of one another; they raised barriers which impeded trade and intercourse, and for the most part went their separate ways and failed dismally to pull together. Men of discernment saw that the absence of vitally necessary cooperation between the States threatened to subvert the nation at the outset. George Washington wrote: "Something must be done or the fabric will fall, for it certainly is tottering."

Then, in response to a need so clear and crucial that it could not be denied, the Congress, with George Washington's support, issued a call for a constitutional convention, to amend the Articles of Confederation in ways "adequate to the exigencies of the Union." That convention brought together forty-five delegates from the thirteen States. It did not take them long to decide that the Articles of Confederation were so hopelessly inadequate that they should be completely replaced by a new Constitution.

What followed was one of the greatest and most fruitful examples of cooperation that the world has ever known; the interests to be reconciled and problems to be overcome appeared at times insuperable. Yet for four months the delegates worked together incessantly, in cooperative deliberation and construction, until at length they succeeded in creating the present Constitution of the United States. "The most wonderful work ever struck off at a given time by the brain and purpose of man," was the English statesman Gladstone's superlative tribute in later years to this achievement. Nor did cooperation enter only into the achievement of that extraordinary result. It entered also into the Constitution itself, which embodied the principle of cooperation in the plan which it provided of three co-equal governmental branches—executive, legislative and judicial—which were to work in balanced unison for the welfare of the nation.

After ratification by the States, this Constitution became effective with a Preamble which set forth that "We, the People of the United States, in order to form a more perfect union . . . do ordain and establish this constitution for the United States of America."

Washington, throughout his two terms of office as the nation's first President, personified the spirit of cooperation. In his Farewell Address to the American People, issued near the end of his second term, he offered for the people's "solemn contemplation" and "frequent review" certain admonitions which he said appeared to him all-important to the permanence of their felicity. The core of his message was contained in these words: "It is of infinite moment that you should properly estimate the immense value of your national union to your collective and individual happiness." Those were words of wisdom from the summit—from the Father of his Country to its people.

But what of the people themselves in the nation's early years? How did democracy and cooperation fare among the rank and file?

To answer this query there is available certain testimony which is all the more impressive because it came from a detached observer, a Frenchman of rare powers of analysis and description. This witness was Alexis de Tocqueville, who visited the United States in the 1830's to study its institutions. De Tocqueville wrote a book called *Democracy in America,* which went through a dozen editions and was translated into all the leading European languages. In that comprehensive work he carried his scrutiny of American democracy to its very nucleus, the township. And here is what he saw and reported:

"Many important observations suggest themselves . . . but there is one which takes precedence of all the rest. The social condition of the Americans is eminently democratic; this was its character at the foundation of the colonies, and is still more strongly marked at the present day. . . . Great equality ex-

isted among the emigrants who settled on the shores
of New England. . . . The native of New England
is attached to his township because it is independent
and free: his co-operation in its affairs ensures his
attachment to its interest; the well-being it affords
him secures his affection; and its welfare is the aim
of his ambition and of his future exertions; he takes
a part in every occurrence in the place; he practices
the art of government in the small sphere within his
reach; he accustoms himself to those forms which can
alone ensure the steady progress of liberty; he im-
bibes their spirit; he acquires a taste for order, com-
prehends the union or the balance of powers, and
collects clear practical notions of the nature of his
duties and the extent of his rights."

It would be difficult to delineate a more concrete,
specific, human and convincing likeness of cooperation
in practice than that which is presented in this account
by de Tocqueville of the way in which democracy func-
tioned—and still functions—in the township, with its
natural community of interest and its mutually helpful
interaction between the individual and the local group.

And now back to the nation and its government as
a whole. The next great test of the principle of cooperation came when the Southern States seceded from the
Union. Secession was the reverse, the negative, of cooperation. The nation was engulfed in civil war to
restore the Union, and the Union was restored.

Abraham Lincoln, in his Gettysburg Address, gave

the American people another testament of unity, democracy and cooperation: "Four score and seven years ago our fathers brought forth upon this continent a new nation, conceived in liberty, and dedicated to the proposition that all men are created equal. . . . We here highly resolve that this nation, under God, shall have a new birth of freedom, and that government of the people, by the people, and for the people, shall not perish from the earth."

Today the American nation still holds true, in its political life, to its tradition of democracy. This broad statement is subject to many qualifications, because American democracy is by no means perfect. There is much self-seeking domination on the one hand, much supine servility on the other; much ignorance, inertia, inefficiency and muddle-headedness. But although these obvious imperfections obscure, confuse and obstruct democracy's outworkings, the fact remains when all is said that still democracy prevails. Throughout this whole land of forty-eight States, across whose borders trade and friendly intercourse flow freely, every adult citizen is the equal of every other in the right to vote and in the individual power of his ballot. Electoral campaigns are often vehement, decisions sometimes close and sometimes overwhelming. But whatever the result, it is democratically accepted.

In last analysis the individual citizens through direct and indirect taxation defray the cost of government. And in last analysis the individual citizens with their co-equal votes collectively control the government. We still have "government of the people, by the people, and for the people." Our political life still upholds the principle of cooperation on which the American nation is founded.

3. THE CONSUMER'S PLIGHT

BUT when we turn to the economic side of American life, we see a very different picture.

In the economic field the person who corresponds to the citizen is the ultimate consumer. He is the ultimate consumer or user of goods, as the citizen is the ultimate consumer or user of government.

As the function of government in a democracy is to serve and not to exploit the citizens, so correspondingly the function of industry in a democracy should be to serve and not to exploit the consumers.

That indeed is the only warrant for the whole laborious process of production and distribution, which is justified not for its own sake as an end in itself, but as a means to the end of satisfying the wants of consumers.

Everybody without exception is a consumer of food, clothing, shelter and other material things, and of intangible things which pertain to the heart, the mind and the spirit. Consumers are therefore all-embracing and potentially all-powerful. Either passively or actively they sanction the functions of production and distribution. Most consumers are engaged in production and distribution—sometimes so intently that they forget themselves and their fellows as consumers. But however important their work may be to their own livelihood and the general well-being, it is still essentially a means to an end and subordinate to the end itself, consumption—which in simplest terms means *living*. Production and distribution are mediate, but consumption and consumers are ultimate.

The consumers are industry's final support. As the citizens collectively defray the cost of government, through direct and indirect taxation, so likewise, as will presently appear, the consumers pay all the costs of production and distribution, through their purchase and consumption of commodities.

But there the resemblance between citizen and consumer—under present economic conditions—comes to an end. For the consumer pays not only all the costs of production and distribution, but also the profits of all the producers and distributors. And furthermore, notwithstanding the fact that he pays all the costs and the profits, the consumer receives no part of the net earnings of production and distribution and does not control or measurably share in controlling the price, kind, quantity or quality of the products for which he pays.

In an earlier day this was not true. The relations which then prevailed between consumers and producers were simple and direct. A man who wanted a pair of shoes, for instance, went to the nearby shoemaker and struck a mutually agreeable bargain with him regarding the kind, quality and price of the shoes desired.

Such a face-to-face relationship between consumers and producers continued to prevail very largely until the advent of the sweeping economic change which has gone down in history as the Industrial Revolution.

Increasingly and predominantly, since the rise of the new industrial order in England in the eighteenth century with the invention and introduction of modern machinery, goods have been made not by independent handicraftsmen of many trades, conveniently located among the consumers whom they served, but by dependent wage-workers congregated in capitalistically controlled factories in congested industrial centers.

These drastically altered conditions were well advanced in England by 1800, spread thence to the continent of Europe, and then across the ocean to America. But in this still little developed country the new order did not become fully established until after the Civil War, when the building of our great railway lines made feasible the speedy transportation of raw materials from distant sources of supply to the manufacturing plants, and of finished products from the plants to outlying regional markets. Since that time the American capitalistic system of production and distribution has expanded enormously; and in recent years—until it was struck by the crash of 1929 and the subsequent depression—it has carried mass production to the nth degree.

Of course these radical changes in the industrial system involved a radically changed relationship between consumer and producer. The old direct relationship has for the most part disappeared. Today the consumer, instead of being able to see and consult with the producer as his forefathers could, would have to use a super-telescope to espy the producer afar off beyond a line of middlemen, and would be compelled to stand the expense of a long-distance telephone call for the possible but highly improbable privilege of even a minute's conversation with him. As for watching an article being made, as his forbears could do, if they so wished, in the artisan's shop—that is out of the question unless he is prepared to visit a number of plants in various places in order to follow the process from beginning to end and eventually see emerge from a machine something which he can recognize as the article desired. No, it is all so complex that he throws up his hands. But there is one thing he can do; he can go to the store and buy almost anything for which he is able to pay.

That is what he does. He buys and *pays*. It is doubtful whether he understands very well what he is really paying for, but a concrete illustration will serve to make that clear.

HOW COSTS ACCUMULATE

For this illustration, which follows the sequence of cotton from the plant to the garment, the author is indebted to a well known man, now the head of a large agricultural organization, who has been in the cotton industry himself and knows it from the inside. Here is his outline. First, the cotton-planter picks the cotton from the vine and sells it to the operator of a cotton-gin. Second, the gin-operator separates the lint from the seed (which goes a different route) and sells the lint to a local buyer. Third, the local buyer sells it to a big regional buyer. Fourth, the big buyer sells it to material mills. Fifth, these mills process it into many varieties and qualities of what may be called intermediate material. Sixth, the mills sell the material to manufacturers who dye it and make it up into rolls of cloth. (Sometimes the dyeing is done in separate specialized plants, making an additional stage in the sequence.) Seventh, these manfacturers sell the cloth to jobbers. Eighth, the jobbers sell it to the wholesalers. Ninth, the wholesalers sell the cloth to manufacturers of garments. Tenth, the garment-manufacturers sell the unfinished garments to garment-processers, who take care of necessary hand sewing, buttonhole stitching and other finishing touches. Eleventh, these garment-processors sell the garments to a store. And twelfth, the store sells them to the ultimate consumers.

Be it said that the foregoing cotton sequence of a dozen stages is, if anything, abridged, as there are sometimes other points besides those mentioned where jobbers or wholesalers intervene. It is also a comparatively simple illustration of present-day production and distribution. If the example cited were, let us say, an automobile, it would be necessary to trace separate routes, each one corresponding to the cotton sequence, for most of the numerous parts, even down to nuts and screws, which are manufactured separately in many specialized plants and are brought together only in the final assembling.

At nearly every stage of the sequence, moreover, there is use of banking, credit and insurance, and at some stages there is very conspicuous and aggressive use of advertising and high-pressure salesmanship. And now to consider the matter of costs and profits.

Of course, actual outlay and cost are involved in each stage of production and distribution and in each use of banking, credit, insurance, advertising and salesmanship. At each stage of the sequence the cumulative cost up to that point is passed on to the next stage, and eventually to the consumer-purchaser who thus pays the total cost. Under modern complex conditions there can be no question that many, perhaps most, of these stages and costs are necessary. If all the stages are indispensable and all the costs are kept as low as possible, then the consumer has no reasonable ground of complaint—so far as costs in themselves are concerned. But two questions can and should be raised: are costs kept as low as possible and are all the stages quite essential?

It is true that within each stage of the sequence the producers or distributors who control that stage are spurred to reduce costs by the motive of profit. By reducing costs and selling at the same or slightly lower prices, they have a larger margin of profit per article; or, by reducing costs sufficiently to sell at substantially lower prices, they may increase their volume of sales sufficiently to make a larger total profit. Competition between producers or distributors of the same sort is a further spur toward reduction of costs and prices, though this is sometimes wholly offset by trade agreements. Another tendency which runs counter to cost and price reduction is that which is not uncommon in closely managed corporations, of paying exorbitant salaries to the executives, supplementing their regular salaries by large bonuses, creating a number of semi-sinecure positions for favored persons, and permitting extremely liberal expense accounts. All such things increase the overhead expense, so that even if costs at other points are reduced the increased overhead may counterbalance those reductions. Furthermore, such devices as these are sometimes employed as ways of diverting a large share of the profits of an enterprise from the stockholders to a few insiders in the management, or of disguising or concealing profits for various reasons, including tax evasion. After such diversions of funds have been made it is possible for the management to say with literal truth that the corporation's "profits" were only so-and-so-much, whereas, if those diversions had not been made, the profits—for all except the insiders—would have been considerably larger.

Those are the factors which affect costs in any given stage of the sequence which, as noted, is controlled by the producers or distributors who handle that stage. As regards the whole sequence, which in the case of cotton runs to at least a dozen stages, the situation is different. In the instance of comparatively few commodities is the whole sequence from beginning to end controlled by one management. As a rule, each stage is managed more or less independently of the others. So even though costs and prices might be reduced within each stage, it is still possible to add additional stages or functions and thereby to increase the total cost which the consumer must pay at the end of the line. In fact the profit motive tends to bring that very thing about. People who are looking around for new profit opportunities are sometimes able to create such opportunities by muscling in on the production and distribution sequence of various commodities. They may, of course, render a new service which is really valuable. Or they may render very slight service and simply add to the length and the cost of the sequence. This is apparently the case with some of the numerous jobbers or sub-wholesalers, and with some of the still more numerous advertising agents, solicitors and salesmen. And the consumer pays the total bill.

PROFIT PROBLEMS

What has been said about costs applies by implication to profits. When a consumer buys a cotton garment at the store, he of course knows that the price he pays for it includes a profit for the storekeeper, which is sometimes reasonable and sometimes unreasonable. But he may not realize, at least, not very fully, that the price he pays also includes, besides the cost and the storekeeper's profit, a long chain of profits for all the producers, processors, distributors, bankers, credit men, insurance companies, advertising men and salesmen who have had anything to do with the material in that garment in its tortuous course from the cotton-planter to himself. But this is undeniably the fact; and there is no way, other than amending our present system of production and distribution, that the consumer can escape paying all the profits.

Each middleman, in selling the product at his stage to the next middleman, must cover in the price he gets not only what he paid for the product plus the actual cost of whatever he does to it, but also a profit for himself. Unless he adds such a profit he would be in the position of doing his part for nothing, which is hardly customary or feasible. In short, as the saying goes, he is not in business for his health. So he adds a profit for himself, which is included in the price that the next man pays him. Then the next man, in turn, adds to that price and to his own current costs another profit for himself, which is likewise passed on. And so it goes to the end of the line when the consumer comes along and pays a price which includes all these cumulative profits from start to finish.

Reflection on this fact quite naturally raises two questions in the consumer's mind. The first one is the same as that which was raised before regarding costs, namely, are all these stages, all these incidental services and all these middlemen, involving profits for someone at every point, really necessary? If not, then the consumer is paying unnecessary profits as well as costs.

The second question strikes deeper. Granted that a certain number of stages and auxiliary services are necessary in the complex modern process of production and distribution, is there some practicable way in which consumers (who pay all the bills and are themselves the reason behind all production and distribution) can by controlling production and distribution transform what are now profits for a few people into savings for all the people, by turning back to the consumers whatever remains at the end of the sequence, over and above actual costs involved in the process?

To the extent that this could be effected, the middlemen would, of course, lose their profits. But anent that bare statement several things may be said. The great majority of consumers, although engaged in production and distribution, are not so engaged on a basis of profits. They are workers who receive wages, salaries, or professional fees; and farmers who have a roof over their heads, earth from which they can extract a living, and sometimes with good luck something more. As compared with this great majority of basic producers, the profit-basis manufacturers and middlemen, though numerous, conspicuous and influential, are a small fraction of the whole. They too are consumers, but consciously or unconsciously they believe they can get more for themselves by means of their profits, which consumers collectively defray. It comes, then, to a question of what serves the greater good of the greater number.

By the same token there is also a question as to whether the present profit-system serves the best interests even of those who are directly dependent upon it. Competition for profit, whatever may be its merits in promoting efficiency, reducing costs, spurring invention and generally contributing to what is commonly called progress, is responsible for constant and frightful wreckage in the form of business failures, bankruptcies, suicides, unemployment, poverty and misery. It is also true that while some men reap large profits, many more make barely enough to keep going, and some get nothing but losses.

This being true, it is altogether reasonable to believe that if by amending the present system of production and distribution a way can be found of putting on a basis of assured salary or fee payments producers and middlemen who render some essential service, this would work out advantageously for the majority of those who are now dependent on precarious and often non-existent profits. It would probably be welcomed in due course by all except the few, comparatively, who are reaping the big profits under present conditions. And if thereby the business and industrial wreckage which now results from acute—not to say cut-throat—competition for profit could be eliminated or largely reduced, the community and the nation would be that much better off. Under modern industrial conditions the sequence of production and distribution necessarily involves a number of stages and services, which means that a series of producers, processors and middlemen would still be required under the amended system. It would not be a matter, therefore, of removing the means of livelihood of such intermediaries, but simply of amending the basis of their compensation for services rendered, with a view, as has been said, to the greater good of the greater number.

PRODUCTION UNCONTROLLED

So much for the consumer's interest in transforming profits for a few into savings for all. But there are other equally or more important ways in which under present conditions consumers suffer disadvantage. They have no definite control over the kind of things, the quantity of things, or the quality of things which are produced and for which they are expected to pay. It is true that they do have a great variety from which to choose and that if they cannot find what they want they can decline to purchase. Usually, by shopping around, they can get what they wish—but by no means always. Not infrequently one has the experience, after having become attached to a particular article or kind of goods, of being told it is no longer available but "here is something just as good." For this particular purchaser it may not be just as good, for values are psychological and flow partly from habit and sentiment.

Besides not always being able to find what they want, consumers are confronted by a vast and varied array of things that they have certainly never thought they wanted. These things are of two classes. One class consists of goods which serve some useful purpose, filling some need not fully realized before, or meeting some need more satisfactorily than it was met before. Such things, in connection with which science, research and invention play so large a part, are of course a boon. The other class, however, consists of things which can be described only as impositions which people would be better off without, such as cheap gew-gaws and the innumerable and widely advertised patent medicines and drugs. There is a constant tendency to put out such new and often worse-than-useless things in order to create new opportunities for profit. And as against the consumer's latent right of refusal to buy, the profit-seekers utilize alluring and expensive advertising and high-pressure salesmanship—for which the consumer pays—to batter down "sales resistance." If the consumers themselves, who are interested not in profits but in savings, had some effective control over the kinds of things produced, it is safe to say that the output of trash would be at least appreciably reduced.

As regards the quantity or volume of production, one is told that the law of supply and demand takes care of that problem. It does to some extent, but only in a nebulous, negative, dilatory and wasteful way. For the only way in which production and distribution as now carried on can attempt to gauge the consumers' demands and adjust the supply to them is by more or less intelligent guessing. Under our present system there is no organized way in which the consumers themselves can definitely register their wants and obtain a commensurate supply to meet them. As a result of the highly competitive conditions which prevail, much of the supply of goods is based not even on guessing the demand, but is put out simply to be sold. And then the salesmen are told to go out and sell it before competing firms get ahead of them. When prospects of sales look good to the producers and distributors, there is overproduction and waste; then, in the consequent reaction and depression, when prospects look poor, there is underproduction and want. Under present conditions, in short, the quantity of things produced is outside of the consumers' control.

And what may be said regarding the quality of goods produced? If all the advertisements which crowd the newspapers and almost fill the magazines, which clutter the city streets and the countryside, which are blazoned forth at night in brilliant lights, written by airplanes in the sky and borne everywhere by radio through the air—if all of this advertising for which the consumer duly pays were to be taken at its word, then it would indeed be foolish to raise any doubt or question about quality. For the ads carry assurance that everything is superfine. No matter how credulous a person may be, he can hardly help recognizing that if all the superlative statements of one such advertisement were true, then obviously the equally superlative and almost identical things which competing advertisements say about the products cannot be true. If all the ads for competing brands of a given commodity were ranged alongside in parallel columns, where the consumer could survey and compare them all at once, they would come pretty near to canceling each other out, and the consumer would have left for his guidance only a great big question mark.

Of course, there are many products which are excellent in quality and all that they are represented to be, and many firms which take pride in maintaining high standards. But that there are also many products which are inferior in quality and far from what they are represented to be is a by-word. Many other products are good for a time, while the business is being built up and getting a well-merited reputation, but begin to deteriorate when the responsible head of that firm passes on and is replaced by others who lack his standards and are out for profits first and last. All in all, goods of poor and fictitious quality are so common that the most pertinent observations regarding them are, "Things are not what they seem," and, "Let the buyer beware."

HELP ALONG THE WAY

To an increasing extent, government departments, commissions and investigations, federal, state and municipal, and some non-governmental organizations, are aiding the consumer directly or indirectly. Of the federal agencies which are rendering such assistance, the one which ranks first in stature and scope is the Department of Agriculture. This includes many divisions and bureaus charged with research, experimentation, laboratory tests, inspection, regulation and publication. Though, of course, its activities apply immediately to farms and farm products, they greatly benefit consumers by maintaining and improving the quality of the main food supply of consumers throughout the country. More will be said about some of these activities at a later point. Here it is fitting to mention especially the Food and Drug Administration, also connected with the Department of Agriculture, which affects consumers more directly through its enforcement of laws and regulations applying to the quality of basic foods, and the ingredients and labeling of processed and packaged foods and patent medicines and drugs. The most direct and extensive contact with individual consumers is made by the Consumers' Counsel of the Agricultural Adjustment Administration, through its bi-weekly magazine the *Consumers' Guide,* which anyone may receive free, simply by making the request and supplying name and address. This is a substantial, practical and interesting publication, the character of which may be indicated by citing the following articles which appeared in a recent issue: "Your Money's Worth in Shoes"; "Know Your Fabric"; "Cold Storage Locker Plants"; "Your Food Supplies"; "Consumers' Bookshelf"; and "Consumers' Queries and Comments." Individual consumers may also make inquiry and obtain specific information from Consumers' Counsel, and are doing so in large and growing numbers.

The Federal Trade Commission is doing vigorous and effective work in combating dishonest or unlawful advertising of products and monopolistic or price-manipulating trade practices. Other federal agencies which serve consumers' interests, though mostly in indirect or less immediate ways, include the National Bureau of Standards, which functions for government-buying primarily and is otherwise available to conduct tests of products on a fee basis, but whose findings are not issued to the public; also the Bureau of Labor Statistics and the Consumers' Project of the Department of Labor, which carry on general and special studies and publish reports of great value, having to do with standards of living and consumers' activities of the kind which will be discussed in the present volume.

Among state agencies, the state agricultural colleges and experiment stations are doing invaluable work, along lines similar to and closely related with those of the federal Department of Agriculture and of course touching more closely the farmers and, mediately, the consumers of their respective States. Working quietly, modestly and without fanfare, but incessantly and efficiently, these agricultural colleges are a great constructive force in bettering the chief supply of grains, vegetables, fruits, milk, eggs, butter and meat available for consumers. The state departments of agriculture and markets are law-enforcing and regulating agencies, which usually include milk control divisions that are charged with watching over conditions of milk production at the source, on farms and in dairies, and with inspecting and safeguarding the purity of milk retailed to consumers. The state departments of health have like supervision over sanitary conditions affecting milk and other foods. At still closer range, the municipal departments of health and of markets conduct supplementary local regulation and inspection.

Some of the ingenious cheating devices with which these agencies have to cope may be illustrated by reference to a recent review in the *New York Herald Tribune* of the activities of the Department of Public Markets, Weights and Measures of New York City. A butcher, for example, had the habit of inserting in each chicken, before weighing, a strip of salt pork containing a pound and a quarter of lead shot. Another trick was that of using a 20-pound scale with a 25-pound face, which robbed the customer of more than a pound out of each five. Last year 7,703 violations of various kinds were reported and penalized. This department maintains a Division of Consumers' Service. "The average housewife," says the review, "is seldom aware of the many factors which determine the price she must pay for food —the daily fluctuations of supply, the little profits all along the line from producer to consumer. Behind that screen of ignorance springs up a long chain of abuses ranging from downright criminal racketeering to legitimate but irrational practices that have nothing but custom to recommend them." Through the press and the radio the Division of Consumers' Service disseminates much useful information and gives daily and weekly market reports, telling what varieties of food are most seasonable and abundant in the city and therefore the best bargains. The success of this Division has been such that the Department of Agriculture has recommended that similar bureaus be set up in every large city.

Of the principal non-governmental agencies which work to assist consumers, the first in point of time is Consumers' Research, of Washington, New Jersey, which was organized in 1929. It conducts research and laboratory tests which include a wide range of products, and issues its findings in monthly, special and annual bulletins. Its "subscribers" (this being the term used rather than "members") are stated to number at present about 60,000. Its scope, as defined in its circulars, is that of a research and educational organization which "studies and reports on goods and services from the point of view of their selection, purchase and use by the ultimate consumer, and solely for the ultimate consumer's use and profit."

A new but rapidly growing organization is Consumers Union of United States, of New York City, which was formed in February, 1936, as the aftermath of difficulties and disagreements which developed between members of the working staff of Consumers' Research and the management. That controversy aroused considerable public interest at the time, and was taken up at a hearing before the National Labor Relations Board which, in January, 1936, issued an intermediate report adverse to the management and recommended that it reinstate the complaining staff members who went on strike. As the points at issue could not be adjusted with mutual satisfaction, however, a group of former employees of Consumers' Research and of people in sympathy with them proceeded to organize the Consumers Union on a membership basis. It began with 148 members, its circulars state, and now has more than 50,000. The membership fee includes subscription to its monthly reports and annual buying guide. These publications provide information and recommendations based on research and laboratory tests and cover a broad and expanding field. Besides dealing with quality and prices of foods, clothing and household supplies, it gives special attention to patent medicines from the viewpoint of safety and health and proposes to go into medical care, insurance, investments and the reliability of advertising. It also investigates and discloses labor conditions in the industrial plants where products originate. Its own advertising, it states, "is being refused by more and more publications now that CU's work is beginning to make itself felt. Commercial interests which dislike an open statement of the truth about products may be expected to bring their big guns into play in an effort to stop it. But the work that CU has undertaken is bound up with too many American people to be stopped."

Two other organizations which are still in the early formative stage are the Consumers' National Federation, which was formed in May, 1937, with headquarters in New York City, and the Consumers Foundation, which was announced tentatively about the same time but was not definitely organized till January, 1938. The former's executive is Miss Persia Campbell, economist and author of *American Agricultural Policy*. The organization has already shown vigor in getting consumers' groups together at meetings in New York to consider practical ways and means of combating high retail milk prices and gas and electric service rates. The Federation is composed mainly of societies and institutions in the New York district and other parts of the country which are interested in consumers' problems and activities from various angles, and it also includes individuals as associate members.

One of its major purposes is to "establish criteria by which bona-fide consumer organizations may be identified." That is by all means a timely and important object, inasmuch as a growing number of wholly commercial enterprises, recognizing the degree to which consumers are becoming aware of themselves, are beginning to call their businesses "consumers'" this-and-that, in order to create the impression that they somehow represent consumers and have their interests deeply at heart. In general, the Federation will conduct an information and education service on consumer problems and aim to become a clearing house to coordinate activities which are designed to protect the consumer.

As regards the Consumers Foundation, there was some intimation in the press last spring that it might undertake research in economic, legislative and tax questions affecting the consumer, for the purpose of enabling consumers and consumer organizations to "take a definite and vocal stand upon legislation, taxes and economic developments, particularly as they affect the field of distribution." If any such program is undertaken it will be vitally important, as the Federation has emphasized in the statement quoted above, to identify bona-fide consumer organizations and keep clear of interlopers with ulterior motives.

In cooperative circles there appears to be considerable question as to just what this Foundation's aims and character really are. A press release emanating from the Cooperative League of the U.S.A. and dated January 13th cited Dr. William Trufant Foster, the Foundation's president, as authority for stating that its initial grant of $25,000 came from the Institute of Distribution "which is supported by chain stores, variety stores and mail order houses," and that while individual consumers will be accepted as associate members at one dollar a year they will have "no voice in the control of the organization." This release further states that Mr. Donald E. Montgomery, Consumers' Counsel of the AAA, to whose excellent service I referred a little way back, withdrew from participation in organizing the Foundation because he doubted whether it would operate in the consumer's interest. *Business Week* of January 8th is quoted as follows: "Contributions will be accepted from individuals, foundations and other sources for research. . . . All of which sounds like an A-1 opportunity for business to win the consumer over onto its side."

In one press account it was said that the Foundation would begin by looking into the reasons for success or failure of the "Consumers' Councils" which were formed under the late NRA, sixteen out of a hundred and fifty of which are still functioning under "private auspices." Results of such inquiry "will point the way for similar consumer advisory groups which may be formed in various sections of the country."

Dr. Foster is also director of the Pollak Foundation for Economic Research, and jointly with Mr. Waddill Catchings is the author of a number of books on business, money, production and profits. It will be very interesting to see how the new Consumers' Foundation develops and what attitude it adopts toward the consumers' cooperative movement.

The foregoing agencies have been described at some length not only because of the work they are doing but also because of what they signify, what their general effect is, and what they cannot possibly accomplish for consumers but must necessarily leave to more direct and complete action by the organized consumers themselves. What they signify is that consumers are waking up. Their most important effect, transcending the detailed service they render, is that they are contributing very appreciably to the consumer's growing consciousness of his plight, his rights and his powers. But they necessarily stop at the point where they have supplied the consumer with a bewildering array of facts, figures, tests, recommendations and problems—things, moreover, that do not stay put, but change from day to day.

What can the individual consumer do? He may have some notion that he can surround and master all this material, make himself into an encyclopedia of commodities, ingredients, qualities, grades, prices, et cetera, and keep this self-encyclopedia calendared, classified, and in good working order from day to day. But unless he has the leisure and means to devote all his time to the task, he is likely before long either to throw up his hands in despair or to recognize the practical fact that what he must have is another kind of consumers' organization, in which he and his fellow-consumers will tackle this job together and see it through to the finish. They must provide themselves with such quarters, equipment, management and personnel as are essential to keep abreast of conditions and buy goods of assured quality at the best prices possible. And they must take such further measures as may be required to give consumers, who pay all the costs and the profits, some effective control over production and distribution and over the apportionment of proceeds.

THE UPSHOT OF IT ALL

The consumers' claim to their share in the proceeds rests, furthermore, upon their indispensable economic contribution, which is this: that by their purchasing and consumption they impart value to commodities. In other words, the consumers provide and constitute the market for commodities. Without a market commodities would have no value at all. This is shown from time to time when some of the more quickly perishable farm products, such as apples, melons and tomatoes, are brought forth by nature in such quantities that the available market cannot absorb the supply. Under these circumstances there is no market for the surplus, which is therefore valueless and is left to rot upon the ground. Or again, when there is overproduction of manufactured goods, especially those which are affected by changes in habits and styles. Or when the trouble is not primarily with overproduction but with insufficient buying power on the part of consumers. Overproduction or underconsumption is a question of terms and relativity, but in either case the result is reduction or cessation of commodity values.

But this vital contribution of consumers is unrecognized and unrewarded in our present scheme of industrial organization. The factors in production are commonly held to be capital, management and labor. As between capital and management on the one hand, and labor on the other, there is a good deal of conflict. Capital and management regard themselves as the chief contributors, who provide the funds, assume the risks and responsibilities, and should therefore come first in allocation of proceeds. Labor challenges this attitude, contends that its human contribution is more important than money, that it also takes risks and responsibilities when it casts its lot with any industrial enterprise, and that it should at least have a more fully recognized and organized part in the determination of wages. But neither capital, management nor labor shows much concern for what the consumers give or get. It therefore devolves upon the consumers themselves to assert their interests and their rights. They are compelled to conclude that in order to do so in an adequate way they must have recourse to consumers' cooperation.

As they survey the field of production and distribution, they see no end of cooperation of one kind or another among producers and distributors. They see local, state, national and even international Chambers of Commerce, innumerable Boards of Trade, Merchants Associations, Wholesalers and Retailers Associations, Banking, Credit and Insurance Associations, Railway and Shipping Associations, and Associations of Advertising men and Salesmen. They discover holding companies and superholding companies, interlocking directorates, trade pacts, pressure groups, gentlemen's agreements and plain unadorned understandings. In fact there appears to be so much cooperation of sorts among producers and distributors, and especially among big financial operators that the actual if not the nominal control of banking, credit, capital and industry is effectively diverted from the communities and districts where the profits are made, and concentrated in the hands of a comparatively small number of men in a few financial centers.

This situation has just been recognized in such a remarkably frank and wholesome way by an outstanding business man that I will quote him briefly. The man is Mr. W. Averill Harriman, chairman of the board of directors of the Union Pacific Railroad and head of the Business Advisory Council of the Department of Commerce. The statements which I quote are taken from a news report in the *New York Times* of January 28, 1938 of an address by Mr. Harriman the day before at a luncheon of the Bond Club of New York at the Bankers Club. A perfect setting.

"We have been hearing a lot recently about holding companies and about interlocking directorships and about the sixty families and about the concentration of control in the hands of a few people, the concentration of control in New York," said Mr. Harriman. "There isn't anything particularly new about this subject, because there are plenty of people who talked about it a generation ago, but it is in the political arena today. We resent the fact when people bring that to the attention of the public, and yet we don't hesitate to say it when we resent the concentration of control in Washington, when we think it goes beyond what is in the public interest and what is socially desirable. I think we should frankly analyze what this concentration of control in New York and the interlocking of directorships means. We ought to do one of two things—either justify it or else change it."

"We all know of cases of companies that came to New York with their headquarters because, for one reason or other, they thought they would get national prestige, or that they would be financed better if they had headquarters here, or maybe for the personal likes of the president or his family." Urging decentralization, Mr. Harriman continues—"If your business is moved back you will be getting in touch with the local people. Those local towns would have a stake in that industry. They would feel they had a greater stake than they have today. . . . I think New York would be better off with that decentralization of management. We wouldn't have the load to carry here of justification of why there should be so much of the business of the country centered here. . . . Your interlocking of directorships is distorted by those who want to throw darts at someone or another and you get around so that people say there are a few thousand people who control half the industry of the country."

So the producers, distributors and financiers can hardly object, with grace and consistency, if consumers after taking due account of all the facts and facing the whole situation, decide at last to cooperate among themselves. In undertaking such cooperation, however, consumers have interests and aims which far transcend their immediate material objects. True, they want first to transform profits for a few of the people into savings for all of the people. True, they want to reduce and if possible eliminate the constant waste and wreckage of our present industrial system. True, they are concerned with the price, kind, quantity and quality of the goods for which they pay.

But not alone with material goods. Still more with those unmaterial goods of the heart, the mind and the spirit, which enter into the pursuit of happiness—that inalienable right with which, along with life and liberty, our American forefathers declared that all men are endowed by their Creator. What everyone most desires in living is the enjoyment of life. But under modern economic conditions the enjoyment of life is for most people inseparably interwoven with the cost of living. That is why consumers are interested in the material things *first*—not last. With consumer control of those material things as the practical foundation, they can then provide more fully for the other things they seek in their pursuit of happiness—the cultural, intellectual, spiritual, intangible and limitless things which are envisioned in human aspiration and have to do with all man's being and becoming.

4. CONSUMERS' COOPERATION: THE WORKING PLAN

NOW we come to the practical means by which consumers not only propose to solve, but in substantial and growing measure are actually solving, the problems which were outlined in the preceding chapter. The plan of social-economic organization which is known specifically as "Consumers' Cooperation" is well advanced in America and most of the other civilized countries of the world. It began in America as early as in any other country, though in a different way. In some fields of activity it has now attained much larger stature in America than in any other country. And in this country the movement as a whole and in certain features has developed in a distinctively American way.

AN IMPORTANT DISTINCTION

In order to understand the basis and character of consumers' cooperation clearly, we must first distinguish it from another form of cooperation which antedated it in the United States and most other countries, but which though it has played an important pioneering part and had some success, has in the main proved impracticable and is comparatively small in its present extent. It is known by various names in various countries but can best be differentiated by calling it workers' productive cooperation.

In the previous chapter something was said about cooperation of sorts among producers and distributors, but there the term was used in a general sense as applied to the numerous associations and combinations in which manufacturers, merchants and middlemen join forces, more or less, to promote their common business interests. In a succeeding chapter something will be said about the extensive development and characteristics of marketing cooperatives among farmers. In speaking of workers' productive cooperatives at this point, reference is had only to groups of industrial workers who organize themselves on a cooperative plan, undertake to own and operate an industrial plant, pay themselves wages as workers, interest as shareholders, and divide the profits among themselves in proportion to their individual contributions of work or on some other equitable basis.

In the beginning such workers' productive cooperatives were largely an effort on the part or in behalf of workers, especially handicraftsmen, to combat the displacement of independent workmen by machines and mass production. Later, when it had to be recognized that modern machinery and factories had come to stay, the leading motive became that of gaining for workers a share of the profits and at the same time preserving their independence.

This movement arose first in France as an outgrowth of the French Revolution of 1789 and enthusiasm for its principles of liberty, equality and fraternity. Workers were filled with hope that these principles could be applied to the field of industry. Many cooperatives of this sort were formed at that time and subsequently, and on the whole they have fared better and attained more influence in France than in other countries, but there they have had the support of government subsidies. Across the channel in England this workers' movement was first espoused by philanthropists and idealists, and most notably by the wealthy humanitarian mill-owner Robert Owen. In that country the plans were at first more ambitious and took the form of so-called self-supporting communities, partly industrial and partly agricultural, and including cooperative stores, with the expectation that these communities would become completely self-sufficient and independent outside of the rapidly-growing capitalistic organization of industry. Several hundred such communities or less grandiose workers' cooperative groups were launched between 1820 and 1830, but within a few years nearly all of them had failed and vanished from the scene. They had been fostered philanthropically from above. In later years other workers' groups were organized on a more truly self-supporting basis at the outset. The majority of these have either died out, become ordinary business enterprises, or been aided by consumers' groups and carried along as producer-consumer co-partnerships. They have a federation of their own in England which is distinct from but affiliated with the general Coopera-

tive Union. The story of workers' productive cooperatives in Germany and other countries is much the same.

In the United States groups of this sort, including
communal projects like Brook Farm and the Oneida
Community and workers' craftshops and factories, were
formed in the same early period and have appeared
from time to time ever since then. Today an interesting
variety and respectable number of them can be found
here and there in most sections of the country, but they
have no general federation among themselves and are
not an important industrial factor.

By and large it may be said that a few workers' productive cooperatives have been notably successful and
that this movement is by no means extinct. It has latent
possibilities which under certain circumstances, such
as a strong wave of labor sentiment or a pronounced setback in labor's general policy of collective bargaining
with management and capital, might be revived and
made more directly fruitful. But in any event the workers' cooperatives must be credited historically with
having first broken ground for the idea and principle
of cooperation and planted some of the seed from
which the consumers' cooperative movement came
forth. In fact the workers' cooperatives by their very
failure in the main, and by the evident reasons for such
failure, paved the way for discovery of a sounder basis
of cooperative organization, free from the inherent
weaknesses by which they were for the most part un-
dermined.

Those weaknesses were chiefly three, if we exclude

others which were incidental or which apply generally to any industrial undertaking. The first was the almost inevitable internal dissension which resulted from invidious comparisons, jealousies and bickerings among the workers about the amount or quality of work which each one contributed and the wages and profits which each should receive. Each worker, being a joint owner and operator on the ground, where he could watch the others, felt that he had a right to criticize and object. Quarrels with the worker-manager were frequent, and dissension often ended in disruption. The second weakness of these productive groups was the necessity of selling their products in the general market without an assured patronage. Their own numbers were too small to take more than a fraction of their output, and to supply themselves was not their purpose. The marketing of products is a job in itself, which lies outside of the mechanical operation of an industrial plant and calls for different experience and abilities. Lack of success in solving this problem frequently accounted for financial failure. The third weakness of workers' cooperatives, and the one which proved to be most insidious, was their motive of making a profit over and above wages and interest on capital. If no profit was realized the workers became discontented and discouraged. They naturally asked, "If the big factory-owners can make a profit, why can't we?" Sometimes in order to make themselves bigger they borrowed money which they were unable to repay, and lost their business to the money-lenders. Sometimes when they did operate at a profit, a few of the cleverer and more acquisitive of their own members contrived to get control and eventually became the owners. Thus many workers' cooperatives, bravely launched, found the profit lure was their undoing.

CONSUMERS' COOPERATION SOUNDLY BASED

But consumers' cooperatives, not because of any difference in the human nature of their members, but by virtue of certain fundamental differences in their basis and motive, have precluded these obstacles more fully, it would appear, than any other form of economic organization has succeeded in doing. The definite means which they employ will be described in due course. Suffice to say at this point that the motive of consumers' cooperatives is not profit, but saving; that the apportionment of savings to their members is made in such an automatic and plainly equitable way as to leave no room for dissension on that account; and that these cooperatives have their own constituency or market of consumers to whom they distribute their goods.

In order to approach consumers' cooperation with an adequate appreciation of its character and scope, we must clearly define "consumer" and "consumption." As has already been noted, everyone without exception is a consumer. But most people are also producers of either material or intangible goods, and thus have a dual role in economics. So the question of just where these two roles separate, and wherein consumer and consumption differ from producer and production, requires some consideration.

A consumer of food and drink is of course the person who eats the food and drinks the drink. A consumer of wood or coal fuel is the person who burns this fuel up in the stove or furnace. But food, drink and fuel are the only commodities which are consumed in this simplest and most immediate sense of the word. Clothing and shelter, man's next most rudimentary necessities, last for some time in use, and yet they are "consumed" in the economic sense of this term. In economics, as the 1934 latest edition of Webster's Dictionary explains, a consumer is "one who uses (economic) goods, and so diminishes or destroys their utilities." Or as the New English Dictionary states in slightly different words, the consumer is "one who uses up an article produced, thereby exhausting its exchangeable value." Consumption, according to Webster, is "the use of (economic) goods resulting in the diminution or destruction of their utilities." According to the latest edition of the Encyclopedia Britannica, "The economist means by consumption the satisfaction of wants, the using up of utilities in the satisfaction of demand."

It is evident, therefore, that consumption has a broadly inclusive scope. It applies not only to those things which in business vernacular are commonly called consumers' goods, such as food, clothing, comforts and luxuries, which directly satisfy man's more primary or personal needs. It extends to any and all goods whose utility or usefulness is diminished or exhausted in either direct or indirect satisfaction of the whole range of human wants and demand. This is something to be kept in mind. At the moment it may be left in these rather abstract terms, but in due course it will be applied concretely.

With the ground thus cleared we may outline the general working plan of consumers' cooperation and then go on to its major principles and policies.

Consumers' cooperation has an economic base and a social character and vision. It begins in the economic field and gradually augments its resources and expands its scope to include a wide range of constructive social and cultural activities.

RETAILING—WHOLESALING—PRODUCING

Its economic beginning usually takes the form of self-organization of a group of individual consumers as a cooperative association to supply themselves with commodities. As the most practical means of serving that purpose they set up a retail store, for which they themselves provide the initial capital by share-subscriptions, and which they themselves own and control. Unlike workers' cooperatives, however, they do not employ themselves in the store but engage competent management and working personnel on a basis of salaries and wages. The employees, as *consumers*, usually become members of the cooperative in due course, and thus share its benefits. This store, using its initial capital for operating equipment and purchase of goods, then proceeds to distribute the goods to the association's members. As a matter of practical procedure it sells goods to the members, usually at current market prices, and periodically returns to the members, in proportion to their patronage, that part of the store's proceeds which remains over and above actual cost of the goods and necessary reserves for continued operation and up-building. This of course means that the final net figure at which the individual members obtain their goods is less than the price which they paid at their store and which the general public pays at commercial stores.

At first these cooperative retail stores have to buy their supplies from the commercial wholesalers. But when a substantial number of stores are under way in a given region they federate among themselves, and for the purpose of more satisfactory operation proceed to organize a cooperative wholesale of their own, sub-scribing the necessary share-capital to set it up. Just as the individual local consumers own and control the retail stores, so likewise (although this original or stand-ard plan has been considerably modified in practice) these retail stores own and control the regional whole-sale which now begins to supply them with the goods they retail.

The wholesale likewise sells its goods to the local stores at current wholesale prices and periodically re-turns to them, in proportion to their patronage of the wholesale, that part of its proceeds which remains over and above actual cost and requisite reserves. Thus the final net figure at which the local stores obtain their goods is less than the price which they paid the wholesale and which other stores pay commercial wholesales. This means an additional saving for the local stores, as compared to what they were able to save before they had their own wholesale. The stores pass this additional saving along to their own individual members, whose net outlay for goods is thus still further reduced.

Regional wholesales in due course form a national wholesale, and at the apex of this cooperative structure there is now an international wholesale, which is still in its infancy.

At first the wholesales have to buy all of their supplies from commercial producers. After a time, however, when their resources have grown sufficiently, they find it advisable for the purpose of obtaining their supplies more satisfactorily, to enter the field of production themselves. (In the meantime ambitious local cooperatives may have undertaken on their own account some of the simpler forms of production, such as bakeries, dairies, meat-processing and canning, in which there is a substantial local demand for the output.) Of course the wholesales cannot cover the whole productive field at once, but usually begin with things which they are obtaining least satisfactorily, in terms of price and quality, from the commercial producers. After cooperative production of these commodities has been well developed, the wholesales add others—and so on in gradual succession.

At this point someone may interpose a query: "But didn't you say that cooperative production had generally proved unsuccessful?" Ah, but that was another kind of cooperative production, in which the *workers* tried to own and operate the plant themselves and sell their product to the general public. *Consumers'* cooperative production, on the contrary, is assured of its market before it starts. In other words, when a wholesale decides to set up a manufacturing plant, it does so only to meet more satisfactorily the already existing and approximately known and measured demand for some commodity, on the part of all cooperative retail stores which own the wholesale and the entire body of individual consumers who own the retail stores. Thus the otherwise difficult and often disastrous problem of marketing the product is precluded—solved in advance. That is the great advantage of consumers' cooperative production as contrasted with either workers' cooperative production or ordinary business production. Those forms of production have to guess at their market as best they can and take the chances. But consumers' cooperation does not have to guess. It *knows*—and adjusts its production to this known demand.

The cooperative processing plants and factories are set up on their own feet, so to speak, by one or more wholesales who provide the initial share capital and own and control the enterprise. The factory sells its products to the wholesales at the general market price, and periodically returns to them the difference between its gross proceeds and the cost of manufacture plus reserves. This means a saving for the wholesales, as compared with what they previously had to pay commercial manufacturers for their supplies. The wholesales pass this saving along as a further saving to the retail stores, who in turn pass it along to the individual local members, and thereby reduce still further the final net outlay of these local consumers for the goods they obtain.

Such is the usual retailing-wholesaling-producing sequence of consumers' cooperation which deals with the distribution of commodities. There are other fields in which consumers' cooperation deals with the distribution of services. Those fields include, for instance, insurance and credit, so organized as to meet more economically and satisfactorily the needs of individual consumers and the larger needs of cooperative industrial enterprise. Cooperative organization applies likewise to housing, restaurant, laundry, medical, burial and any other kind of service in which consumers find it advantageous to engage. In these fields likewise cooperation yields further savings to consumers. In the case of insurance and credit the savings are especially large.

Such services are sometimes initiated and conducted separately, through cooperative associations formed for the specific purpose in view, as, for example, housing. More often, however, they grow out of the mercantile and productive activities which have been outlined, and are maintained as departments of the parent association or federation, with accumulated resources which are set aside for such use. That is also the way in which the educational program is carried out. Cooperative education does not attempt to duplicate or replace the existing schools, colleges and other educational institutions. It is supplementary and deals with the nature of cooperation itself. Recreational and cultural activities are developed in close relation to education, and likewise as an integral part of the whole movement.

From what has been said it is evident that consumers' cooperation has two aspects and two contiguous lines of advance. One is economic and the other social. On the economic side, as already noted, cooperatives are joined in regional, national and international wholesales. From the viewpoint of more broadly social interests, they are federated in regional, national and international leagues which devote themselves to the movement's general promotion. In both working divisions of the field, cooperative education is omnipresent. The wholesale federations and retail units which are engaged in production and distribution bring education to bear primarily upon matters of economics, efficiency and industrial success; while the leagues and local associations, which are more immediately concerned with the movement's social aims and values, utilize education primarily to promote a fuller understanding of cooperation's principles and methods on the part of its members, its present and prospective working personnel, and the public at large.

TO YOU, WHOEVER YOU ARE

On the threshold of cooperative principles, which the ensuing chapter will present, let us pause a moment and think of ourselves as individual consumers who are naturally interested in the general idea of consumers' cooperation, and would like to learn more about it.

Some of us are married men and women with sons and daughters growing up and budgetary problems of making both ends meet. Some of us are single, perhaps not from choice but because we lack the wherewithal and the security of employment and income which we feel would justify us in asking another person to share our lot. Some of us are young people just starting out in life, filled with aspiration and ambition but perforce with doubt as we face the world in its present unsettled state of wars and rumors of wars, dictatorships encroaching on democracy, and in our own country economic depression, industrial strife between capital and labor, and entrenched privilege and exploitation clamoring in the name of "Liberty" to be let alone.

As consumers and potential cooperators our daily needs are such as would relate us in practical ways to cooperative stores; to cooperative bakeries, restaurants and housing; to cooperative health and medical service; to cooperative credit and insurance; and all along the way to cooperative education and recreation.

Let us then keep all these facts of interest in mind—
not abstractly *as things which pertain to that remote and
bloodless creature called the "economic man,"* but
concretely *and* personally *as things which concern us
ourselves, as living human beings with heart and head
and spirit. Keep this close and individual interest in
the forefront of your thought throughout the following
chapters. Look at consumers' cooperation not distantly
and detachedly but intimately, receptively, critically if
you will—and always in relation to yourself and your
own circumstances. Bring your own native common
sense to bear upon it, pro or con. Just common sense
applied to your own consumer problems is all you will
need, because there is nothing abstruse or mystifying
about cooperation. So view it humanly and simply but
with broad vision, taking due account not only of its
material benefits but of its vital significance in terms of
economic democracy.*

*As you reflect upon that final aspect of cooperation,
consider these two "Thoughts" of America's poet of
Democracy, Walt Whitman:*

"Of ownership—as if one fit to own things
    could not at pleasure enter upon all,
    and incorporate them into himself or herself."

"Of Equality—as if it harmed me,
    giving others the same chances and rights as my-
        self—
    as if it were not indispensable to my own rights
    that others possess the same."

5 · THE PRINCIPLES
AND POLICIES

THE governing principles of consumers' cooperation are somewhat differently named and assessed by different exponents of the movement. But there is general agreement as to their substance: the three basic principles which may well be called the A B C. They are like the three sides of an equilateral triangle, bounding common ground in which they come together and are unified. Principle A is Constructive Savings and Patronage Returns. Principle B is Limitation of Returns on Capital. Principle C is Democratic Control. How important these principles are, and how basically different they are from those which govern commercial business, will become clear when they are examined.

A. CONSTRUCTIVE SAVINGS
AND PATRONAGE RETURNS

In outlining the usual retail-wholesale-production sequence of consumers' cooperation we noted how it works from the bottom upwards and at each stage effects savings which are passed down until they reach individual consumers. But that is far from being the whole story. There is more to be said on this score.

First of all, this kind of saving is very different from

penny-pinching parsimony. Parsimony is negative and static. It means non-use or niggardly use of resources. But the saving which results from consumers' cooperation is positive, dynamic and constructive.

Consumers' cooperation eliminates the economic waste which in profit business results from supporting such middlemen and services as are really unnecessary. As was noted, commercial business is largely unable to make such eliminations because each stage of the sequence between producers and consumers—as in the cotton illustration—is separately conducted and controlled. Unified control of the whole sequence is the exception and not the rule. Under these conditions various jobbers and other middlemen, who are not essential but are seeking opportunities for profit, contrive to muscle in. But consumers' cooperation has the advantage of a unified line of control from retailing at the bottom to production at the top. Cooperative organization is therefore able to shorten the sequence. It finds that wholesales, as an intermediate stage between production and retailing, fulfill a useful function. And of course it needs such essential services as insurance, credit and banking. At all these points, however, it turns back to consumers what would otherwise go as profits to middlemen. And at other points it can and does eliminate stages, middlemen and services which are unnecessary and therefore uneconomical.

This applies especially to extravagant advertising and inflated salesmanship. From the viewpoint of a commercial producer or distributor, large outlays for advertising and salesmanship may be advantageous in enabling him to sell his product in the competitive market at a profit to himself. But of course he shifts this expense to the pocketbooks of consumers by adding it to the sales price of his product. For the consumers, therefore, this is simply an addition to their cost of living. From the viewpoint of consumers who are cooperatively organized, such exorbitant outlay for advertising and salesmanship is mostly outright waste, because in distributing goods to themselves to meet their own known and measured demand, they do not have to expend large sums in overcoming sales resistance.

Owing largely to the marked growth of consumer-consciousness and consumers' cooperation, a good many commercial stores and other business concerns are now saying that their first interest is to serve the consumer. But that claim cannot stand up in face of the fact that the first interest of commercial business is and must be profit. It is true that profit-business is waking up to the necessity of doing something for consumers; but the utmost that can truly be said about its endeavor is that it is a means to the end of profit, and at best comes next after profit in line of consideration. If service to consumers were actually the first consideration, the consistent thing to do would be to reorganize the business as a consumers' cooperative. Then it would really be serving consumers as fully as possible.

That is what consumers' cooperation does and what *only* consumers' cooperation does. It reduces costs by eliminating unnecessary stages, middlemen and services and then returns to consumers the difference between actual cost and the selling price, which in commercial business goes to producers and middlemen as profits.

This return to consumers is made not in proportion to their ownership of shares, but in proportion to their patronage of the business, whether the business be a retail store, a laundry, a bakery, an insurance company or any other kind of cooperative enterprise. So it is known as the patronage-return. In the true sense of the word "radical," which applies to something that goes to the roots of a situation, this plan of replacing profits for a few people by savings and patronage-returns for all people (since all are consumers and eligible to participate in consumers' cooperation and share in its benefits) is thoroughly radical. It is a concrete and substantial recognition of two fundamental economic facts which, as previously noted, are not thus recognized in commercial business. Consumers' cooperation recognizes the fact that the essential object of production is consumption, and it therefore replaces production for the profit of producers and middlemen by production for the use of consumers. It recognizes that consumers by their purchases impart actual value to commodities which, without the market that consumers constitute, would have no value at all; and that the consumers or patrons who buy the goods or services of any given business undertaking thereby build up and support that business.

True, some initial capital is necessary in cooperative business. This is supplied by the members themselves.

Such subsequent capital as is required for expansion is drawn very largely, as will presently appear, from savings-reserves made possible by growth of patronage. Therefore, consumers' cooperation holds that after paying fair salaries to management, fair wages to labor and fair compensation to capital and incidental services, consumers are entitled to get back the residue as savings effected through cooperation, and thus to obtain their goods in the end at actual cost.

CONSERVATION VERSUS WASTE

Here several queries may naturally arise. "Is there any real difference between profits and savings? When consumers return to themselves as savings what would otherwise go to producers and distributors as profits, are they not merely calling profits by another name and engaging in profit business themselves?" "If cooperative business returns its net proceeds to consumers, how can it provide for its own growth and expansion? Commercial concerns are constantly plowing part of their profits back into the business." "If by means of patronage returns consumers can obtain goods through their cooperatives at actual cost, and if cooperation does grow and expand, will not commercial concerns which are run for profit and make no patronage-returns be forced out of business by cooperative competition?" Let us consider these queries in turn. The answer to each of them will go quite a way toward answering the next one.

There is as much difference between savings and

profits as there is between the North Pole and the South Pole. They are opposite ends. To reach either of them from a middle point would mean going in exactly the opposite direction from that required to reach the other. To obtain a profit a person must sell something to someone else for more than it cost him, and he tries to sell it for as much as he can get. In doing so he is quite likely to expend time, energy and material resources in dressing it up, proclaiming its merits, and keeping its demerits in the background. From any viewpoint except that of the sellers' own profit, such expenditure is largely waste. If we assume that the thing sold is worth what it cost the seller and that he succeeds in selling it at a profit, that profit is a deduction from the resources of the buyer. It is simply impossible for a person to make a profit from himself. He must necessarily make it from someone else.

To effect a saving, however, a person tries to get something at minimum expenditure and with maximum conservation of time, energy and material resources. That is the antithesis of waste. Furthermore, he can effect a saving in producing things for himself. In the old pre-machinery days farmers' wives made homespun clothes for the family with homegrown wool. By increasing their skill, care and economy of material, these housewives could make a saving in their own production. Although this saving was not measured in money or exchange it was none the less actual. When consumers organize cooperatively to supply themselves with goods, and especially after they begin to produce their own goods in their own plants, they are saving on a large scale in virtually the same way in which the farmers' wives saved on a small scale with their spinning wheels and weaving looms. In other words, they are engaged not in waste expenditure but in the constructive conservation of resources.

This implies the answer to the next query, as to how cooperatives can return savings to consumers and still provide themselves with the wherewithal for their own expansion. Of course, the savings which are thus returned substantially augment the purchasing power of consumers. With more money in hand they can buy more goods. Increased demand calls for increased supply, which in turn leads to enhanced industrial efficiency in terms of larger output from existing plants, and to such expansion of plants as may be required. Meanwhile increased purchasing power and growth of patronage have resulted in a larger total of savings and thereby provided such additional capital resources as are needed for expansion. The procedure is simple. Before the cooperative distributes patronage returns in cash, it sets aside from savings whatever reserves are considered necessary for successful operation and expansion. Such reserves tend to become larger as retailing adds wholesaling and wholesales move on into production. Sometimes additional shares are issued to patrons against their individual portions of savings thus reserved, and sometimes the reserves are treated as undivided patrons' equity.

Cooperatives are constantly building up their resources in this way. There are some wholesales whose entire working capital from the outset has been drawn from savings, and many cases in which the bulk of capital has been thus obtained. Conclusive proof of the ample spread between the actual cost of goods and the prevailing prices at which they are sold is had in this fact that cooperatives, selling goods in the first instance at these market prices, are able to pay patronage returns to their members and still have sufficient savings available to take care of expansion. Such use of savings takes the place of what commercial concerns call plowing profits back into the business. But there is this tremendous difference. In the case of commercial business the consumers, who buy its products and thereby support it, do not share at all in its ownership and control or in its proceeds. In the case of cooperatives, on the other hand, the consumers own and control the business completely and get back its net proceeds as savings.

UPBUILDING VERSUS DEPLETION

This brings us to certain differences between the results of cooperative and commercial business which are vitally important not only for individual consumers, but for the communities, states and regions in which they live. In the case of many stock companies—probably most of those which are large and extensive—the great majority of stockholders are absentees as regards living in the communities where the stores, stations or plants of these corporations are located. As noted earlier, such stock companies divert profits from those localities to other parts of the country and very largely to a few financial centers, where they are used in financial operations which may be of no benefit whatever to the communities, states and regions where the profits were made. Chain stores, for example, have no roots in the communities where they ply their trade. They do not put their profits to use in building up those communities but transmit them to the chain's headquarters in New York, say, which uses the funds thus acquired to launch other stores in other places. Then the new stores proceed to divert profits from those other places in the same way.

The shareholders and patrons of cooperative stores, however, are residents of the community in which the store is established. This is necessarily true, because the store is not plopped into the community from outside but is organized by local consumers to supply themselves with goods. When the savings are returned to these local consumers, the community's resources are thereby increased. When the retail stores in a given region organize a wholesale, the additional savings made by the wholesale go back through the retails to all the local communities in that region. And when the wholesales federate and set up productive plants to serve a still larger area, the further savings thus effected are turned back to the wholesales and by them to the retails for distribution to consumers, thus eventually augmenting the resources of every community throughout the area. This means that the proceeds of cooperative industry are not bottle-necked and controlled at a few points by a few people, but are constantly being returned to promote the well-being of the localities where they originated.

Surely this is a new way of plowing back resources. It is an aspect of consumers' cooperation which merits, and is receiving, more and more attention from discerning people who recognize that under our present economic system many communities are not being built up but depleted, and that there is an ominous trend toward economic delocalization and centralization. Nor is this trend solely economic. It is also social and political, involving transiency of residence, shifting of large numbers of people from one part of the country to another in hope of getting on better, a general movement toward the industrial centers, and deterioration of local initiative, independence and self-government. As consumers' cooperation grows it helps very definitely to counteract such tendencies. By enabling local consumers to own and conduct a business which is part and parcel of their own community, it enhances their sense of participation, responsibility and self-respect, helps them to put down roots in the community and remain there, and is an influence in substituting content for discontent. Something will be said a little later about its strengthening of democracy.

SECURITY AND ECONOMY

Of the three queries which were posed we have now answered two, by pointing out the difference between saving and profit and explaining how consumers' cooperation obtains capital reserves for its own expansion. The third query is whether as cooperation expands and continues to supply goods to consumers at a saving, its competition will put an increasing number of profit-dealers out of business. The answer is partly this: "No, it will not necessarily put them out of business, but it will no doubt put many of them *out of business for profit.*"

This answer carries the implication that cooperation holds out to men and women who are now engaged in business for profit, opportunities to come into the co-operative movement as executives, managers, consultants, et cetera, on a basis of fair and assured compensation for their service. For many business men, especially among those who are struggling to maintain modest proprietorships against the competition of big chains and combinations, such a change would probably prove to be for the better. Profits, though alluring, are precarious. Over a substantial period only a few people, comparatively, manage to keep on top in the rough and tumble. As was earlier observed, profit business leaves a constant stream of wreckage in its wake. Failure, bankruptcy, closing-down and unemployment involve not only the people at the head, but the subordinates, the white-collar workers and the labor force. And that means enormous economic waste. Consumers' cooperation, free from the unsettling and often disastrous lure of profit, must of course as it grows enlist men and women of ability and experience in business affairs. Many of its present leading executives and other members of its working personnel have been drawn from fields of commercial business.

The rest of the answer to this query is that in so far as cooperatives by virtue of their saving to consumers may replace business concerns which are run for profit, the losses affecting commercial dealers who are thus replaced will be far outweighed by the gains which will accrue to the community as a whole. If commercial concerns fail on account of inefficiency and waste, of course they *should* fail under any rational system of economy. If others which are efficient from the profit viewpoint fail because consumers prefer to obtain goods through cooperatives and receive patronage-returns, instead of patronizing dealers who are reaping profits for themselves, the community will benefit likewise from such failures. The question here presented is much like that which arises from technological progress in industry. It is true that many inventions of labor-saving machinery have the incidental effect of displacing many laborers from their accustomed employment. But it is also true that technological inventions open up new fields of production and employment. No doubt some of the laborers who are displaced are for various reasons unable to readjust themselves to the changed conditions. That by-effect of invention is unfortunate in itself and calls for study of practical means of dealing with the problem. But if, as is generally accepted, the main results of technological progress are of benefit to society as a whole, an attempt to stop such progress because of its incidental displacement of labor would be going counter to social well-being. Essentially the same consideration holds as regards any residual displacement of profit-makers by the growth of consumers' cooperation.

What has thus far been said about constructive savings and patronage-returns has been confined to lessening the cost of goods to consumers in terms of cash. That is the most obvious and easily recognized kind of saving. But there is another form of saving in consumers' cooperation which is equally or even more important. That is the saving in terms of quality. Consumers generally have not yet come to realize the full meaning and value of superior quality as measured by utility-in-use. Consumers of modest buying power are inclined to regard goods of better quality as rather in the luxury class, at least for them, and to look not so much for quality in what they buy as for price bargains. But when some goods are superior to others in utility, the choice lies between real and apparent economy. Suppose a person needs a pair of shoes. Is it better for him to buy a pair, at, say, $5.00, or to pay $7.50 for another pair which will wear twice as long and no doubt more comfortably? This is simple enough when it is figured out. In buying the first pair instead of the second he saves $2.50 in cash immediately. But in buying the second pair he gets twice as much usage, that is, five dollars' worth more of utility-in-use than the first pair would yield. Subtracting from this $5.00 the added

$2.50 which he has to pay for the second pair, he is still $2.50 better off at the end of the wearing period by having bought the better shoes.

But when the buyer sees two pairs of shoes thus differently priced, how can he know—unless he is an expert on shoes—that the difference in quality is commensurate with the difference in price? He has had so many disillusioning experiences to the contrary that he is skeptical, and feels it is safer to save the cash and let the quality go. When consumers distribute goods to themselves through their own stores, however, they naturally do not go in for fooling themselves. Their store managers and directing boards are charged with the duty of obtaining goods of assured quality and marking these goods in such a way that their quality can be dependably known. True, cooperative stores usually carry goods of several grades, but the grades are plainly indicated and the consumer takes one or the other knowingly.

Up to the point where cooperatives undertake production themselves through their own plants, they have to rely largely on selecting the best of commercial products. An intermediate stage between such selection and their own production is that of having goods processed or manufactured for them under contract and according to specifications which the cooperative wholesales lay down. As direct production has to be developed soundly and therefore somewhat slowly, this intermediate contract plan is widely used. It gives the cooperatives opportunity to explore various fields, study the conditions which affect quality and prices, and then choose for direct production those commodities which are most difficult to obtain from commercial producers satisfactorily, as respects quality and price combined. Once the cooperatives enter upon production of their own, they are of course in the much stronger position of being able to control the quality of goods themselves. They can then provide their members with a maximum saving of utility-in-use, as distinguished from the more immediate saving in cash.

Such saving in quality tends to come more and more to the front, as a result partly of cooperative education and partly of cooperative success in lowering the general price levels of many commodities in areas where the movement is large and active. As prices are thus lowered the spread between cost and price is reduced, and consequently the margin for immediate cash savings by cooperatives is narrowed. At the same time the tendency of cooperatives to make larger savings reserves for expansion reduces further the amount which can be paid out in cash returns. But returns in better quality of goods are constantly increasing. Consumers are learning what they can accomplish in this regard by collective action and resources. As was remarked in the preceding chapter, it is humanly impossible for the great majority of individual consumers to devote the amount of time, thought and eternal vigilance which is required to keep abreast from day to day with the multitudinous matters that have to do with prices and quality of goods, and with the ingenious and endless misrepresentations and subterfuges which are employed by many commercial producers and distributors to sell things at prices which, though they look low on their face, are really high when judged by the inferior and sometimes worthless quality of the product. The market is glutted with all sorts of stuff which is cheap only in the worst sense, and for which the word "goods" is a misnomer. Purchase of such trash by consumers not only wastes their money but has a cheapening influence on their standards of living and character. The cooperatives, by serving as agencies which distribute to consumers goods of superior quality and dependable utility-in-use, are rendering a great social service. They are helping to raise not only the standard of living, but the cultural and spiritual standards of life.

B. LIMITATION OF RETURNS ON CAPITAL

Consumers' cooperation is not opposed to capital. It recognizes that the use of capital is necessary under any system of economy. But it treats capital not as the owner and master of industry but as an instrument, and holds it strictly to that function. For the use of this instrument it pays the lender a fair hire, and limits the returns on capital to that compensation.

At first glance this second principle of consumers' cooperation may not appear to be so radical, when compared with commercial business practice, as the first principle—which as we have seen leads to the ownership and control of industry by consumers, whose wants give rise to industry and whose patronage supports it. But if that first principle is to be applied fully and effectually, it is necessary to transfer to consumers such ownership and control of industry as are now vested in capital, and to limit the returns on capital. On closer examination, therefore, the second principle is found to be no less radical than the first (again in the true sense of radical, as something which goes to the roots). The matter of control of industry will be taken up further when the third principle is discussed. At this point the question is that of ownership and returns, and the difference which applies to cooperative practice may be brought out best by describing, in contrast, the practice of profit business.

In profit business it is taken for granted that capital owns the business. In stock companies capital is represented by the stockholders, who own the company through their ownership of stock. At the outset of a corporate enterprise, when the first stock subscriptions are made to provide the initial capital, many of the subscribers and presumably most of the larger ones have a close and constructive interest in the enterprise. Such interest, and the expectation of profits, are the reasons why they subscribe for some part of the capital stock. Even at the beginning, however, if all the stock is not privately subscribed but is open to public subscription, there are usually some people who buy stock only in hope of profit, and knowing or caring very little about the enterprise in and of itself. Then later, if the undertaking does prove profitable or appears to have good prospects, the current market price of its stock is likely to rise considerably above the original subscription price and to become attractive not only for investment but for speculation. Some of the original subscribers of capital may sell stock, new stock may be issued and, especially when shares are listed on the Stock Exchange, there is a good deal of wholly speculative trading. This means that many of the stockholders are temporary and transient, having no close and continuing interest in the business, but concerned only with stock-market profits. And yet these people, to the extent of their holdings, are the legal owners of the business for the time being.

As regards the returns on capital, profit-business holds that capital by virtue of its ownership of business is entitled to the entire net earnings over and above expenses and reserves. Stated thus broadly, the returns on capital in profit business are unlimited. But more specifically the situation is that on certain classes of capital the returns are limited, while on others they are not. Capital is obtained mostly through bonds, preferred stock and common stock. Bonds bear a fixed rate of interest, which comes first. Preferred stock carries a fixed dividend (sometimes with provision for sliding-scale additions) and comes next. But to returns on the common stock, there is no fixed limit. Sometimes a company may issue only common stock from the outset. Sometimes it may get on a common stock basis by retiring preferred stock and bonds. In any event, the common stock is entitled to all earnings over and above operating expenses, reserves, and any interest or dividend payments on prior obligations.

The dividends, on both preferred and common stock, are paid to whoever owns the shares on the dividend date of record. Thus people who have bought stock merely for speculation receive these dividends if they happen to own shares at that time. But their contribution to the actual upbuilding of the business is nil. Consumers, whose patronage does build up and support the business, receive no part of the earnings whatever.

In contrast, consumers' cooperation limits the returns on capital to a fixed interest, usually about 5 percent, which it regards as a fair hire paid to the owners of capital for its use as an instrument of industry. The people who provide this capital are resident patrons who have a close and constructive interest in the business. As a rule, the shares are priced very low, and any one person is allowed to subscribe for a few shares only. This helps to keep his interest as a shareholder subordinate to his interest as a patron. If, for example, a person holds five shares in a cooperative grocery, of $5.00 par value each and bearing 5 percent, he receives at the end of the year $1.25 in interest. If, as a patron, he buys $250 worth of groceries during the year and patronage returns are at the rate of 5 percent, he gets back at the year's end $12.50 in savings. Or put in another way, the consumer by using $250 in purchasing supplies gets currently the groceries which he needs and also a patronage return equal to what he would have received if the $250 had not been used for living purposes but lent at 5 per cent as capital.

Shares are usually redeemable at the wish of the owner on due notice, and likewise at the discretion of the cooperative if the owner moves out of the community or if share capital can safely be contracted and interest thereby saved. Redeemability, combined with low, fixed interest, insures stability of value for the shares and keeps them immune from speculation. Cooperative shares are not subject to trade on any stock market.

New shareholders, it is important to note, come in largely through the door of patronage, by having their savings credited to cover purchase of a share. The members of a cooperative have a dual role in the enterprise, that of patrons and that of shareholders; and because these roles are enacted by the same persons the line which divides them is well-nigh invisible. To keep it so is of the essence of cooperation. Nevertheless, there is a line; and if we can imagine the members as standing behind and in front of that line at the same time, they would stand at the rear as owners of capital, receiving limited returns for its use as an instrument of industry, and to the fore as consumers who hire capital, own and control their business, and distribute its savings not to property but to people.

C. DEMOCRATIC CONTROL

The third major principle of consumers' cooperation is that of democratic instead of plutocratic control of industry. To insure democratic control each share-holder, irrespective of the number of shares he owns, has only one vote. As further safeguards against the rise of control by property rather than by people, voting by proxy is prohibited. Two provisions mentioned above in the discussion of capital are also pertinent in the present context. Pricing the shares of local coopera-tive units very low, usually around five or ten dollars, enables people of slender means to own them; and re-stricting each member to a few shares, forestalls the rise of large holders who might contrive to exercise undue influence indirectly.

Again, the practical bearing of these regulations may be most fully appreciated when they are compared with those which govern voting in commercial stock compa-nies. In a stock company each stockholder's votes are commensurate with the number of shares he owns. If he owns only one share he has only one vote, but if he owns a thousand or ten thousand shares he has a thou-sand or ten thousand votes. Shares are often priced so high in the original subscription, or get so high in the stock market, that people of slender means cannot ac-quire very many at best. On the other hand, the only limit to the number of shares which a person of large means can acquire is the limit of his own resources and the total number of shares available. Furthermore, vot-ing by proxy is freely permitted and practiced.

Under these conditions it frequently comes about that a few stockholders (or even a single stockholder) of very large means acquire a majority of the shares and thus control the company. For example, in a given company with, say, a million shares of common voting stock outstanding, a combination of five stockholders owning 500,001 shares between them (or one person owning that many shares alone) could effectually veto the total votes of a maximum of 499,999 stockholders owning one share each. As a rule, moreover, it is not necessary for the combination or the single stockholder to own an actual majority of the shares, because control which is practically as certain can be obtained by the simple and innocent-looking device of proxy voting. Here we are not dealing with the motives, which may be good or bad, but simply with the matter of control. A committee of stockholders who are really, though not nominally, acting as agents of the combination or individual seeking control, circularizes the numerous small stockholders and offers to serve as proxy in voting the stock of those who do not expect to attend the annual or special meeting at which certain questions are to be brought up for action. To many of these small stockholders this looks like an opportunity to express themselves indirectly and make their votes count, and so they are quite likely to sign and return the proxy forms. The proxy votes thus obtained add up to a large total which, when added to the total votes which the combination already has through ownership, insures an open-and-shut control of the meeting.

Plenty of small stockholders have gone to such meetings, at which some important issue was to be submitted to a vote, with the expectation possibly that they could be of some effect in the decision; but when the votes were counted and the meeting was ended they have realized that neither their votes nor their voices have had any effect at all. On some occasions there is a large attendance of little stockholders and a general howl of criticism on their part; an innocent bystander would conclude that nothing short of a drastic reorganization of the business must result. But when the issue is put to a vote the result is something like this: for the proposal recommended by the combination, 1,377,377 votes (including proxies) ; against the proposal, 1,313. And the little stockholders make their exit with the feeling, "What's the use!"

It may be said that the large stockholders, being so heavily interested, are likely to know much more than the little stockholders about the company's affairs and how they should be run. That is undoubtedly true. Sometimes it is true in the best sense, in that these large stockholders try to have the company run as honestly and efficiently as possible. But sometimes it is true in the worst sense, when these large stockholders knowing so much more about the company's affairs and its prospects, good or bad, turn such inside information to their own financial advantage and the disadvantage of those who are not on the inside.

Of course it is conceivable that small stockholders could manage somehow or other to obtain equally complete information about the business. But suppose they made themselves veritable authorities on its affairs— what good would that do them without the votes? They are simply out of the picture so far as control of the enterprise is concerned, and if they get something that appears to be fairly good in the way of dividends, most of them do not try to be Don Quixotes, but let the big fellows run things.

In short, corporate profit business is not democratically but plutocratically controlled. This is undeniable.

Consumers' cooperatives however are, as we have said, organized on the basis of equal voting power for each shareholder. That is the broad and solid foundation of control on which they are built. The shareholders elect from among themselves the usual officers and a general committee or board of directors, which is responsible to the shareholders and charged with carrying out the program and policies on which they decide. The directors employ a manager, who is responsible to them for the day-to-day operation of the business. For this position they try to find someone who, with competence and successful experience in the particular field of business, combines full accord with cooperative principles and, when possible, familiarity with cooperative methods. The manager, in consultation with the directors or a smaller executive committee, employs the operating personnel and labor force who, according to the size and nature of the business, are responsible either directly to him or to assistants whom he designates.

This is virtually the same line of responsibility which applies to corporate profit business, but the way it works in cooperatives is considerably different. Their shareholders' meetings function democratically. Shareholders ask questions, make criticisms, and thrash things out as fully as they wish. The officers, directors and manager submit to questioning and explain anything which needs explaining. Then the shareholders vote with *equal voting power,* and a human rather than a money majority decides the issue.

All this may sound somewhat amateurish and inefficient to the management and controlling stockholders of commercial corporations. That is because they have a different point of view and a different scale of values, in which property and profits rank first. With cooperatives, living men and women are the first and last consideration. As they are working to replace the present industrial system by one which better serves the greater good of the greater number, they realize that it is vitally important for the individual consumers to acquire education and experience in dealing with economic problems and the control of business affairs. They believe that such affairs are no mystery beyond the ken of ordinary people, but call mainly for commonsense— which is not necessarily confined to business men. Rank and file cooperators have proved by constructive results that they possess sufficient commonsense for the purpose, and that they understand the practical need for concentrated direction and management within due limits but do not allow them to run amuck.

In local cooperatives, whose members live in the community, full discussion and direct control by the individual shareholders provides at the base of industry an economic counterpart of the New England town-meeting in its prime. In the case of cooperative whole-sales, which as previously noted are owned and controlled by the retail stores in the given region, the meetings are composed not of individual shareholders as a rule, but of delegates elected by the local units. As regards productive plants established by a federation of wholesales, their meetings are composed of delegates elected by the wholesales. Thus the working plan of consumers' cooperation combines democratic control at the bottom with representative government above. It is thereby in harmony with the American constitutional system of political government; and in giving American consumers opportunity and experience in the directing of economic affairs it is at the same time equipping them to take a more informed, intelligent and constructive part as citizens in shaping the political life of the nation.

SUPPLEMENTARY POLICIES

Supplementing these three basic principles of consumers' cooperation, which have here been called its A B C, there are certain other characteristic features which may be regarded as prevailing policies. These policies grow out of the principles, and especially out of the third principle of democratic control.

One of these policies is that of voluntary, open and unlimited membership. This means that no one shall be compelled to join a cooperative—as laborers are sometimes compelled by the check-off plan to join a labor union. The cooperatives want only members who join of their own free will because they believe in cooperation. Open membership means that there are no sectarian, racial or political restrictions, and that anyone who wants to join may do so. Unlimited membership means that the door is never shut—that cooperatives, unlike many stock companies, seldom become closed corporations confined to a few people who got in on the ground floor. A person may join a cooperative in its infancy, its youth or its maturity, either by purchasing a share outright or by patronizing the cooperative and being credited with patronage-returns until these become sufficient to pay for a share, after which the patron has the status of a member entitled to patronage returns in cash. As a rule, cooperatives permit members of the general public to purchase the goods or services which they distribute primarily to their own members. Such patrons are under no compulsion to join the cooperative, but after they have had personal experience with its fair prices and good quality they frequently do join of their own accord. In this way, as well as others, the ranks of cooperators are continually augmented.

Consistently, and almost necessarily, open membership involves an attitude and policy of political, religious and racial non-partisanship or neutrality on the part of cooperatives. They realize that if they are to unite people of various political affiliations, religious creeds and racial stocks as consumers, they must keep clear of partisanship or prejudice themselves, while leaving their members free in their own individual affairs. Political neutrality, however, does not mean political passivity. On the contrary, consumers' cooperation aims to secure consideration of its merits by all political parties, with a view not to receiving special favors or subsidies but to obtaining such recognition and legislation as are essential to assure a fair opportunity for the movement, free from discrimination against cooperation as compared with the prevailing profit system. In this respect they have a constant uphill job, by reason of the open or covert opposition of profit-seeking business and the endless legislative, legal and administrative obstacles which it contrives to put in the way of cooperative progress.

Gradually to overcome such opposition by public enlightenment is one of the objects in view in another general policy of cooperatives—that of reserving a certain percentage of their savings for education in cooperative principles and methods. Reference has already been made to the omnipresence of education throughout the cooperative movement, and more will be said later about concrete educational activities.

SOUND OPERATION

Finally, there are several policies which have to do with sound business operation. One which it is very difficult to maintain in the face of commercial competition, especially in the United States, is that of selling goods for cash and not extending credit. That is partly a matter of simple equity to members. It is not equitable to the members who pay cash to give other members credit and thereby diminish, temporarily at least, the operating resources; also the patronage returns which can be paid out safely. Consumers generally do not realize that commercial concerns which extend credit add a certain surcharge to their prices in order to cover tie-up of funds and losses. Customers who pay cash at such places are therefore paying more than they would have to pay if the concern were run on a strictly cash basis. Cooperatives have to contend with the widespread commercial practice of not only granting but encouraging credit and installment buying; but business on a cash basis is their standard. Of course, the savings which they return to patrons can be set over against the credit lure. In constantly educating their members to buy for cash and pay as they go, the cooperatives are rendering another economic and social service for which there is ample need in the United States.

Likewise for reasons of sound operation, the cooperatives make substantial reserves from savings for depreciation, contingencies and expansion. A companion policy is that of frequent audits and very full and complete financial statements. It is a by-word that the financial statements of some stock companies are puzzling, to put it mildly. Nor is it an uncommon commercial practice to withhold important figures from the public and even from stockholders on the plea that to give such information out would be detrimental to the business. That may or may not be true in an immediate sense. Sometimes it is merely a pretext for concealing conditions or operations by insiders which are extremely detrimental in themselves. But even if such concealment or withholding is beneficial to the business for the time being, it is questionable whether it is a wise policy in the long run from the viewpoint of building up confidence, understanding and goodwill. Cooperatives, because they believe it is unwise in the end and also because their members expect and demand full information, pursue the opposite policy of making their annual, quarterly and often monthly statements so complete and detailed that the members can see exactly what the current situation is, and can take up at once any financial problems which they feel require attention.

Lastly—and we might say first, too—comes the prevailing cooperative policy of selling goods, ordinarily, at the general market prices for such goods. Of course, the patronage returns mean that the final net prices which cooperative patrons pay are below the general market prices, and coincide with the actual cost of goods, except as part of the savings are reserved for operation. Then why not sell at cost in the beginning, it may be asked, and thereby eliminate the bother of calculating and distributing the patronage returns? Well, that apparently simple plan was tried in the early days before the present plan was adopted, and is still attempted from time to time and in some quarters. It has usually proved to be impractical and unwise as a business practice, for reasons which, once clearly understood, are convincing.

In the first place, it is next to impossible to know exactly in advance what the actual cost of goods is going to be. A cooperative retail store, for example, must include in its costs not only what it pays for the goods, but its operating expenses. If it is to continue operating it must also set aside reserves. It must allow for fluctuating prices of supplies, spoilage, and losses in transit. And only at the customary time of inventory and audit can it be sure of just how much its costs have been. If, therefore, it has sold the goods for only what it paid for them, it might find itself confronted with a deficit so serious that it would have to shut up shop. In fact, that is what most of the cooperatives who tried this plan were compelled to do. It is practicable only in the case of pool-buying for immediate distribution, with little or no overhead expense, or in other rare cases where the overhead can be figured exactly in advance. On the other hand, the plan of selling at market prices, figuring actual costs at the end of a given period, and then returning to patrons the difference between cost and the prices they paid at the store, keeps clear of all these difficulties.

A second and equally practical reason for selling at prevailing market prices is that this policy is less likely to arouse opposition on the part of profit-dealers. If a cooperative store were to open up in a certain neighborhood and begin to sell milk, butter, eggs, bread and other groceries at prices considerably below those at which commercial stores in the same neighborhood were selling the same things, it might very naturally expect that the commercial dealers would take offense and would be more than likely to make reprisals through concerted under-cutting. Indeed, they resort to such tactics even when the cooperatives sell at market prices. But they would certainly do so still more aggressively if the cooperatives sold below the market. This same consideration, of course, applies in a larger way to cooperative wholesales and productive plants, which likewise follow the policy of selling at market prices and handing back the savings.

My statement that this is the general cooperative policy was qualified by the word "ordinarily." At times and under circumstances where it becomes necessary for cooperatives to wage the most positive and effective warfare against monopolistic prices, or prices which have been run up to exorbitant heights by some form of commercial exploitation, they will sell at what they know to be reasonable prices in order to break such monopolistic control or exploitation. Most of the cooperative wholesales and productive plants, and many of the larger local units, have been compelled to do this from time to time in the interests not only of their own members but of all the consumers in their areas. Such action has usually resulted in lowering the general market prices for the commodities involved, with advantage to consumers generally. When the cooperatives are satisfied that prices have been brought down to a reasonable level, they return to what may be called their normal policy of selling at the market. Some of their greatest services, however, have been rendered by such emergency departures from this normal policy.

In conclusion, it should be clearly understood and emphasized that we have been dealing in the present chapter with the general principles and standards of consumers' cooperation, that is, with cooperatives more or less in the abstract. There is no assertion that all cooperatives embody these principles in the same way and to the same degree, or that all of them come fully up to these standards. In the ensuing chapters we shall deal with American cooperatives in the concrete and find interesting variations from the general pattern:— some cooperatives which embody the basic principles with practical completeness, others which incorporate them partly, some which measure well up to the standards, and others which in certain respects fall short. We shall see that in giving any particular con- sumers' cooperative its rightful place in the scale of values, the final and decisive question is that of the quantity and quality of its actual service to consumers.

In the comparisons which have thus far been made between cooperative principles and practice on the one hand, and those of profit business on the other, there has been no contention that all or a majority of the commercial concerns which are engaged in business for profit resort to practices which may rightly be called abuses. Nor is it a matter primarily of criticizing the individuals who are conducting business for profit, but rather the profit system itself. On that score, what one is willing to say without reservation is that in the profit system there is an inherent tendency for the profit motive to lead into profiteering, and from profiteering into racketeering of either respectable or unrespectable appearance. Business men of integrity and high standards keep these tendencies latent, so far as their own control extends. But the inherent tendency is still present, and unless it is thus held in leash it is liable to get away to an opportune start and keep going.

Consumers' cooperatives, though unescapably subject to frailties of human nature, preclude the profit motive, and thereby eliminate the tendency toward profiteering and racketeering as far as is humanly possible. Human nature is a constant factor in human affairs. Cooperators are human beings. By and large they constitute a representative cross-section of the community and the nation. But two things may be said about them which are undeniable. First of all, the very fact that they are engaged in *consumers'* cooperation, which is open to *everyone,* witnesses in itself that they want to work with and for their fellow human beings. In the second place, their working plan and the principles and policies which they adopt are such as are most likely to permit and promote the expression of those attributes and potentialities of human nature which best serve the common good.

IN THE TIME DIMENSION

Cooperatives to be measured adequately must be measured in four dimensions: length, breadth, thickness—and time. Their length (or what corresponds to length in a physical object) is the extent of their membership. Those which have a small membership are short and those of larger membership are longer. Their breadth is their cooperative vision, which is partly embodied in their present activities. In this respect some are narrow and others are broad. Their thickness consists of their capital and operating volume. Without sufficient thickness, in due proportion to length and breadth, they may be so exceedingly thin and bony that they rattle in their shoes and are shaky on their feet.

But even though a given cooperative qualifies in terms of length, breadth and thickness, its real and lasting success depends on its attainment of the time dimension. If a cooperative attains only a few years of that dimension it amounts to little more than a flash in the pan, no matter how bravely it started off and how impressive or promising its other dimensions were. But when it attains a time dimension of twenty-five, fifty or a hundred years, it is then soundly established on a foursquare foundation.

In the following chapters, therefore, I am going to describe American cooperatives from the viewpoint of their time dimension as well as their length, breadth and thickness at the moment. Some chapters which may appear at first glance to be historical are not such in the usual sense. They do not deal with what is past and gone, or with what is important only by way of background. On the contrary, they are meant to bring out what is not only present *but* indispensable, *namely, the time dimension which American cooperatives have now in various degrees attained. If I were merely to describe current cooperative activities, that would be not only inadequate but misleading. Such activities may be here today and gone tomorrow. In fact one of the chief faults of urban cooperatives in the past, as compared with those of rural character, has been that they have made a momentary splurge and fanfare, issued proclamations, launched projects and jumped into all sorts of activities which could be described most thrillingly—soon to fold their tents and vanish from the scene. But the rural co-operatives, starting quietly and sometimes almost unnoticeably, and going on in rather matter-of-fact fashion and without undue pretension, have successfully attained the time dimension which now at last the urban cooperatives are beginning to give real promise of attaining for themselves.*

Another virtue of the time dimension is that it runs into what we call the future as well as into what we call the past. As you follow its line of direction from the past to the present, you can look along that line and somewhat foresee or discern its future projection. Specifically, in the case of a given cooperative or the cooperative movement as a whole, this means that when you have for your guidance not only its present membership, volume and vision, but also its time dimension up to the present, and when you find that its other dimensions have grown along with that of time, you can then look ahead and with reasonable assurance forecast continuity and trend.

I would accordingly suggest to readers who wish to evaluate the American cooperative movement and form some estimate of its future, that they themselves bring this test of time to bear throughout the following account. The preceding chapters have simply posed the consumer's problem and outlined the working plan and principles of consumers' cooperation. Those which follow will tell the factual story of what American cooperatives are accomplishing.

6. AMERICAN FARMERS
LAY FOUNDATIONS

AMERICAN farmers laid the foundations of consumers' cooperation in the United States. That was fitting and auspicious. Farmers, as colonists and pioneers, had laid the foundations of the American nation itself. They cleared the wilderness, tilled the soil and brought forth sustenance for the nation's growth. From the Atlantic they pushed the nation's frontiers continually westward across the continent to the Pacific. They settled and cultivated that vast expanse, and by their brawn and brain, their patience, industry and enterprise, brought America to a place of primacy among all nations in the abundance of good things of the earth.

America, from the winning of its independence down to the time of the Civil War, when the Industrial Revolution's onward sweep put capitalists at the helm in this young land as well as in Europe, was a nation predominantly of farmers. George Washington was one of the largest and most progressive farmers in the original thirteen States. He taught his fellow-farmers in Virginia to rotate their crops and to plow a sloping field crosswise instead of up and down, in order to save the top-soil from being washed away by the rains. Thomas Jefferson and most of the founding fathers believed that

America would always remain a nation of farmers. Although they did not foresee the rise in later years of enormous cities and industrial centers, and the eventual preponderance of urban population, they were nevertheless right in the substance of their expectation. Farmers still constitute the nation's base. Town and city dwellers are dependent upon them for the raw materials of their food and clothing. Cities constantly draw fresh and invigorating blood and leadership from the rural areas. No element of the American people commands higher respect than its farmers. Nor is anything pertaining to "the state of the Union" more generally and whole-heartedly recognized than this fact, that the welfare of the nation's farmers is vitally essential to the sustained welfare and progress of the nation as a whole.

The ways in which American farmers have laid the sound foundations of consumers' cooperation in America will be shown in ample measure as we proceed. It is a story full of interest and importance not only for the farmers of today and tomorrow but for all Americans, because all alike whether farmers or townspeople are consumers. In the opening chapter I referred to consumers' cooperation as a mutation of capitalism, something in process of evolution as a new species of social-economic organization. Now we are about to observe the first stage of that evolutionary process in America.

It began among the farmers in a rudimentary way as soon as they found that they themselves needed the help of their fellows. The farmer is by training and tradition a rugged individualist, self-reliant, beholden to no employer, independent, something of an isolationist, a monarch in his own domain. But he is compelled to realize that he is pitted against another monarch of far greater power—a monarch whose name is Nature—and that in this unequal contest he cannot solve all of his practical problems by his own unaided efforts.

His first source of help is that which is nearest at hand, in his own family. Farm families take for granted a routine day-to-day cooperation to which city families are not commonly accustomed. The influence of city conditions on family life is centrifugal, while that of farm conditions is centripetal. How much the farmer's wife contributes is proverbial. Hers is a perpetual round of housework to the refrain of three square meals a day for the supposedly even harder working menfolk. As for the children, they are welcomed into the world for their own sake and as helpers, who almost as soon as they can toddle begin to take some little part in the daily chores. The older boys work in the fields with their father, the girls lend a hand around the house with their mother. Everyone has something to do.

Neighbors are always helping one another out with man, horse or tractor power, aiding one another to harvest crops, joining in groups to buy threshing machines for use turn and turn about, and so on. Nor is all such neighborly cooperation confined to matters practical and prosaic. Corn-huskings and barn-raisings end in recreation, with dancing to the fiddler's call, with

doughnuts, apples and sparkling cider. Farmers play as
well as work together.

COOPERATIVE FIRE INSURANCE

Rudimentary and occasional cooperation among
American farmers in the early days served as a kinder-
garten in preparing them for larger and more continuous undertakings. About the year 1820, or nearly a
century and a quarter ago, they began to apply the
cooperative idea to dealing with the losses caused by
fire in destroying farm buildings, stored crops and livestock. At that time there was little or no rural equipment for fighting fires; such equipment is still comparatively simple in farming areas. Once a fire got started
in a farm building there was slight possibility of saving
that building, and the main hope was to keep it from
spreading to adjacent buildings. The commercial business of fire insurance, which now bulks so large, was
then in its infancy, farm property was deemed a poor
risk, and consequently the rates quoted by commercial
companies for rural insurance were for most farmers
prohibitive. Under those circumstances farmers had to
stand their losses from fires as best they could, and
sometimes they were completely wiped out. So they
fared badly until they brought cooperation to bear
upon this problem.

About 1820 they began to organize local fire insurance groups of their own, within the area of a township
or sometimes a county. So far as available records show,
they did this spontaneously and independently in each

locality, and not in response to any central direction or in conformity with any general plan. It appears to have been a case of necessity being the mother of invention. There was a serious need and here was a practical way to meet it. No doubt the first group of this sort was formed on the initiative of some individual, and then the good news was circulated and the same idea took hold in other places.

At that time the term "cooperative" as applied to a specific form of organization was barely beginning to emerge. As noted in an earlier chapter, some cooperative communities and workshops were appearing—in most cases soon to disappear. Another quarter-century was to elapse before the Rochdale Pioneers opened their little store in a weavers' community in England and demonstrated the way of success for consumers' cooperation in the distribution of commodities. The American farmers of the 1820's undertook the distribution of a *service*—insurance. Had they chosen the term "cooperative" to describe their working plan, that would have been altogether suitable because, as we shall see, these self-serving insurance groups were fully cooperative in organization and operation. But they chose a term which was better known, especially in connection with insurance, the term "mutual," and called their groups farmers' mutual fire insurance companies. One practical reason for taking that name was that they could obtain charters and become incorporated as *mutual* insurance companies, whereas the laws of this country did not then—nor do they yet—provide for the incorporation of insurance companies to be known legally as *cooperative*. Companies of this nature must still be incorporated as mutuals in name, though there is a great deal of difference between them and some of the commercial companies which call themselves mutuals but are only partly so in fact.

Whether a company which is mutual in name is cooperative in fact, depends on the degree to which it applies the principle of mutuality, not only in its form of organization but in the actual control of its affairs and distribution of its benefits.

In traveling about the country I heard a good deal about the farmers' insurance groups and came upon them in many localities, especially in the Middle West. In order to get a well rounded view of them I talked with farmers who know them from the inside, with other people who come into contact with them in various ways, and with officers of commercial insurance companies who see them from something of a competitive standpoint. I have also discussed them rather fully with Dr. Victor N. Valgren, a Principal Agricultural Economist in the Cooperative Division of the Farm Credit Administration at Washington, who has carried on research in this particular field for many years and who generously assisted me with historical and other essential data. Further information regarding some interesting recent developments has been obtained from Mr. Harry P. Cooper, Secretary of the National Association of Mutual Insurance Companies, an organization whose activities will be mentioned later.

A COMPOSITE PICTURE

Without going into numerous but incidental variations of local detail in the farmers' companies themselves, and many differences in the state laws and regulations which apply to them, I shall try to sketch a sort of composite picture which will bring out their typical and salient features. It will have to be a telescoped motion picture as well, showing their beginnings, their geographical spread, their growth in number, their remarkable achievements, and their present importance and potentialities from the cooperative point of view. To trace each stage of their evolution from 1820 till today would be tedious and confusing. Suffice to say broadly that with the passage of time and the aid of state legislation which they themselves were mainly instrumental in securing, the companies have tended to grow larger in size, to expand their areas of operation from townships to counties or groups of counties, to include lightning and sometimes hail, windstorm and other risks, to extend their operation to village, town and even city property, to strengthen their operating resources and reserves, to improve their methods and results, and to join forces among themselves in cooperation on a larger scale.

A group of from twenty-five to fifty leading farmers living in a given township or county and owning between them insurable property worth $50,000 or more, would form a mutual company to provide insurance in that area. These farmers were familiar with local conditions and property values, and knew a good deal about the character, habits and trustworthiness of the other local farmers. The company could decline to issue policies to individuals who bore a poor reputation for carefulness or honesty, and it could depend on its policy-holders generally to play fair. Thus it was able to minimize what is known as the moral hazard, and save itself very largely from outlay on account of fires resulting from deliberate neglect or arson on the part of owners. That in itself gave the local company a big advantage in economy as compared with outside commercial companies having no such community status and incurring considerable losses on this score. The local company protected itself further by limiting the amount of each policy to two-thirds, or at most three-quarters, of the actual value of the property.

Overhead expenses were extremely modest. Except for a small per diem allowance for specific requirements such as attending meetings, the officers usually served without pay. Different farmers took turns in rendering such service and thus evened things up. It was not necessary to maintain an office, at least not until a company grew somewhat large. Solicitation of policies, which in the case of commercial companies entailed liberal outlay for commissions, was handled very simply. Farmers who wanted insurance often applied of their own accord. Sometimes an officer or other policy-holder would broach the matter to his neighbors. Gradually the practice grew of assigning a representative of the company to the task of soliciting, and allowing him to retain as compensation a small fee which was collected from each new policy-holder.

By thus reducing expenses and outlay to a minimum, the farmers' mutual was able to provide insurance at amazingly low rates, compared to those which commercial companies with their large expenditure for salaries, commissions, legal services, rent and incidentals, were able to offer. Furthermore, the farmers' company, instead of collecting premiums in advance like the commercial companies, usually waited until a fire occurred and a claim had to be settled, and then collected the necessary amount by a pro rata assessment of all the policy-holders who, at the time of taking out their policies, had accepted liability for such assessment. In fortunate years when no fires occurred or fire damage was small, the policy-holders got their insurance for little or nothing, and in any event they retained the use of their money themselves until it was needed. In later years, however, it became a rather common practice to collect estimated normal assessments on an annual basis in advance and make supplementary assessments from time to time if necessary. The only reserve maintained was a safety fund to cover operation and contingencies. That fund was created by setting aside a certain percentage of the fees and assessments, and tended to become more ample with experience. It was virtually the company's working capital, which cost it nothing and was deposited in a bank at interest.

There were no stockholders. The policy-holders were themselves the members of the company, and they

owned and controlled it. As a rule they had only one
vote each. They elected a board consisting usually of
nine directors, three of whom retired each year. The
board elected a president, vice-president, secretary, and
treasurer. The president, secretary and treasurer served
together as an executive committee. Annual meetings
were held at a fixed time. Special meetings could be
called by the directors or by petition of a certain proportion—usually a fourth—of the members. General
attendance of meetings was encouraged, and the individual policy-holders usually asserted themselves and
took an active part in the company's affairs.

SPREAD AND GROWTH

The movement began in the New England and Middle Atlantic states, spread westward through New York,
Pennsylvania, Ohio, Indiana and Michigan, reached its
maximum development in Illinois, Iowa, Minnesota
and Wisconsin, and overflowed into the Dakotas, Nebraska, Kansas, Oklahoma and Texas. Comparatively
few companies appeared further west and those were
widely scattered. That was likewise the case in a large
part of the South. In all probability a due percentage
of the companies eventually failed or ceased to exist,
owing to inadequate management, over-extension of
risks, disagreements or other factors. But statistics or
records of such mortality are almost wholly lacking,
especially for the early period when most of these farmers' mutuals were incorporated under special charters
and left to shift for themselves, without benefit of any

central help or guidance and without requirement of reporting to any State authority. So the demise of any which failed to survive went unrecorded. But by and large the companies appear to have shown remarkable vitality and persistence.

During the first half-century of their history their growth in numbers was not large. But after 1870, when the Grange (which will presently be described) got behind the movement, it gathered size and momentum. According to figures given me by Dr. Valgren, the number of companies which were formed in each decade from 1820 to the present, and which are still in operation, is as follows:

1820-1830	2
1830-1840	6
1840-1850	37
1850-1860	63
1860-1870	85
1870-1880	471
1880-1890	328
1890-1900	433
1900-1910	221
1910-1920	157
1920-1930	71
1930-1935	49

Total operating in 1935   1923

About the year 1880, largely through stimulation by the Grange, the local farm mutuals began to form voluntary and loosely organized State associations. There are now twenty-seven of these associations, though only two—those of North Dakota and California—include all of the local groups in their respective States. They hold annual meetings which usually last two days and take up matters of common interest, especially such joint action as may be necessary to forward favorable legislation in the state or resist hostile or competitive attempts to impede the movement's progress. These annual gatherings have helped to broaden the viewpoint and modify the over-independence of local groups, and to bring about a growing acceptance of methods and standards which make for increased efficiency. Further influence in the same direction has been exerted by the National Association of Mutual Insurance Companies, which was organized in 1896, mainly but not entirely by representatives of the farmers' fire insurance companies; and in ways similar to, but more sustained and extensive than, those of the State associations, has had an important part in furthering the advance. This national organization also includes a few large urban mutuals, and by bringing the farmers' groups into regular contact with them it has fostered better understanding and closer cooperation between rural and urban elements.

EXTRAORDINARY RESULTS

Today there are approximately 2000 of the local farmers' groups in the United States—1941 to be exact —with a total rural membership of about 3,000,000. This means that about 44 percent or nearly half of all

the farmers in the United States—that is, of the heads
of farming families—are policy-holding members of
these groups of their own creation. The average membership, including some small units at the bottom and
a few very large ones with exceptionally large areas of
operation at the top, is about 1500. The membership
of four-fifths of the companies is under 2000, and of
those which appear to be most typical in size it ranges
from 500 to 1000 persons. The amount of insurance
which all these companies combined now have in force
has reached the almost incredible total of $11,000,-
000,000. The fact that about 12 percent of this total
consists of insurance on village, town and city property
bears witness to the disposition of the farmers' groups
to expand their operations and give urban dwellers the
benefit of their service. The strictly rural insurance now
outstanding covers well over half of all the fire-insurable
farm property in the United States. It dwarfs the volume of any corresponding form of farmers' fire insurance in any other country in the world.

The assessment or premium rates of the farmers' companies are as a rule less than one-half of the rates
charged by commercial companies, and very frequently
they go still lower. One of the lowest costs is that of
the Svea Mutual Life Insurance Company of Orion,
Illinois, which provides insurance at eleven cents per
$100 and has some $30,000,000 of insurance now in
force. This company operates in three counties and
holds its annual meetings in each of them by turn, with
a big picnic on each occasion by way of neighborly

commingling and celebration. The representative of a
commercial company with whom I talked in Minnesota
mentioned one of the farmers' mutuals in that state
which charges twenty cents per $100 for the first year,
and after that—except as additional funds are needed—
no premium at all. The average cost for all the companies combined was in 1935 about twenty-four cents
per $100, as compared with commercial rates ranging
from about fifty cents to two dollars per $100. These
extraordinarily low costs not only save the three million
policy-holders an enormous amount of money, as compared with what they would have to pay commercial
companies for the same volume of insurance, but have
enabled a considerable proportion of these three million farmers, who otherwise could not have afforded to
carry insurance and would have had to stand fire losses
themselves, to protect their property and save themselves from such impoverishment. Of course, it is well
nigh impossible for the commercial companies with
their large overhead to compete with such low costs.
They look upon the modest farmers' groups with min-
gled feelings of admiration and envy, and are inclined
not to waste sales efforts in districts where they are
active but to devote their attention to other districts
not yet so fortunate.

With regard to the future of the farm mutuals, Dr.
Valgren's opinion is of special interest. He believes that
"the possibilities ahead of them far exceed, in economic
and social significance, what already has been accomplished." The opportunity which he stresses most

strongly is that of positive and constructive work in *preventing* farm fires, by such means as periodic and thorough inspection, systematic advice to and assistance of farmers in safer construction and upkeep of buildings, installation of water tanks and chemical fire extinguishers, and constant lessening of such common causes of fires as defective flues, soot accumulation in chimneys, rotting roofs and absence of lightning rods. Such stoppage at the source would, of course, save the companies themselves from many or most of the fire losses which they now have to stand, and would thereby still further reduce their rates. What is even more important, it would save the individual farmers and the townships, counties, states and nation, from vast losses in material property and human well-being. When fires destroy farm buildings, stored crops and livestock, those things are gone forever and cannot be recalled. Payment of insurance to the farmer simply helps him, to the extent of three-quarters of his loss, to begin again. The money which he receives is not newly created but only transferred from the insurance company to him. By working to prevent fires, however, the farmers' mutuals will conserve the wealth of the community and the nation.

THOROUGHGOING COOPERATIVES

In concluding this presentation of the farmers' mutual companies, which have carried on so quietly and simply that their achievements are not generally known and appreciated, I submit that they must be credited

with having laid the first solid and enduring foundations of consumers' cooperation in America. Consumption, as previously defined, means the using up of
utility in the satisfaction of wants. Assuredly the policy-
holders of these companies, from away back in 1820,
have been consumers of the utility or service rendered
by insurance on their homes and other farm property.
The working plan by means of which these American
farmers provided themselves with insurance was in substance the working plan of consumers' cooperation.
Large savings were effected and these savings were distributed to the patrons or policy-holders in the form
of exceedingly low costs. Those savings were the patronage returns. There was no profit for anyone. Limitation
of returns on capital was carried to the extreme of
zero, in that no stock was issued and no interest whatever was paid. The safety fund belonged to the company and was interest-free. The policy-holders with
equal votes owned and controlled the company. Nor
was such control merely nominal—as it is in the case of
most of the large commercial "mutual" insurance companies. Making due allowance for exceptions, the great
majority of companies were and are conducted in a thoroughly democratic way.

Hear what one of the farmer-leaders of this democratic insurance movement has to say about it. This man
is Mr. H. P. Hostetter of Illinois, who presided at the
National Association's session in Philadelphia on October 13, 1936, at which the progress of the farmers'
mutual groups was the special topic of the day.

"Only a city like Philadelphia replete with historic landmarks could have furnished such an opportunity to refresh in our minds those great historical events that attended the founding of our Nation," said Mr. Hostetter in opening the meeting. "Here we should have an opportunity to express our patriotism and thus restore confidence in our American institutions as they were conceived and dedicated in the founding of our Republic. Along with the Declaration of Independence and our Constitution mutual insurance was born. Mutual insurance has been the Declaration of Independence of our people from the great capitalistic organizations whose principal object has been to make a profit on the protection they had to sell. Without the competition of our mutuals these profits would have been unlimited. Our farmers were among the first to be exploited by these organizations. The farmers without redress from these exorbitant charges were forced to go to their legislatures and obtain special charters to organize their own companies. . . . The stock company agents sought to belittle and ridicule these local farm organizations, but they could not be stampeded by such tactics."

With regard to the remarkable record of solvency of the farmers' mutual groups during the current depression, and their stupendous volume of insurance, Mr. Hostetter continued: "How did these companies, without capital, without assets, without surplus, accomplish this miracle, as it were? They had something the stock companies did not have. They had a responsive membership. A membership that during the worst depression in history, met their obligations and paid their neighbors' losses. . . . Let us remember that the strength of mutual insurance lies in the loyal and responsive membership. By keeping fresh the ideals of our founders our farm mutual companies will continue to serve and protect their membership in the future as they have in the past. The spirit of neighborly helpfulness must be maintained."

It is clear beyond question that though these farmers' insurance groups are known as mutuals, they are fully cooperative in character and embody the essential principles of *consumers'* cooperation. In fact, it would be impossible to find, I think, any more completely cooperative groups than these are in every way. They are a native American growth, and began to appear in this country a quarter-century before the advent of the Rochdale Pioneers in England. The wide expanse of territory over which they extended is roughly the same as that in which the American cooperative movement has subsequently made its most impressive headway. They have served as the primary school of American cooperation, and have done much to prepare the soil and pave the way for its general progress. Today they constitute an extraordinary achievement in themselves and a massive foundation for cooperative building. Because of their own modesty, these groups have been somewhat overlooked by younger and perhaps more aggressive members of the American cooperative family. But by virtue of seniority and total accomplishment, they are entitled to a place at the head of the board.

7 . GRANGE PIONEERING

SHORTLY after the close of the Civil War, the first national organization of American farmers came into being. It was called the Order of Patrons of Husbandry, but became popularly known as the Grange. The word "grange" means a farm, or more especially the farm home and its cluster of buildings. Used by the Patrons to designate their local, state and national bodies, it came to serve as a short and simple name for the Order as a whole. From its beginning to the present day the Grange has been a great social, educational and economic force among American farmers, and has become a deeply rooted institution and tradition whose beneficence and permanence are taken for granted. In relation to other organizations of farmers which arose in later years, the Grange occupies the respected place of a progenitor that is living, vigorous, and of commanding stature.

Grange pioneering marked another stage in the evolution of consumers' cooperation in America, and was responsible for its progress from the distribution of insurance to the distribution of commodities. The story of why and how that pioneering was undertaken and what it accomplished, is so important that it should be told; and to be told at all adequately, calls by way of background for some reference to conditions in the

United States at that time and for at least an outline drawing of the Grange itself. This is one of the most humanly interesting and warm-hearted societies in America, and its story is a national epic to be cherished.

Up to the time when the conflict between North and South threatened to split the American nation apart, agriculture was the dominant influence in the country's economic and political life. The power of Northern capitalism and industrialism, however, was steadily growing. The Industrial Revolution, already far advanced in Great Britain and continental Europe, was getting ready to go full steam ahead in America. Under war conditions the manufacturing and commercial interests got the upper hand and have kept it ever since. Farmers became increasingly aware of this deep-reaching change in the situation and its practical bearing on their own well-being, notwithstanding the fact that for agriculture as well as for business and industry the decade which ended in the panic of 1873 was a period of tremendous expansion. Eastern farmers, especially the younger men who were growing up and others who were looking for fresher ground or felt the stirrings of adventure, migrated westward to the prairie states and established themselves on free homesteads granted by the federal government. A great influx of European immigrants helped to fill the wide open spaces. This agricultural expansion in itself stimulated the minds and energies of the country's farmers and made them more assertive in their protests against capitalistic and commercial exploitation.

Their bill of grievances, omitting details and incidentals, consisted chiefly of the following complaints: The railroads, while of course they enabled farmers to ship their crops to distant markets, charged excessive and discriminatory rates; and the middlemen who bought the crops paid too little for them. So the farmers did not have much to show for all their effort. The so-called protective tariff was framed for the benefit of the manufacturing and trading classes, and enabled retailers and commission men to charge exorbitant prices for the goods which farmers had to buy. Farmers were caught and squeezed in the vise of credit, and were burdened with farm mortgages on which they paid high rates of interest to Eastern money-lenders who sent agents out to drum up loans. Powerful business interests controlled state and national legislation. All in all, farmers and agriculture were relegated to an inferior place and the cards were stacked against them.

Feeling thus oppressed, and pondering what they could do about it, the farmers observed that the business interests whom they held accountable for their hardships were well organized. This turned their minds toward the idea of applying organization to their own situation. An illuminating comment on their reflections is made by Dr. S. J. Buck in his book, *The Granger Movement*. "In casting about for a remedy," he says, "it was but natural that they should look for examples to those other classes of society which had been forging so rapidly ahead. The one thing which presented itself again and again in almost every other industry, but which appeared to be lamentably lacking in agriculture, was organization—the organization and cooperation, for their mutual advantage, of those whose interests coincided. The manufacturers were united into stock companies and more or less vague associations; the merchants had their commercial organizations; the bankers and brokers, their stock-exchanges and clearing houses; and even the laboring men were beginning to find and assert their common interests in trade unions."

The time was therefore ripe for some program of concerted action among farmers. There was real need for a national organization, and a plan was brought forth to meet that need. In its origin that plan was an imaginative invention; it proved well suited to its purpose. The leading inventor was Oliver Hudson Kelley, a New Englander by birth and a Minnesota farmer by migration, who was appointed to a clerkship in the agricultural bureau at Washington and in 1866 assigned to travel through the South and gather information regarding agricultural conditions. During that field trip he conceived his plan for a national society of farmers. As he was a member of the Masonic Order he naturally pictured a society which would have the character and color of a fraternity, with certain rites, ceremonies and degrees. The following year he began to develop that plan and enlisted the cooperation of half a dozen other government clerks, some of whom owned farms at the time and all of whom had been born and reared on farms. These seven men—a Biblical number—met in Washington on December 4, 1867, constituted themselves the National Grange of the Patrons of Husbandry, and elected Kelley as secretary in charge of further organization.

The structural plan included local, county and state Granges heading up in the national body, seven graduated degrees for men and four for women. One feature which was remarkably progressive for that day was that the Grange proposed to admit women on a basis of full equality with men. That was a richly merited recognition of the part which farmers' wives have in farm economy and rural life. Such full participation of women in the Grange has always been one of its greatest sources of strength. The annual dues were set very low so that anyone could afford to join. The provisions regarding eligibility were so liberal that not only farmers but other people who were in sympathy with the objects could be admitted to membership. The primary objects were social and educational—to provide American farmers and their friends in each locality with a social nucleus and gathering place, where they could come together for respite from the toil and tedium of farming, enjoy simple, neighborly recreation, and through lectures and discussion educate themselves to become better farmers and better citizens. Meetings were to begin with a business session, which would train members in orderly methods of procedure; to pass from that to the lecture hour, "with discussion of vital questions"; proceed to the Degree Work, which "beautifully illustrates the seasons and symbolizes the loftiest ideals in human living"; and conclude with the social hour of "wholesome association of helpful people" by which "members are enriched in proportion as they contribute." Regular meetings of this kind were to be supplemented by fairs, suppers, dramatic events, debates, contests and community service projects—"all calculated to set the members doing a variety of things" on the principle "that a busy Grange is an achieving Grange."

The first local Grange, Potomac No. 1, was set up at Washington, D. C., to serve as a testing ground and training school in ritual and methods of organization. It is still in existence and has a distinguished membership of national farm leaders and government officials who are especially interested in agriculture. The first unit composed of rank and file farmers was launched at Fredonia, N. Y. But it was in the Middle West and some sections of the South that the Grange movement first took hold vigorously and attained volume. Thenceforth its growth was phenomenal. By the close of 1873 there were some ten thousand local units distributed through all but five of the states, thirty-two State Granges were in operation, and the total membership was about half a million. At the sixth session of the National Grange in that year the original organizers, Kelley and his associates, feeling that they had fulfilled their task, handed the reins over to the "dirt farmers," who from that time on have directed the Grange as a fraternity of American farmers in their own right.

Meanwhile, under stress of commercial exploitation and in face of the panic of 1873, local and state Granges

were more and more insistently pressing the national
body to sponsor a program which would help to
relieve their economic hardships and improve their
material condition. In response to that widespread demand the next session, held at St. Louis in 1874 and
called the "most representative gathering of farmers
which had ever taken place in the United States,"
adopted a "Declaration of Purposes of the National
Grange" which has stood from that day to this as the
Grange platform, and the principles of which have been
largely incorporated into the platforms of all subsequent farmers' associations in America. It was a rather
long document, from which, within limits of present
space, I can cite only those parts which pertain most
closely to the subject in hand. Those particular sections
put the Grange on record as "opposed to excessive
salaries, high rates of interest and exorbitant profits in
trade" and as discountenancing "the credit system, the
mortgage system, the fashion system, and every other
system tending to prodigality and bankruptcy." The
Grange, this statement declared, was not an enemy of
capital but was against "the tyranny of monopolies."

On the positive side, as a means of mitigating the economic problems, the Grange proposed "to foster mutual
understanding and cooperation" through "buying together, selling together, and, in general, acting together,
for our mutual protection and advancement, as occasion
may require." "For our business interests we desire to
bring producers and consumers, farmers and manufacturers, into the most direct and friendly relations possi-

ble. Hence, we must dispense with a surplus of middle-men, not that we are unfriendly to them, but we do not need them. . . . All our acts, and all our efforts, so far as business is concerned, are not only for the benefit of the producer and consumer, but also for all other interests that tend to bring these two parties into speedy and economical contact. . . . For we seek the greatest good to the greatest number."

COSTLY EXPERIENCE

But these broad declarations lacked specifications. No definite working plan was put forward as a practical way of accomplishing the desired results. In its progress toward sound cooperation the Grange had not yet gone farther than obtaining trade discounts on the basis of pooled orders. To that end the national body had for a couple of years been distributing among state and local granges lists of merchants and manufacturers who would sell goods to them at wholesale prices if ordered in large lots. The local and state units, however, had already begun to buy in that way themselves, without any guidance from the national headquarters, and they were getting into difficulties — especially the state Granges.

Such buying as was done directly by the local and county units was comparatively modest, and worked out fairly well when the orders were assembled and for-warded by a Grange member who rendered this service without compensation, other than sharing in the savings thus effected, or for a small salary. Purchasing at wholesale prices or special discounts, in bulk lots which were locally apportioned, Grange farmers throughout the country saved themselves an amount of money which in the total must have been very large. The transactions were simple and easily handled.

But there was pressure for operations on a larger scale. The state Granges undertook more ambitious projects. At first, in order to avoid drawing on their own treasury funds, they appointed state agents—who sometimes were not Grange members or even farmers themselves—to serve them on a brokerage or commission basis. Under that plan the state agent assembled orders from the local units in that state, bought the goods at wholesale or special prices, and then distributed them to the Grange constituency at prices which included brokerage or commission fees for himself but were still below prevailing retail prices. On its face this procedure looked expedient, but it proved to be pernicious, particularly when the agents were not members of the Grange, or had joined it with ulterior motives. Under such circumstances the agents tended to conduct their operations not primarily for the benefit of the Grange but for that of their own pocketbooks. Those whose standards of integrity were deficient found opportunities for additional profit in deals with merchants and manufacturers, and were lenient in the quality of goods which they distributed. Abuses became more flagrant in certain cases where the state Granges selected commercial firms as their agents, or morally guaranteed them as dealers for Grange patronage. When some of these firms went into bankruptcy or became otherwise discredited, the Grange shared the stigma and lost prestige.

Meanwhile the state organizations were plunging in still deeper. They had been casting envious eyes at a reserve of $100,000 which the National Grange carried in its treasury. They persuaded the national body to distribute half of that sum among them, in amounts proportionate to their size, and with the funds thus freely obtained they expanded their operations and undertook the manufacture of farm machinery. Some of these enterprises did very well while they were held within reasonable limits. Headers, harvesters and other machines were supplied at about one-half of the commercial prices. But such initial successes led on to excesses of overproduction which, combined with underservicing and some bad failures in quality and workability, resulted in quick financial failure of those manufacturing adventures.

By that time the credit and debit account of the Grange stood about as follows: On the credit side, the local, county and state Granges had by means of pool-buying and manufacturing saved their members a tremendous amount of money, and in doing so they had unexpectedly demonstrated that the methods which they followed were unsound. Of course, the second result did not look like a gain, but nevertheless it was, because it pointed the need and opened the way for better methods. On the debit side there was a long and sorry list of entanglements, errors, failures and fiascos. No

doubt the generally depressed conditions brought on by
the panic of 1873 were partly blamable for Grange
disasters, as they were for many other business calamities at that time. But after making due allowance for
those conditions, it remains true that unsound methods
were responsible very largely for Grange catastrophes,
which were so numerous and widespread that they in
turn, along with the depression and natural reaction
from too rapid growth, had much to do with a sudden
decline of Grange membership and resources that began
in 1875. In some states the organization completely
disappeared. The national body, with a reduced treasury and shrinking income, was compelled to retrench
heroically.

MOMENTOUS ACTION

But at that very crisis in its fortunes came the positive,
constructive and enduring contribution of the National
Grange to the advancement of sound cooperation in
America. This momentous action was taken at the
annual session in November, 1875, in Louisville, Ken-
tucky. It proved to be so decisive in furthering the
evolution of the American cooperative movement that
I have gone back to the Grange journal of proceedings
for the year 1875 in order to be sure of the facts.

First the National Grange roundly condemned the
brokerage or commission plan to which most of the state
Granges had resorted and recommended the abolition of
all commission agencies still existing. The following
Resolution was adopted: "That in the opinion of this

Executive Committee the commission system in business is at variance with cooperative principles, and that its results, as conclusively shown to this committee, have disappointed the expectations of our members."

This conclusion may well be pondered today by some cooperative organizations which have adopted the brokerage or commission plan. The immediate and rather alluring advantages of that plan are that it enables an organization to carry on a large volume of operation with comparatively small resources in the form of fixed assets and working capital. By obtaining goods from commercial dealers on consignment without purchasing them outright, and then transmitting to the dealers the proceeds from the sale of their goods, with a liberal commission deducted, an organization can apparently fare pretty well with little investment on its own responsibility. But an organization which follows this plan is liable to get more and more deeply involved in the disadvantage of serving merely as a distributing agent for the commercial dealers, and may eventually find itself so fully in their power, through extension of credit, favors, and inside understandings which the organization would dislike to have known, that it has to tread on eggs for fear of offending these dealers, and hardly dares to call its soul its own. I have encountered several organizations which are in that sorry fix, and which I would not feel justified in describing as cooperative in the full sense. This observation applies not only to the distribution of commodities, but to that of insurance and other services.

After denouncing the commission system, the National Grange called for the adoption of a uniform cooperative business system throughout the organization. This system included local cooperative stores and district wholesales, and laid down rules or principles to govern their organization and conduct. Shares at $5.00 each were to be subscribed by the individual members, but no member could own more than a limited number. Returns on the shares were restricted to a fixed interest. Each of the shareholders was to have only one vote, regardless of the number of shares he owned. Goods were to be sold for cash and no credit extended; and were to be sold not at cost but at prevailing market prices. Finally the net savings were to be distributed not to shareholders but to patrons, in proportion to their patronage.

In substance, though evidently not in direct derivation, these rules may be regarded as an adaptation, for use in the cooperative distribution of commodities, of the simple rules which from 1820 onwards had proved so successful among American farmers in the cooperative distribution of insurance. The Grange had found that movement well under way and got behind it. Feeling that such farmers' insurance groups were well suited to its purpose, it encouraged Grange members to organize them in every locality where the order flourished. The figures given in the preceding chapter showed how suddenly and sharply the number of such companies increased as soon as the Grange took hold. In so far as the Grange sponsored and furthered that movement, the results can be put in the front rank of its successful achievement. How far it analyzed the inherent reasons for the strength and progress of the insurance groups, and consciously applied the same principles in working out rules for the stores, cannot be said with certainty, though we may reasonably presume that such a demonstration before the very eyes of Grange members and leaders must have influenced their thought.

But things which appear obvious in retrospect are often unnoticed at the time. The cooperative plan of providing insurance could not have been applied exactly as it stood to the distribution of commodities, but would have required some translation and amendment. Democratic control by policy-holders would have had to be translated into democratic control by shareholders, and patronage returns in premium savings into patronage returns of cash savings. A cooperative insurance group proceeded immediately to sell a service which it did not have to buy but created, and therefore needed little or no initial capital. A store had to buy a stock of goods and some equipment before it could begin to operate, and therefore had to obtain working capital at the outset through share subscription. These differences in appearance may have obscured the likeness in substance between cooperative distribution of insurance and cooperative distribution of goods.

In any event the records indicate that the Grange based its system for cooperative stores upon the successful development of consumers' cooperation in England after the Rochdale Pioneers opened their little provisions shop in 1844. Grange leaders were in correspondence with leaders of the cooperative movement in England, in 1875, and representatives of the English movement visited a number of Grange centers in America about the same time. But the journal of proceedings makes it clear beyond question that the system which the National Grange outlined and recommended was the product of long and careful study on the part of the Executive Committee, and that it embodied many provisions born of Grange experience and an understanding of American conditions.

In outlining the proposed system to the Grange assembly, the Executive Committee's spokesman stated that this committee had been making a study of the subject for about five months; and was unanimously behind the plan now submitted for consideration. He then proceeded to read the document which the committee had drawn up, and which was so comprehensive and detailed that it filled seven closely printed pages in the journal. It was certainly a thorough-going job, that anticipated and made specific provision for about every imaginable requirement or eventuality. My own summary will be sufficient only to show its character and tenor. It was in three parts, namely, "Advice to Members," "Preface," and "Rules." The advice stressed the necessity for sound business procedure, especially competent management, frequent and full financial statements, and strictly cash operation: "Never depart from the principle of buying and selling for cash." The preface reiterated that principle: "Successful cooperation is dependent upon quick exchanges for cash and *cash only*." It noted that selling at cost instead of at prevailing prices was likely to arouse commercial prejudice, and indicated that the proposed system looked to economies which could be effected and working capital which could be provided through cooperative purchasing.

The rules were arranged in the form of a full set of regulations or by-laws for a cooperative store dealing in "merchandise, farm products and machinery, for the mutual benefit of its shareholders and customers." All in all, there were forty-four of these rules, the last one concerning amendments. As I mentioned the most important features in an earlier paragraph, I need not repeat them. Consideration for needs and exigencies of members was shown by ample provision for redeeming shares and permitting members to withdraw up to twenty-five dollars of their share capital on demand and more on ninety days' notice. But there was no softness in the matter of credit; once again cash operation was specified. There were to be quarterly meetings and quarterly audits. Income was to be applied first to operating expenses, depreciation and interest on shares; net proceeds to building up working capital, forwarding educational or provident objects, and making distributions to patrons in proportion to their purchases. Patrons who were not Grange members would receive such distributions at one-half the member rate. The reserve for education was set at $2\frac{1}{2}$ per cent of the net. Surplus capital of local stores could be invested in cooperative wholesales. Salaries of officers were to be determined not by the directors but by the members. To forestall undue control by management it was specified that no employee could serve as a director or auditor. Once a store was set up in a given district, no other Grange store should be organized in the same area. In other words there was to be cooperation among the cooperators.

Several days after this human document was placed before the Grange assembly and printed for study, the matter was brought up again for final action. Up to then there had been no mention of Rochdale, but at this session the Executive Committee's spokesman "explained at length the system of cooperation known as the Rochdale plan, on which the system reported by the Committee is based." After some discussion, the National Grange approved the cooperative system which the Executive Committee had formulated. In adopting that plan the Grange showed that it had profited from its own experimentation sufficiently to be willing and able to incorporate and naturalize the elements of a successful experiment in another country. It sponsored and interpreted the composite plan, disseminated it in printed form among Grange members throughout the country, and proceeded through local and state Granges to demonstrate its feasibility.

Hundreds of cooperative stores were organized by local, county and state Granges in communities which had not been hit too hard by the previous failures. Many of these stores, however, embodied the right principles only in part and violated them in other ways, such as selling goods at cost instead of at market prices, extending credit, and permitting voting by shares of stock instead of on an equal footing. In this connection it should be said that the laws of some states made it impossible to organize stores on a completely cooperative basis and necessitated following the stock company plan of voting and dividends. With comparatively few exceptions the stores which did not or could not adhere to the Rochdale rules soon failed or lost their cooperative character. Of those which did stick to the rules, some failed on account of the depression and others through poor management, but the number which succeeded was sufficient to prove that the plan itself was as sound in America as it was in England.

In Texas, for example, cooperative stores began to appear in 1875 and in three years grew strong enough to form the Texas Cooperative Association to serve as their wholesale. By 1887 the wholesale's capital had increased from an original $250 to $50,000, its annual business was upwards of $500,000, and yearly savings passed back to the retail stores amounted to $20,000. In the same period the number of stores had grown to 150 with a combined capital of $750,000, annual sales of $2,000,000 and yearly savings to members of $250,000. In fact these stores were making such remarkable headway that competing commercial interests got together about that time and obtained legislation which prevented the formation of any more cooperative stores in that state until recent years. In New England, New York, Pennsylvania and Delaware, similar stores did well in a smaller way. Clear across the continent, in

the states of Washington and Oregon, another cluster
kept on sturdily.

By and large, a goodly number continued for as long
a time as the usual life-span of commercial stores, and
then passed away under the same wear and tear, hard
times and vicissitudes which took toll of business generally. But even today, some sixty years after their
inception, a respectable residue of those early stores are
still in operation here and there over the country,
though the fact that they were originally launched by
the Grange is not always known to the present generation in their communities. In this new land sixty years
is a long time.

CONSTRUCTIVE INFLUENCE

Although the espousal of consumers' cooperation on
a sound basis did not come soon enough to save the
Grange from a difficult period of recession and rehabili-
tation, the cooperative activity and results which grew
out of that espousal did save the organization from what
would otherwise have been a still more severe setback,
and helped it gradually to renew its prestige and resume
its progress. Today it is established in thirty-five states
and has a total membership of about three-quarters of
a million men and women. It is still primarily a social
and educational fraternity devoted to the advancement
of agriculture and rural life, and is now strongest in
New England and the North Atlantic states. Through
its constant activity in educating its own members and
the public to a better understanding of social and eco-

nomic problems, and its sponsorship or support of state and federal legislation designed to cope with these problems, its influence has been brought to bear, down through the years, in a broad and constructive way.

The Grange is not a radical organization in the loose but common usage of that term. It is not wild or revolutionary in its character and objects. On the contrary, it is truly conservative, in that it stands for the preservation and application, in the nation's social, economic and political life, of fundamental American principles. "We desire a proper equality, equity and fairness"; the Grange Creed declares, "protection for the weak, restraint upon the strong; in short, justly distributed burdens and justly distributed power. These are American ideals, the very essence of American independence, and to advocate the contrary is unworthy of the sons and daughters of the American republic."

For its challenge of privilege and championship of democracy, under the changed conditions of industrialization and capitalistic domination which have prevailed in the United States since the time of the Civil War, the Grange merits a high place in American history. Judged by tangible and growing results, its pioneering in the field of consumers' cooperation must be put in the forefront of its accomplishment. That pioneering advanced the evolution of cooperation in the United States from provision of insurance to distribution of commodities. It implanted sound principles of consumers' cooperation in American soil, and opened up that field to Grange members and to other rural and urban groups, who in recent years as we shall see have tilled and reaped exceedingly well.

The cooperative banner which the Grange unfurled in its early years still flies from its ramparts. A recent conclave of the National Grange, which brought leaders and representatives together from all parts of the country, voiced this clarion call: "For fifty years the Grange has led the way in doing the educational work for cooperative organizations, and we should at this time emphasize the importance of cooperation in buying and selling. . . . Cooperative associations have continually been fought by those who for selfish reasons seek their destruction. . . . We must rededicate ourselves to this cause." This was meant not for the Grange alone, but for all Americans who have ears to hear.

PEREGRINATION

One way to get an impressive sense of the place which farming holds in our national life is to pay a visit to the vast and imposing edifice of the Department of Agriculture in Washington. If you do so on a boiling day in midsummer, as I did last August, the impression is almost overpowering. But whether the weather be hot or cold, to behold and explore that great temple of husbandry is an unforgettable experience. It is a majestic building, not crowded in among others but standing spaciously by itself, as though in symbolization of the farmer's rugged independence of character.

When you enter this edifice, gaze down along the interminable corridors, espy cross-corridors in row after row, see galaxies of elevators going up-up-up, and realize that the floor on which you stand is only one of many which are just as bewildering, or maybe more so—well, you forthwith decide, as one usually does in a big art museum, to confine your exploration to a limited area for the time being and leave the rest for another time. Nevertheless, in a helpless and desultory sort of way I wandered around a bit, perhaps a mile or two, and fell to wondering how many days it would take an able-bodied pedestrian to cover all the ground on every floor, and how far into space all the longitudinal and latitudi-

*nal corridors would extend if they were stretched out
end to end.*

*After encountering so many Bureaus, Divisions, Proj-
ects and What-nots that my eyes fairly swam with them,
I eventually arrived in the South Building, Wing 7,
Room 1768, and there found Mr. Donald E. Montgomery, Consumers' Counsel in the Agricultural Adjustment Administration. I found him friendly, unassum-
ing, unhurried, discerning, and withal a very human
being. Here is an excerpt, not in quotes but in substance, from the conversation which ensued.*

*Mr. Montgomery, I asked, when so many people and
interests are banging away at the farmer to think of
himself only as a producer and agricultural capitalist,
so incessantly that he is often unable to think of himself
in any other way, how comes it that right here in the
Department which is the farmer's stronghold one discovers the only public Consumers' Counsel in the entire
country? Are you perhaps trying to save the farmer from
himself, and from those who call themselves, or think
they are, his friends? Is this the Adjustment part of the
Triple A?*

*Well, he replied, I guess that's about it. What we're
working toward is to help the farmer to become more
conscious of himself and his rights and potentialities as
a consumer. Of course, all farmers are consumers, like
everybody else, and as a matter of fact they are in a better position than urban consumers to recognize the
spread between the prices they get for what they sell and
the prices they have to pay for what they buy. That is*

especially true when they sell their crops through marketing cooperatives, because they have to sell at wholesale prices, and unless they buy through purchasing cooperatives they have to pay retail prices for the farm supplies and household goods they need. But they are learning from experience, and coming to see things more and more from the consumer's point of view. Our Consumers' Guide *now has a circulation of more than one hundred thousand. The fact that this is about equally divided between rural and urban people is significant of the trend.*

When farmers attempt to better themselves through cooperative marketing alone, Mr. Montgomery continued, that is like trying to cut cloth with shears of one blade. Furthermore, when farmers confine themselves to a program of serving their interests as sellers, they may thereby defeat their own interests as buyers. Because probably one-third of the money which farmers spend in the purchase of commodities is spent for goods originating on other farms. Farmers are one another's customers. Organization for marketing alone may serve to divide them. But when they organize to buy cooperatively, they have a purpose which serves to unite all *farmers in a common cause.*

This commonsense fact, he concluded, is gradually coming to be more fully understood. Farmers are beginning to see that after all their income from farm produce is a means to an end, and that the end is increased consumption of tangible and intangible goods which will raise their standards of living to permanently higher levels. From this viewpoint they are also beginning to see that there is no real conflict of interests between farmers and urban consumers. The better off urban consumers are, the more farm products they can buy, and their increased buying will make the farmers better off. The most vital thing of all which both rural and urban consumers are coming to comprehend is that consumer's cooperation can restore to the individual citizen a genuine opportunity for the exercise of his initiative and influence in the control of his own and the nation's economic affairs.

8. CURRENT TRENDS

THE inherent soundness of cooperative purchasing and its remarkable progress in recent years will stand out more clearly if at this point we differentiate it from another kind of cooperation, namely, cooperative marketing, and consider the latter sufficiently to appreciate the relationship, incidental resemblance, and fundamental unlikeness of these two forms of cooperative activity.

Their relationship has been one of common origins and close association, but of divergent character and aims. Like cooperative purchasing, cooperative marketing in America has developed mainly among farmers, as a means of selling their produce more advantageously. Here, of course, we are still using the term cooperation in its specific sense, which does not apply to so-called cooperative combinations of chain stores, merchants, manufacturers, and middlemen of one sort or another. Such things are more in the nature of trusts or trade agreements, which follow the accustomed lines of commercial business. For that matter, there is such a wide variety of structure and methods among the farm marketing organizations themselves that it is sometimes hard to tell, without close scrutiny, which are really cooperatives and which are not. To pass muster as a cooperative the organization should at least have a foundation of democratic control and should distribute its net proceeds among those who make use of its services, in proportion to their patronage. The patrons of a marketing cooperative are those whom it serves by marketing their produce.

A few small and scattered marketing cooperatives appeared among American dairy farmers as far back as 1810, and among grain-raisers about 1850. Around 1870 the marketing movement began to grow in a much larger and more widespread way. That was the time, it will be recalled, when the Grange came on the scene. The Grange went in for marketing along with buying, and was largely responsible for a spurt in marketing activity. But its early marketing adventures did not fare any better than its first false starts in purchasing through commission agents. The fact that the same agents handled buying and selling may have been one reason why both caved in. These are distinctly different operations, which have different objects and call for different methods and abilities. Though subsequent experience has shown that they can be conducted by the same organization and that this is sometimes expedient for reasons of convenience and overhead economy, experience has also shown that in such cases it is advisable to handle these operations through separate departments, and that the major tendency is toward completely separate and specialized organizations which devote themselves either to marketing or to purchasing. The Grange agencies were set up too haphazardly and were too short-lived to be departmentalized. After those hit-or-miss attempts went on the rocks the Grange appears to have eased off somewhat on the marketing side and turned its attention to cooperative purchasing through stores organized on the Rochdale plan of consumers' cooperation.

Most of the marketing cooperatives which came into existence after 1870 were small local affairs, handling livestock, grain, fruits and vegetables, milk and processed dairy products. About 1890 these local units began to form district and regional federations which undertook marketing on a larger scale, arranged transportation, collected payment for produce and distributed the proceeds, formulated and supervised regulations for local grading and packing, and in general worked to standardize marketing operations and promote their success. Such federations, owned and controlled by the local units, held the field until about 1920. Then a burst of promotional activity by some new and enthusiastic leaders resulted in the meteoric rise of many highly centralized and ambitious marketing associations. These were not federations of local units, but enlisted great numbers of individual farmers—fully six hundred thousand altogether—over areas so large that regular contact between the central headquarters and the members was practically impossible and autocratic management was almost inevitable. These associations, specializing in major agricultural products, aimed at "orderly marketing" to the point of complete control of supply and dictation of price. In short, they wanted to become monopolies. But though they expended an enormous amount of money they did not succeed in the attempt. Within a few years this soaring movement was deflated, leaving widespread disappointment in its wake.

Those were tough years for farmers, because the depression struck agriculture about ten years before it extended to industry and was acutely felt in the cities. The Agricultural Marketing Act was adopted in 1929 as a measure of relief through government assistance. Large-scale marketing operations were resumed, and advanced from regional to national magnitude. The most grandiose project launched at that time was the Farmers National Grain Corporation. It had been preceded by three similar undertakings which failed: U. S. Grain Growers, Inc., born 1921, died 1924; Grain Marketing Co., born 1924, died 1925; and National Farmers' Elevator Grain Co., born 1925, died 1928. The fourth structure was erected on an underpinning of twenty-seven regional associations. This new corporation was financed by government loans which enabled it to open offices in Chicago and the other principal grain markets and to engage in operations of extraordinary scope. But now it is evidently going the way of its predecessors. On November 22, 1937, its directors adopted a resolution which called for dissolution of the Farmers National Grain Corporation, with the understanding that its marketing operations would be taken over by regional associations for "geographic areas covering the entire grain of the country." This action was duly ratified by the stockholders on January 25, 1938. An account which appeared in the *New York Times* of December 1st stated that the Corporation had not operated at a profit in any of the eight years of its existence, and estimated that the government's total loss in the venture might run to twenty million dollars. "Today's action," says a *Times* dispatch in referring to the stockholders' ratification, "brings to an end the eight-year-old attempt to establish a successful national system of cooperative marketing for grain producers."

But although the death-rate of marketing cooperatives has been high, their birth rate has been still higher. In the peak year of 1920 no less than 1779 of them came into existence. Today they bulk large in number, membership and operating volume. According to the latest figures available, which are those for the 1935-36 marketing season, there are 8,388 farmers' marketing cooperatives in the United States, ranging from small local units, mostly, up to countrywide bodies, with a total membership of about 2,710,000 and a combined operating volume of approximately $1,586,000,000. In order of volume the agricultural commodities which they market are milk and dairy products, grain, livestock, fruit and vegetables, cotton, poultry and eggs, wool and mohair, tobacco, nuts and miscellaneous items.

The foregoing figures speak for themselves as regards the quantitative importance of cooperative marketing in America. Its political influence is commensurate with its stature. In fact, such federal and state encouragement as has been extended to cooperation in this country in the form of legislative and administrative assistance, has until late years been given only to cooperative marketing. It is an interesting fact, some reasons for which will presently appear, that marketing cooperation and its aid by the government have met with comparatively little opposition from commercial business. In recent years rural cooperative purchasing has been a co-recipient, though in lesser measure, of political benevolence toward farmers, but it has had to overcome and still encounters resistance on the part of profit business. Growing urban cooperation is now the chief butt of attack.

FEDERAL CREDIT AID

Federal agencies for assisting farmers' marketing and purchasing cooperatives, and also individual farmers, by means of loans at low interest, are remarkably complete and efficacious. These agencies are integrated in a closely coordinated system under the Farm Credit Administration. That system was explained to me by Mr. J. E. Wells, Jr., Vice-President and General Manager of the Central Bank for Cooperatives, and Mr. S. M. Garwood, Commissioner of Production Credit Associations. It is so important in practical application and results that some description of it is essential in considering the progress of farmers' cooperatives. In my own necessarily brief outline I will not take up the Federal Land Bank, which provides loans mainly for the purchase, improvement or refinancing of farms, though of course such loans have much to do with a farmer's ability to maintain his position and take part in co-operative activity, and thereby affect cooperatives indirectly. I will outline the functions of the Banks for Cooperatives, the Federal Intermediate Credit Banks, and the Production Credit Associations and Corporations, which relate more specifically to agricultural cooperative activities.

There are thirteen Banks for Cooperatives, including the Central Bank at Washington and regional banks in each of the twelve Federal Land Bank districts. There are twelve Intermediate Credit Banks. The latter are authorized to make loans to cooperatives, but are gradually withdrawing from the field of making such loans directly and, instead, concentrating upon the discounting of loans made by Banks for Cooperatives, and upon making loans to Production Credit Associations and Corporations. The Banks for Cooperatives make no loans to individual farmers but only to cooperative organizations, for what are called "facility," "commodity" and "operating" purposes. Facility loans finance the purchase or construction of plants; commodity loans enable marketing cooperatives to advance funds to members pending sale of delivered products, and help purchasing cooperatives to carry their inventories pending receipts from retail distribution; operating loans cover a miscellaneous assortment of operating needs. The regional banks may lend to or borrow from each other as conditions require. The Central Bank makes exceptionally large or otherwise important loans to cooperatives, lends to or borrows from the regional banks, and discounts loans made by the intermediate credit banks. The original capital for all these banks was subscribed by the Governor of the Farm Credit Administration from the revolving fund authorized by the Agricultural Marketing Act of 1929. Additional capital is obtained through the issuance and sale to the public of debentures, amply secured.

The Production Credit Corporations were emergency agencies which are now being liquidated as rapidly as possible, giving place to the Production Credit Associations as permanent bodies. These are exceedingly interesting in their present service and the way they are being developed into farmer-owned credit cooperatives. They were established under the Farm Credit Act of 1933, to provide a source of low-cost short-term credit to farmers and stockmen in every agricultural county of the country. Five hundred and fifty of these associations are now in operation, with a total membership of some two hundred and fifty thousand individual farmers. They are organized as cooperatives, and make loans only to their own members. Every borrower must subscribe for one $5.00 voting share of stock for every $100 that he borrows. Under a definitely worked out plan, the farmers are gradually acquiring ownership of all the shares. Thus far, in some four years of operation, they have acquired $12,000,000 of the total voting-share capital of $84,000,000. They are encouraged to attend and participate actively in the annual meetings. They elect their own governing boards and pass upon very complete statements of finances and management. They have equal voting power, with only one vote each, and allow no voting by proxy. In other words they are fully cooperative in form of organization and procedure. Up to last September, the enormous sum of nearly $700,000,000 had been lent by these associations to their members, at the low interest rate of 5 percent. As the associations themselves can borrow from the Intermediate Credit Banks at 2 percent, they have a good margin for saving and are building up strong reserves. What a tremendous factor they have already become in the farmer's life is evidenced by the figures I have cited, and what they are capable of becoming eventually as independent cooperatives on their own feet challenges one's imagination.

Now several significant facts emerge from this description. One is that all these agencies were established primarily and mainly for *marketing* cooperatives and *production*. The very name "Production" Credit Associations carry this implication, although in fact farmers are *consumers* of the service which these Associations render, and use the loans for home and family upkeep as well as strictly agricultural objects. The second fact is that the farmers' purchasing cooperatives have also, howbeit secondarily, worked their way in. The third and most significant fact of all is that this entire system of credit agencies is for the benefit of farmers and farmers *only*. Urban cooperatives and urban consumers are not permitted to share in the system's beneficence—even the crumbs that fall from the table. *Why?* I will leave that question with you, gentle readers, as food for thought.

Here are a few practical observations anent the matter. Loans from the Banks for Cooperatives have been of great assistance to many of the farmers' purchasing cooperatives which are now in the strongest position. That is all to the good. Loans from the Production Credit Associations are available to farmers for the purpose of paying their bills at cooperative stores, instead of asking for credit. The farmers ought to be expected to utilize such loans, if necessary, in order to pay cash, and the cooperative stores ought to clamp down on credit and insist on cash as long as such facilities are available. This credit problem, I may as well say at this point, is a constant and serious and sometimes disastrous one with cooperative stores, which are up against acute competition on the part of commercial stores that extend credit (though not *freely* by any means) and actually encourage installment buying—at what cost? The only way for cooperative stores which are not already on a cash basis is simply to go on that basis forthwith without fuddling. They can point to the Production Credit Associations in full warrant for a firm stand.

But the urban cooperatives, which will presently be described, are apparently out in the cold so far as borrowing from federal agencies is concerned, nor can they point to any such source from which their individual patrons can obtain funds to pay for goods. In this respect the urban cooperatives may lay claim to *uniqueness*. Profit business can borrow (and has borrowed in a liberal and life-saving manner) from the Reconstruction Finance Corporation, which (according to a statement by the chairman, Mr. Jesse H. Jones, reported in the

New York Times of February 11, 1938) has authorized industrial loans aggregating $201,616,000. The amount actually disbursed, he added, was $105,000,000. To quote the dispatch—"The most trouble, he said, had developed over loans to the textile and coal mining industries. There the experience of the RFC had not been very happy. . . . The RFC, he said, already was giving a form of insurance by agreeing to participate to the extent of 50 percent in loans which banks were willing to make, thus sharing the risk." Well, well!—profit business can't complain—*but it does.*

So far as the Federal Government is concerned, it is to be highly commended for all it has done to provide farmers' cooperatives with loans,—but in failing thus far to provide similar loan facilities for urban cooperatives it is certainly lagging behind considerations of equity and the welfare of urban consumers. Whether the scope of the Banks for Cooperatives could be thus broadened without amendment of the original Act is presumably doubtful, but such an amendment could be recommended or some other legislative or administrative means of meeting the credit needs of urban cooperatives could be devised. There is no justice or consistency in excluding them from facilities which profit business and rural cooperatives now enjoy. But perhaps the urban cooperatives themselves will beat the Government to it, by providing themselves with funds through resources accruing from cooperative insurance. There lie some great potentialities, of which I shall have something more to say later.

Many of the leading marketing cooperatives are represented and served by the National Cooperative Council, with headquarters at Washington, D. C., of which Mr. Robin Hood is the secretary-treasurer and moving spirit. This organization was formed in 1929, after an earlier one called the National Council of Farmers Cooperative Marketing Associations had run into trouble and been dissolved. It publishes a bi-monthly organ, the *Cooperative Journal,* which succeeded or virtually continued *The Cooperative Marketing Journal* that Mr. Hood and an associate had started several years earlier. The National Cooperative Council includes 53 regional and national bodies, all but a dozen of which are marketing associations. According to a recent statement in the *Journal,* about 4000 cooperative units with a combined membership of approximately one and a half million farmers, are affiliated with these 53 constituent associations. The latter are classified into thirteen voting groups, one of which is composed of the dozen purchasing associations and the other twelve of marketing associations which handle various agricultural commodities. Of the Council's four "permanent objectives" three are concerned with promoting favorable or opposing unfavorable Congressional legislation and governmental action, and the fourth with providing "a forum or conference body through which cooperative views might be harmonized, bonds of friendship developed and experiences exchanged." Mr. Hood, with whom I had a particularly interesting interview in Washington, is an outstanding and influential exponent of what may be called the *business* school of cooperators who, by and large, advocate going along with the profit system, sharing its benefits, and keeping clear of principles and policies which challenge that system and antagonize commercial interests. That, I would say, is the prevailing attitude of marketing associations as a class.

BASIC DIFFERENCES

This brings us to the basic difference between marketing cooperatives on the one hand, and purchasing cooperatives on the other. Up to a certain point their results are similar. Marketing cooperatives, to the end of obtaining better prices, have done a great deal to improve the quality of farm products. They promote the use of better seeds, fertilizers and methods of cultivation; combat plant and animal diseases; raise breeding standards for livestock; safeguard the cleanliness and purity of milk and dairy products; and develop more careful and efficient harvesting, packing and transportation of crops. In thus improving the quality of agricultural products upon which consumers are dependent, marketing cooperatives are at one with purchasing cooperatives and similarly benefit consumers.

It is also true that in so far as marketing cooperatives dispense with smaller middlemen and sell to large buyers, or sometimes directly to packing plants and manufacturers, they eliminate unnecessary steps in distribution and thereby effect economies. But their object, of course, first and last, is to make a *profit* on the products which they sell. This means that their chief purpose is diametrically opposite to that of purchasing cooperatives, which aim to replace profits by savings. As was shown in an earlier chapter, profits and savings are opposite ends, different in nature and approached by different roads. Savings are effected by conservation of energy and add to the sum of social resources. Profits are obtained by competitive expenditure of energy, and do not add to the total sum of social resources but simply shift a portion of those resources from some hands into others.

However natural and necessary marketing cooperatives may be as means of obtaining more for the farmer than he might otherwise obtain, they are subject to certain inherent disadvantages and limitations in comparison with purchasing cooperatives. The latter do not compete with one another injuriously. In fact the more they compete with each other in distributing goods to purchasers at a saving, the more they increase the buying power of purchasers and thereby help each other. To the extent that they lower the prevailing price levels, they benefit purchasers and all purchasing cooperatives still more broadly. But marketing cooperatives compete with one another for profits, and sometimes this results in gain for some and loss for others. Associations in various regions which handle the same product, be it oranges, apples or turkeys, frequently compete with each other to dispose of their supply in the big central markets at New York, Chicago and elsewhere. Some succeed in selling their entire supply satisfactorily, but unless the demand exceeds the total supply available, others have to sell unsatisfactorily and sometimes at a price which leaves them slight profit, if any. Such competition for markets is bound to occur.

A marketing cooperative is also at a strategic disadvantage in dealing with commercial buyers. It has a commodity which it wants to sell. This commodity may be perishable, and in any case its retention involves storage cost and deferment of proceeds. The buyers, on the other hand, have a *unique* commodity, *money*, which is exchangeable into anything else and which the sellers are extremely anxious to acquire because of its exchangeability into the various goods they need. The buyers are well aware of this advantage on their side, and they can also play one marketing cooperative against another and enter into gentlemen's agreements among themselves regarding the amounts they will buy and the prices they will pay. It is not difficult to understand how the marketing cooperatives may lose out under such circumstances and be compelled to take whatever they can get. At a meeting which I attended last summer I heard the sad story of just such a case, in which the marketing cooperative had a practical monopoly of a highly specialized crop and thought it could dictate to the buyers—but was forced to change its mind and suffered badly.

In that respect again the purchasing cooperatives have a decided advantage, because when they buy from commercial dealers it is they who can offer that unique commodity, money, for what the dealers have to sell.

Even under the most favorable conditions, when marketing cooperatives succeed in getting commercial buyers to pay them higher prices, the resulting *net* benefit to farmers is rather dubious. The higher prices which the buyers pay are simply added, as costs, to the prices which ultimate consumers have to pay for farm products after they have been processed or manufactured into food and clothing. And inasmuch as farmers are themselves consumers, they find that although they got more for the crops they sold, they have to pay more for the goods they buy. In olden days the farm family raised its own food and made its own homespun clothing, but under present-day conditions most farmers raise staple crops for market, and except for a few incidentals like milk and eggs, they purchase their food, clothing and household supplies. So when they have to pay higher prices for these things, they feel the pinch just as urban consumers do. Furthermore, they observe that when they get more for their crops and are known to have more money temporarily in their possession, commercial dealers are disposed to relieve them of the surplus by raising the prices of farm supplies—machinery, fertilizer, feed, et cetera. In the end, when the farmers come to balancing their accounts of income and outgo, they may not find much left on the *in* side.

If marketing cooperatives could sell their products directly to consumers' cooperatives, equipped with plants in which these products could be processed and manufactured and then distributed to consumers through wholesale and retail stores, that would be mutually advantageous. Such direct dealing between agricultural producers on the one hand, and both urban and rural consumers on the other, would eliminate the costs and profits of many middlemen and intermediate stages. The savings thus effected would permit a joint board, representing producers and consumers, to allow prices for farm products above those which farmers now obtain from commercial buyers, while still enabling consumers to obtain farm products at prices below those which they now have to pay to commercial dealers.

Direct relations of this sort between producers and consumers are unquestionably the goal toward which marketing and purchasing cooperatives should advance in a gradual, experimental and pragmatic way. In some of the European countries as, for example, England, Sweden and Switzerland, such relations have been worked out on a considerable scale with good results. In the United States there are as yet only a few scattered instances, which are nevertheless important as evolutionary beginnings. Some of these will be mentioned later when particular organizations are described. As consumers' cooperation continues to expand, through regional and national federations, wholesales and manufacturing plants, opportunities for direct dealings in a larger way between marketing and purchasing groups will naturally present themselves. The development of such inter-relationships would make for a much more closely knit cooperative family. Under present conditions, however, the marketing cooperatives really have no other choice than to sell their products to commercial dealers as best they can. The dealers on their side are by no means unfriendly to the marketing associations, and value the service they render by assembling farm products at central markets where it is more convenient to buy selectively. So, all in all, these dealers are not averse to keeping the farmers' marketing cooperatives inside the competitive brotherhood of profit-business.

GROWTH OF COOPERATIVE PURCHASING

But now comes a fact of great importance in the progress of consumers' cooperation in America. It is this: Although cooperative marketing will doubtless continue to loom large in bulk, cooperative purchasing shows a far larger *rate* of increase. To use a popular expression, it is on the up and up. It points toward the future. The figures which I shall cite below apply to cooperative purchasing which has been organized and developed by American farmers, but the significance of these figures, as will soon appear, extends to the American cooperative movement as a whole. For the following figures, as well as those cited earlier for the 1935-36 volume of marketing, I am indebted to the Research Service and Educational section of the Cooperative Division of the Farm Credit Administration, Washington, D. C.

During the last twenty-five years farmers' cooperative purchasing has grown tremendously. In 1913, or just before the outbreak of the World War, its volume was a little under $6,000,000. For the 1937 calendar year the volume was $400,000,000. That means the volume is more than sixty-six times greater at present than it was at the beginning of this recent period. The rate of increase becomes still more striking when compared with that of cooperative marketing. Total marketing figures for 1936-37 are not yet available as this is written. But between 1913 and 1935-36 the marketing volume increased less than six-fold while the purchasing volume grew more than forty-fold. In the combined volume of marketing and purchasing, the percentage of purchasing has ascended from 1.9 in 1913 to 13.8 in 1935-36, while the percentage of marketing has correspondingly fallen off. This comparison is not meant to imply that cooperative marketing is going into a quantitative decline. Its bulk is still much larger than that of purchasing. My intention is simply to bring out the far more impressive rate of growth of cooperative purchasing, and the relative trends.

The inner strength and power of this upward movement is shown by the striking growth of cooperative purchasing since 1932 in spite of the stress and strain of the economic depression from which commercial business has suffered so severely. In fact the very conditions which compelled people to practice economy have strengthened the appeal of cooperative purchasing as a means of reducing net expenses. The widespread response to this opportunity is evidenced in part by the rise in purchasing volume from $140,500,000 in 1932-33 to the previously mentioned figure of $400,000,000 in 1937—an increase of $259,000,000 in four years. The present volume is far beyond that of farmers' cooperative purchasing of any other country in the world. Suffice to say that a volume of four hundred million dollars is one of real magnitude. It accounts for not less than one-eighth of all the farm supplies which are purchased in America. Measured in terms of human beings it represents approximately a million farm-heads— about one out of every seven in America—who are now members of purchasing cooperatives. Counting five persons a family, which is roughly the farm average, brings the constituency of farmers' cooperative purchasing to approximately five million people.

Now of course the character and direction of this cooperative activity in which five million people are involved are matters of great interest and moment in their bearing on cooperation's future in the United States. Is farmers' cooperative purchasing essentially different from and not in harmony with consumers' cooperation? Or is it practically a rural form of consumers' cooperation, and therefore an integral part of the consumers' cooperative movement and a source of strength for that movement's future growth? Is its object, like that of cooperative marketing, to make a profit, or rather to effect savings by eliminating the profits of middlemen? Are its weight and influence helping to perpetuate the profit-system and the capitalistic status quo, or to further the evolution of consumers' cooperation as a mutation of capitalism—a new species of social-economic organization?

The general reply to these questions is that they cannot yet be answered with an unqualified and unanimous yes or no. They are the subject of constant and often vehement debate, among rural and urban cooperators and students of the movement. No full consensus of opinion has yet emerged. Opinions differ—decidedly. The underlying reason for this disagreement is that the rural purchasing cooperatives are themselves in a state of flux and transition. Members of the same local group may differ with one another. In state and regional federations and wholesales some of the units lean one way and some the other. This is true likewise of the officers and leaders. In some quarters these inner differences of attitude have become acute. By and large, the field of farmers' cooperative purchasing is now the chief arena in which champions and challengers of the profit system, opponents and proponents of the basic principles of consumers' cooperation, are engaged in a struggle to determine which way farmers' cooperative purchasing will go. This struggle is intensely human. It involves not only the intrinsic issues, but personalities, predilections, prejudices, outside influences, prior commitments and ulterior considerations. But here we are concerned with the actual merits at the core of the conflict. So let us take a coign of vantage in the amphitheater and see if we can discern what the outcome is likely to be.

9. ATTITUDES
AND ORIENTATION

THE position of what I would again call the *business* school of cooperators was pithily expressed by Mr. E. J. Coil, Jr., economist with the Rural Electrification Administration in Washington, in a statement which appeared in the *Cooperative Journal* of July-August, 1937, as an advance excerpt from an article written by Mr. Coil for another publication, *Plan Age*. I will quote from this statement sufficiently to convey its substance:

> Although all cooperative societies may have their origin in the aspiration of their members for economic betterment, cooperative purposes and policies differ widely. If one is to secure clarity and precision of definition, it is necessary to look to the economic interest of the group of persons who establish the cooperative and who constitute its members.
>
> One form of economic society is based on private property and production for profit; another form is based on collective property and production for use.
>
> Farmers who organize a marketing or selling cooperative do so in order to increase their efficiency as profit-seekers. If they organize a purchasing cooperative to buy raw materials for farm production,

they do so in order to lower their costs of production and widen their margin of profits. Even though they may also buy some items of foodstuff and clothing for consumption through the same purchasing organization, the tone and attitude is set by the fact that the major objective is production for profit.

On the other hand, consumers or workers who organize a purchasing cooperative to provide themselves with the necessities of life at the lowest cost, wish to eliminate profits to middlemen and to outsiders . . . their interest is that of production for use from collectively owned, not privately owned, means of production.

.   .   .   .

It may be concluded, therefore, that any cooperative society whose members are interested in the private ownership of property and in production for profit may be termed producer cooperatives, regardless of the particular service performed; and that any society whose members are interested in non-profit production for use may be termed consumer cooperatives. . . . Producer societies are capitalistic; consumer societies are collectivistic.

This statement appears to draw a line between farmers on the one hand and consumers on the other, and to accord farmers only the status of producers. It does not recognize adequately the fact that they are also consumers. By asserting that all forms of farmers' cooperatives have as their guiding motive production for profit, it ties them up tightly and exclusively with the profit system. It passes too lightly over the further fact that the immediate and specific object of farmers' purchasing cooperatives is to effect savings by eliminating as far as possible middlemen's profits. If indirect and ultimate, instead of direct and immediate aims are to be taken as the test of cooperative purpose, it could just as well be argued that the ultimate aim of marketing cooperatives is by means of the profits thus obtained to improve the well-being and standards of living of farm families, and that therefore marketing associations are really consumers' cooperatives. Mr. Coil's assertion that consumers' cooperatives are "collectivistic," and stand for collective instead of private ownership of property and the means of production, is unwarranted—unless perchance he is using the term "collectivistic" in a sense which can be applied likewise to stock companies and the country's large industrial corporations. These corporations are supposedly owned and controlled by the stockholders. Consumers' cooperatives are owned and controlled by the shareholder-patrons. In both forms of organization the shares are private property, and as for the business itself and its undivided reserves, ownership may be called either collective or private as one chooses to use the terms. So far as numbers are concerned, the big corporations have shareholders in hundreds of thousands where the cooperatives have them in thousands, and are certainly more collective in that respect. Nor can urban consumers' cooperatives be called collectivistic in any sense that does not apply likewise to farmers' purchasing cooperatives, for they are organized on the same structural pattern, the Rochdale plan of consumers' cooperation. It is true that consumers' cooperatives are not committed to the profit system, or to capitalism, which is virtually another name for the profit system. But they are most certainly not opposed to capital, which they utilize, or to private property, which they recognize. Indeed, consumers' cooperation draws upon the private property of its members for working capital, and by its savings to members enables them to acquire more private property themselves.

To bring out the contrast between the business attitude and what I would characterize as the *liberal* attitude regarding farmers' cooperatives, I will quote briefly from a report which Mr. Murray D. Lincoln of Columbus, Ohio, presented at the annual meeting of the Ohio Farm Bureau Federation, a statewide body of farmers, on October 20, 1936. Mr. Lincoln is the executive officer of this organization, and general manager of the Cooperative Association which grew out of it and which is now forwarding a remarkably comprehensive and successful program of cooperative purchasing and inter-related activities. Among liberal leaders in this field no one is more dynamic, influential and highly regarded. He is a practical farmer himself, and in the report from which I now quote he was speaking to a large gathering of his fellow-farmers of the Buckeye State:

In my last year's report I told you that I was coming to the belief, without having any too many reasons for it at that time, that action as consumers was more effective in solving our problems than action as producers. . . . During the past year I believe I have discovered the reasons which enabled me to become convinced of the truth of this premise.

Consumption, of course, means more than just food, but the ability to buy whatever products and services your needs or ambitions may lead you to desire.

As we become producers, we separate into groups, and these groups in general are organized to promote their own welfare. Necessarily, there is much common good bound up in the welfare of any group, but I am beginning to believe that it is this struggle of one group against another that brings about much of the economic and consequently social chaos that we have.

We have arrived at an age of real plenty, as far as production goes. But we have inadequate consumption because of the lack of purchasing power, because of high distributive costs, and because of the profit system with its tariffs, its monopolies, and its other restrictions.

Producer action is, in my opinion, mainly responsible for the deflection of government activity from its basic purpose of serving all, to that of serving the selfish interests of a few.

The more I analyze these two phases of human activity, the more I am amazed at the degree we think of ourselves as producers, largely forgetting ourselves as consumers.

Action as consumers reverses nearly everything I have said about producer action. . . . It has mutuality of interests . . . reduces waste, keeps prices down, avoids duplication of effort and . . . increases real purchasing power.

I am coming to the belief, right or wrong, that as farmers by ourselves, there is not much hope of our licking the present distributive system with its interlocking relationship with finance, its influence in government circles, and its wide economic and political power, and thereby securing our rightful share of the nation's income.

But I do believe that if we can find the proper basis of relationship with the urban consumers, together we can dominate the whole field of economic production and distribution.

This attitude is almost the opposite of the other. It brings to the forefront the farmer's status and well-being as a *consumer*, and broadens the scope of consumption to embrace whatever serves his needs and desires. This broader conception is in line with the standard definition of consumption which was cited in an earlier chapter. Instead of tying the farmers' purchasing cooperatives up to capitalism and the profit-system, and restricting them to a pale of their own, Mr. Lincoln calls on them to join hands with urban consumers in working out an amended and improved system of production and distribution which will replace profits for some people by savings for all people.

These viewpoints are so radically different that humanly speaking it is hard to see how their exponents at the two extremes could come together on principles. But in between these extremes are many gradations and mutual concessions in practice. Is it possible to find common ground on which, without attempting to prescribe and foreclose the eventual future, the differing elements can agree within limits and come together in a constructive working program? I believe that such common ground has been mapped out by a man who holds a rather unique place as friend and counselor of farmers' cooperative organizations. In my extensive traveling last summer I learned that he is held in special esteem by all elements for his moderation, competence and fairness. This man is Dr. Joseph G. Knapp, Senior Agricultural Economist of the Cooperative Division of the Farm Credit Administration, with whom I conferred in Washington on this subject. In an address delivered at the annual Kansas Cooperative Conference on April 17, 1936, which was published in the *Cooperative Journal* for May-June of that year, he outlined the basis for a working program in which farmers and urban consumers could join hands with mutual benefit and understanding. I doubt whether the full import of Dr. Knapp's paper has yet been recognized. He handled the matter in such a considerate way, and made such generous allowance for differences of attitude, that I surmise one school or the other, or perhaps both, accepted what he said as an endorsement of their own position and failed to see or sufficiently appreciate the golden mean which lay between. Present space will not permit reproducing the address in full, but I will summarize as plainly as I can the parts which are most directly pertinent, and quote several excerpts:

1. The term consumers' cooperation "conveys different meanings to different individuals. To some it is another term for cooperative purchasing. To others it is a philosophy for the organization of all economic activity by associations of ultimate consumers. . . . There is, therefore, a twilight zone where the two types of cooperation overlap."

2. Farmers are interested in advancing their well-being as consumers as well as producers, "and it is often to their interest to buy goods for general consumption cooperatively."

3. The growth of consumers' cooperation in America, among rural and urban people or both in combination, would not work to the detriment but substantially to the benefit of farmers and cooperatives which serve them as producers. As to the goods distributed by consumers' cooperatives which are not derived from farm products but which farmers need, there is no possible conflict of interests. Certain things which both rural and urban people require, such as gasoline, oil, motor accessories, and insurance service, are well adapted to joint cooperative distribution. In general, the progress

of consumers' cooperation would shorten the route of agricultural products from producer to consumer, tend to increase the availability in rural districts of cooperative stores handling household supplies, and build up cooperative wholesale associations capable of serving both rural and urban consumers' units.

4. As regards the problem of relationship between consumers' cooperatives which want to obtain farm products as cheaply as possible, and farmers' marketing associations which want to sell them at as high a price as possible, that could be solved through intelligent negotiation, between representatives of both sides, looking to a "price policy which would be satisfactory to farmers while not detrimental to the interests of consumers." "Such joint negotiations would tend to bring home to urban consumers to a greater extent the fact that they are dependent upon the prosperity of the farmers since farmers comprise an important part of the market for products manufactured and distributed in the cities. Consumer associations would obviously come to realize that it would be a shortsighted policy on their part to endeavor to destroy the prosperity of agriculture when it would react on the prosperity of consumers in the towns."

"Moreover, urban consumers' cooperative associations might be able to make a considerable increase in wholesale and retail distributive efficiency and in the elimination of waste. If such organizations could bring about a general increase in the efficiency of retail distributing methods, that would be to the general advantage of agriculture, since the consumption of farm products is to some extent retarded by inefficient retail methods of distribution."

"If consumers' associations can do the job efficiently, there is no reason why they should not displace less efficient distributing machinery. The elimination of waste and profit in retail and wholesale distribution would put more money into consumers' pockets and increase the capacity of consumers to use more products" from the farms.

This is sound, practical and constructive reasoning. To the extent that present differences of attitude yield to the actual merits of the case and are not governed by extraneous factors, these considerations and objectives will, I believe, come to be generally accepted.

Meanwhile, in spite of differences, the farmers cooperative purchasing movement is being broadened and brought into closer community of interest and action with urban cooperation, by forces which appear to be working with the sureness of gravity—only they are not pulling it down but lifting it up. Although the farmers' cooperative stores still deal mainly in livestock feed, seed, fertilizer, gas, oil and motor accessories, they are tending to add family foods and household supplies—things that are commonly known as consumers' goods. Farm women are largely responsible for this development. If farmers in their unremitting round of outdoor labor on the land are naturally prone to think of themselves as toilsome producers, the farmers' wives with their incessant indoor round of housework have ample reason to think of their menfolk as perpetual consumers of food and clothing. "Why not save on such things too?" So the women have been getting more and more of the stores to put in flour, cereals, and other groceries and household conveniences. And they are going to keep right on pushing.

RURAL ELECTRIFICATION

Within the last few years the drudgery and humdrum in the lives of thousands of farm women have been much alleviated, and men's farm tasks eased and simplified, by the godsend of rural electrification. This program is being carried out under the federal Rural Electrification Administration which was set up at Washington in 1935. At that time, amazing as the fact is in a country which boasts of its mechanical progress and efficiency, less than twelve farms out of every hundred in the United States were supplied with electric power lines. In fourteen states the proportion with line service was less than one farm in twenty-five. The two states which made the best showing were on opposite sides of the continent: New Hampshire, with 57 percent of its farms electrified, and California with 54 percent. Altogether, about 6,000,000 farms in a total of 6,800,000 were without electric power. The chief reason for this astounding state of affairs was that commercial electric light and power companies either could not or would not provide electricity for these rural areas at rates which farmers generally could afford to pay. One exasperated farmer expressed himself thus:

"My wife and I are tired of trying to run our farm business with kerosene lamps and smoking lanterns. If we can't get electricity pretty soon we are going into the business of raising lightning bugs."

Now that the federal government has undertaken to remedy the situation, many of these companies have suddenly discovered that they can manage, after all, to quote considerably lower figures than they previously thought they could, and are rushing to pick up such rural custom as they can. Others are accepting the new development in a friendly spirit. But plenty are resisting it to the last ditch by hook and crook, and throwing all possible legal and practical obstacles in the way of the rural projects.

Most of these projects are being carried out through local cooperative groups of farmers organized expressly for this purpose. The most typical groups include about eight hundred member-customers, of whom three-quarters are farmers and the rest villagers. They are scattered over about three hundred square miles of countryside and build about two hundred and fifty miles of line with a loan of around $230,000. When a given project is approved by the REA, this governmental agency lends the local cooperative the funds which are necessary to construct the line. The loans are made at a low rate of interest, under 3 percent, and are payable over an amortization period of from twenty to twenty-five years. The cooperative then contracts locally for the necessary construction and for its supply of electric power, which it usually buys from the nearest commercial company or municipal plant. If it cannot obtain power in either of those ways satisfactorily, it installs a Diesel plant of its own. It then proceeds, though under strict regulation and supervision by the REA, to open an office, engage a modest personnel and begin to operate the line. The minimum charge to patrons is just sufficient to cover the actual cost of power, overhead expense, interest and amortization, and some reserve for working capital and contingencies. The usual range of minimum rates is from $2.50 to $3.75 a month, which is much below the commercial rates.

Including the last quarter of 1937 the REA had allotted funds to build approximately 80,000 miles of rural electric lines, in forty-one states. These allotments were made to 380 local organizations with a total of 200,000 customers. Taking the farm average of five persons to a family, this means that one million persons in forty states share the service. About 5 percent of the projects were carried out by commercial utilities companies who borrowed federal funds, about 20 percent by municipal or other public agencies, and the remaining 75 percent—or 285 out of the 380 projects—by local cooperative groups as above described. On that proportionate basis the total membership of these 285 cooperatives is about 150,000. That figure also indicates the number of farms which have been serviced in the cooperative way.

How much vigor and enterprise the cooperatives will develop in their own right remains to be seen. Before they came upon the scene in response to govern-

ment initiative, there were fifty or more rural electric cooperatives which had been organized and financed by
farmers on their own independent initiative. Generally
speaking, that is the most natural and promising way
for any local cooperative group to originate. But here
was a crying need, and the plan of giving farmers the
opportunity to meet that need through cooperatives of
their own with the aid of government loans, appeared
to serve the double purpose of eliciting local responsibility and insuring repayment of the government's
outlay.

But of course the REA, being accountable for the
success of these projects and for getting the money back,
naturally feels that it has to keep a pretty close grip
on the local groups, and this strict surveillance is liable
to make the cooperatives feel that they are not much
more than dummies or rubber stamps themselves.
I found something of that feeling in most of the localities which I visited last summer, and in talking later
with an REA representative I frankly told him so. In
return I learned that this was by no means news to the
Washington office, and that steps were being taken to
find a middle course which would sufficiently protect
the government's interests and still allow the cooperatives to develop some real character and will of their
own. If they do, they will bring widespread reinforcement to the whole cooperative movement in America,
because these rural electrification cooperatives represent
the farmers not only as producers, utilizing electric
power in various mechanical ways in their farming

operations, but also as consumers, using electricity in their homes in ways that serve the family's comfort and convenience and are especially appreciated by the women.

Mr. John M. Carmody, Administrator of the REA, is confident of the future. "Whole areas have been organized by local men and women," he says in his report for 1937. "They get a new sense of community responsibility and neighborliness. They manage their own business. They take new pride in their citizenship and their community. . . . We here at REA believe in the social soundness of the program set up by the Congress. We believe in the economic wisdom of bringing farm families out of the dark into the light, out of stark drudgery into normal effort, out of a past of unnecessary denial into a present of reasonable convenience. These are giant steps for many people whom we serve."

As soon as the rural electrification program got under way, farm homes were bombarded from all sides with opportunities—to put it mildly—to buy all sorts of electric appliances and undertake such remodeling or new construction, especially for up-to-date kitchens and bathrooms, as was necessary to make best use of the electric current. The Federal Housing Administration offered loans to finance the construction, and the Electric Home and Farm Authority was established to finance the purchase of appliances. The farmers were to buy these appliances direct from dealers; but if they were not able to pay cash they could give notes, and the EHFA would buy these notes from the dealers and hold them for payment. Of course, commercial firms were quick to take advantage of this new market. But so were the farmers' cooperative stores, as well as cooperative stores in towns and cities within handy reach of farming districts. One and all, they stocked up with a marvelous assortment of electrical home appliances, including vacuum cleaners, washing machines, refrigerators, stoves, sewing machines, water pumps and radios. In one local area, for example, where the REA line has been in operation only a year, 84 percent of the homes now have electric irons, 84 percent have radios, 63 percent washing machines, 48 percent vacuum cleaners, 35 percent toasters, 27 percent electric motors, 20 percent refrigerators and 16 percent electric kitchen pumps.

It is easy to understand how delighted farm women were with these devices. So the farmers soon began to buy them, and have kept on buying ever since, as fast as their means or optimism would permit. Homes were transformed. I heard many touching stories from farm women with whom I talked. One comely and competent lass, who kept house for her father, said that now she had time to saddle her horse and gallop over the country roads—which she loved to do and which kept her "as fit as a fiddle." Drudgery gave way to novelty and excitement. And the radios brought no end of new ideas and entertainment. Meanwhile the cooperative stores were doing a brisk and rising business at substantial savings to their patrons, and National Cooperatives (which will be described later) sponsored a line of "Co-op" appliances that have done remarkably well and helped that new and promising national wholesale to get a running start.

These things for the home are assuredly consumers' goods. Their cooperative distribution and their increasing use by farm families have already made farmers and farmers' purchasing cooperatives much more consumer-conscious, and brought rural and urban people closer together in a realization of their common interests. The radio is contributing continuously, we may safely say, to this growing sense of community. For years the ubiquitous automobile has been carrying country folk to the cities and city folk to the country, and making them better acquainted with each other as fellow human beings who are all engaged in the pursuit of happiness and are trying to get more enjoyment out of life from day to day.

A DISCOVERY

But as we remarked some time back, under present conditions the enjoyment of life is closely related to the cost of living. This practical truth is finding deeper lodgment in the consciousness of farmers and farm women, and is leading them into consumers' cooperation. Now comes an interesting discovery which should spur the progress in that direction. I call it a discovery because it reveals a fact which I think is not commonly recognized as yet and the significance of which from the cooperative viewpoint is not fully appreciated. There has been an assumption that farmers spend more of their income on supplies for agricultural production

than they do for consumers' goods, and that therefore
they could save more by purchasing their farm supplies
cooperatively than they could by cooperative purchase
of their household goods. But the following figures indicate that this assumption over-reaches itself.

These figures were obtained from a bulletin of the
Bureau of Agricultural Economics of the Department of
Agriculture, called "Index Numbers of Prices Paid by
Farmers for Commodities, 1910-1935." This bulletin
presents two averaged farm budgets, both of which are
based on area and numbers sufficient to make them
fairly typical or representative, and on prices for the
same recent five-year period so that they are comparable.
One is for farm maintenance, that is, for things used in
production, and comes to $466 a year. The other is for
family maintenance, that is, for consumers' goods, and
comes to $608 a year. Thus it appears that the annual
expenditure for consumers' goods is $142 more than the
annual expenditure for farming goods. As price levels
change somewhat from year to year and the total
amounts may likewise vary, it is better to put this comparison in percentages and say that the farmer spends
30 percent more for consumers' goods than for farming
goods. Put in another way, the home budget comes to
57 percent and the farming budget to 43 percent of the
combined expenditure. This being so, it is certainly
reasonable to believe that farmers can save more by cooperative purchase of consumers' goods than they can
by cooperative buying of farm supplies. And of course
they can save the maximum amount through buying
cooperatively *everything* they need.

For the bulletin cited above, and for some very helpful letters regarding these particular figures and my
conclusions, I am indebted to Mr. O. C. Stine, in charge
of the Division of Statistical and Historical Research of
the Bureau of Agricultural Economics. I have been so
much impressed with Mr. Stine's carefulness and understanding in our correspondence that I want to be
equally careful myself in interpreting these figures, especially because they present the farmer's problem of
expenditure and economy in a rather different light
from that in which he has somehow been led to view
this problem in the past.

The farmer's assumption that the larger share of outlay is for farming goods may be partly accounted for
by the fact that he makes those expenditures *himself*, in
sizable seasonal amounts, while the expenditures for
household goods are usually made by his wife, in little
daily, weekly and intermittent driblets. He leaves those
items to his wife, she leaves the farming things to him,
and perhaps they do not find much time free to total
up and compare their respective outlays. But with these
figures before us, we can make a beginning at least in
their behalf.

Both of the budgets here cited are confined to commodities. Neither one includes expenditure for hired
labor or for services. This means that their combined
amount does not cover the farmer's entire outlay. But
it does cover the things which are now actually or potentially purchasable through cooperatives at a saving.

The Farm Maintenance budget includes annual

quotas of outlay for or depreciation of tractors, trucks, other farm machinery and automobiles (allocating 50 percent of the cost of the latter to farming use). If a farmer buys a tractor, say, in a given year, its entire cost is not included in this representative budget for that one year, but is distributed in equal amounts (as "depreciation") through the budgets of as many years as its estimated life or usability will cover. The rest of this budget consists of strictly annual expenditures for livestock, feed, seed, fertilizer, building material, petroleum products, motor accessories, and incidental and miscellaneous farm supplies. This budget total, as previously stated, is $466.

The Family Maintenance budget includes automobiles, motor fuel and accessories (reckoned at 50 percent for family use), building materials for the house, food, clothing, furniture and furnishings, and incidental and miscellaneous items bunched as "operating expenses."

All the things in both of these budgets are potentially purchasable through cooperatives. In succeeding chapters concrete examples will appear which apply to all of them without exception. But whether a given farmer can actually and conveniently obtain them through cooperatives depends a good deal on where his farm is situated and how far cooperative purchasing has progressed in that particular district. If he happens to be in a section where only a few things, or possibly nothing at all, can be bought cooperatively—well, then it is up to him either to go on paying commercial prices or to get busy with his neighbors and organize a cooperative to do the job more economically and satisfactorily.

Mr. Stine, after taking due account of the relative purchasability through cooperatives of the various commodities comprised in both budgets, expressed his opinion very succinctly as follows:

"It would appear that a cooperative purchasing association handling all types of commodities bought by farmers which are adapted to cooperative buying, might find its volume divided about equally between consumption-type goods and production-type goods."

That puts the matter very fairly, I think, and in conclusion I would stress the fact that there is no necessity of saving on one side only of this fifty-fifty division. Why not make a one hundred percent job of it by saving on both sides?

As the farmers' purchasing cooperatives keep on moving consumerward, in the process of orientation through which they are now passing, it looks as though they will soon emerge from the twilight zone into the sunlight of consumers' cooperation, there to join forces with urban cooperatives in the common cause of bringing to all elements of the American people still better standards of living and more of the joy of life. One of the most enterprising of the farmers' regional organizations already calls itself the Consumers Cooperative Association. In the ensuing chapter we shall see some of the most typical and important of these associations on the march. We will review them not so much as legions of farmers, however, but as cooperative organizations which have laid firm foundations, built solidly and successfully, and are now leading the way to the future.

* * *

Valuable material is just at hand regarding outlay of farmers in New York for family and farming uses. For this I am indebted to Mr. M. C. Bond, Professor of Marketing, State College of Agriculture, Ithaca, N. Y. Bulletin 522, May, 1931, reports a survey made by Helen Cannon of "The Family Finances of 195 Farm Families in Tompkins County, N. Y., 1927-28." Most of the farms were 50 to 175 acres in size; the major group 100 to 125 acres. Some specialized in dairying.

One hundred and nine or 56 per cent of the families had average farm income ranging from $496 to $1883 a year, and spent for *all* purposes (including hired labor) from $878 to $1965. "Probably the families in the low-income groups were reluctant to divulge borrowings and credit which would balance their expenses." Families below $750 income averaged $471 spent for household uses, $333 for farming; $750-1490 income, $646 household, $620 farming; $1500-2249 income, $800 household, $856 farming. From there upward to incomes of $3750 or more, farming outlay showed increasing excess over household expense.

Although these figures cover only 195 families in one county, as compared with some 3,000 widely distributed families covered in the Bureau of Agricultural Economics bulletin I have cited, they nevertheless suggest what I believe is the practical commonsense conclusion of this matter, namely, that farmers of modest farm-income (which probably means the majority for the country as a whole, and an even larger proportion of tenant farmers) spend more for family uses than for farm-operation, and *substantially more* for *household commodities* than for *farm supplies*. In that case, it is safe to say that the country's farmers who are *most in need of saving* can save more (or certainly fully as much) through cooperative buying of household goods than they can through cooperative purchasing of farm supplies. And again the *main* point is that they can save *most* by obtaining through cooperatives everything they need.

10. SOLID BUILDING

IN presenting the cooperative purchasing associations which figure as the dramatis personae of this chapter I shall not go into exhaustive descriptions of them, because that would require a separate chapter for each one. I shall simply sketch their salient and characteristic features and bring out their significance as working examples, from the viewpoint of cooperative evolution in America and the union of rural and urban forces in consumers' cooperation.

The order of presentation is not a simple matter to decide. Some associations of smaller size have larger importance as pioneers. Some of a generally conservative or business cast are in other points among the most advanced. Geographical location is not without influence, though associations which are near together in space may differ widely in attitude, and others which are situated in different parts of the country may be similar in spirit and inter-related in their operations. We cannot isolate or rigidly rank them for inspection. But if we proceed in a natural way from what has gone before, I think we shall find that the line of review will somewhat shape itself. It will be an evolutionary line, with precedence given to current cooperative enterprise which has developed a good measure of the vitally essential time dimension.

GIANT OF GRANGE DESCENT

In an earlier chapter I told the story of Grange pioneering in the seventies and said that in spite of many failures at the time, it implanted the roots of consumers' cooperation in American soil. What would serve better then to present first an organization which has grown from those roots, and grown so lustily that it is now not only the largest farmers' cooperative purchasing association in America but the largest in the world. This organization bears a name which matches its stature. It is the Cooperative Grange League Federation Exchange, Incorporated. The central headquarters of its broad cooperative empire are housed in a plainly handsome building of five stories which tops a hill in the altitudinous town of Ithaca, New York, seat of Cornell University and the State College of Agriculture. From that hilltop the G.L.F.—as it is called for short—commands a splendid panoramic view of the surrounding country, and has reason to think of itself, perhaps, as monarch of all it surveys.

This organization may be best introduced by its own founding-father, Mr. H. E. Babcock. In a recent issue of the *G.L.F. Patron* he told how it was founded, who sponsored it and how it got its imposing name:

> The idea of buying farm supplies cooperatively was kept alive by the New York State Grange for fifty years before the G.L.F. was thought of. Beginning in 1874, the Grange tried to carry out this idea by Grange Purchasing Agents, by Grange stores some-

what similar to our own stores, by a State Grange Purchasing Agency, and finally by the Grange Exchange, Inc., which was set up in 1918.

Two other organizations also had a share in the founding of G.L.F.—the Dairyman's League, Incorporated, and the New York State Farm Bureau Federation. Both of these organizations developed in the period between 1910 and 1920. Both got their big stimulus when the farmers of New York won a milk strike in 1916. Both attempted to serve their members with cooperative buying programs.

The time was just after the close of the World War. For several years, farmers had to contend with rising prices and a scarcity of goods. Now the prices of their own farm products were beginning to slip. They had, therefore, great need for some service which would protect their interests as buyers of farm supplies.

At that moment there happened to be elected as president of the Grange Exchange, a man—W. L. Bean, of McGraw—who was keen enough to realize the vital need of farmers for a better service in the purchasing of farm supplies, and to appreciate that there was no chance of his organization giving it. This bit of analysis by Mr. Bean was of the first importance in determining what happened immediately thereafter.

Early in 1920 Mr. Bean came to the writer of this article, who was then Secretary of the New York State Farm Bureau Federation, and through him presented the whole situation to the New York State Agricultural Conference Board, which is composed of the executive committees of leading farm organizations. . . . The situation was beautifully shaped for a coalition.

It was decided by the Conference Board to set up a farmer-owned, farmer-controlled cooperative with an authorized capital of a million dollars—an unheard of sum in those days. It was decided that the three organizations which had had experience in buying farm supplies would give up their efforts and turn what business they had over to the new organization. It was decided that the original board of directors of nine men would be made up of three members from each of these organizations.

On only one point was there disagreement—a name for the new organization. . . . The conferees haggled for hours over what to call the new cooperative. Finally, they struck an awkward compromise. They decided to name it after all of them: The Cooperative Grange League Federation Exchange, Incorporated.

Plans for the launching of G.L.F. moved forward speedily. A milion dollars' worth of stock divided into five-dollar shares on which dividends were limited to six per cent, and with which went the privilege of one vote per shareholder, was offered to farmers the third week of June, 1920. About three-quarters of a million dollars' worth of stock was sold in five days. The writer had charge of this campaign.

The money from this stock sale put the new organization in funds. It took over the going businesses from its sponsors, mainly from the Grange Exchange. By July 1, 1920, promptly as scheduled, the G.L.F. was on its way.

GREAT ACHIEVEMENT

The first source of strength of the G.L.F. and the first lesson its experience holds for all cooperatives, urban and rural, who want to built solidly, is that it was organized on a broad foundation of assured support—moral and financial. Its second advantage, which any cooperative must have in due measure if it is to succeed, has been that of competent direction. Mr. Babcock is a man of rare vision, energy and organizing genius. For sixteen years, from 1920 through 1936, he devoted himself to building up this organization, as its General Manager, and then retired from the executive post in order to have more time free for research, and for developing the new and momentous Family Foods program which will presently be described. In the autumn of 1936 general management was handed over to Mr. J. A. McConnell, who had demonstrated his capacity during fourteen years of associate service and is now ably and progressively carrying on.

In the last fiscal year which ended on June 30, 1937, the G.L.F. did a cooperative wholesale business of $39,000,000. This consisted mainly of staple farm supplies. The organization's principal grain and feed mill at Buffalo, New York, which I went through last summer, is I understand the largest single mill of that kind in the world. Although it was built in 1930, just as the depression was setting in, it went right ahead with successful production. Including feed mills, fertilizer manufactories, other processing plants and warehouses, the G.L.F. maintains eighteen producing and wholesale distributing centers. All of these plants, except several small ones on lease, are owned by the central organization.

To build, equip and operate them, and to handle a yearly distributive business of steadily growing magnitude, has of course required large working capital. In that respect, likewise, the G.L.F. has set an example which all cooperative associations—and especially urban groups whose zeal often exceeds their foresight—would do well to emulate in measure suited to their needs. After paying out patronage returns for the first few years and finding that expansion of resources and facilities was thereby hampered, it decided to apply all savings to accumulating adequate reserve and working capital. That policy was strictly followed until the G.L.F. had succeeded in building up a fund of five million dollars. About one-third of that total was obtained through the issuance of common and preferred capital shares, but the remaining two-thirds was created from cooperative savings, that is, from savings which the G.L.F. was able to effect by means of its own productive and distributive equipment. This achievement stands as a towering monument to what cooperation joined with directing ability can accomplish.

Put in another way the results are still more impressive. If we take into account the organization's plants and equipment which cost approximately four million dollars, and add to that amount the capital fund of five millions, we get a combined total of about nine million dollars which is being utilized to serve 119,000 G.L.F. patrons. In having such a cooperative medium at their service these 119,000 patrons are $9,000,000 better off than they would be if the G.L.F. as it now stands were not in existence.

Cash distribution to patrons of part of the current savings was resumed in 1936, when $275,000 was thus paid out. In 1937 the amount distributed was $465,000, which was 1⅕ percent on the wholesale volume of $39,000,000. Instead of making bulk patronage returns to its local retail units and leaving to them the allocation of these *wholesale* savings to patrons in their districts, the G.L.F. prepares the individual checks in the central office, and turns them over to the stores in district batches. The stores make out additional checks for savings on *retail* patronage, at rates ranging from 1 to 4 percent, and then hand the two checks out together. Thus the individual patrons receive combined distributions of from 2⅕ percent to 5 percent on their patronage.

As compared with the $465,000 distributed as wholesale savings-returns to patrons, the total dividend payments to common and preferred shareholders came to $90,000. These figures provide concrete evidence of one of the major differences between a cooperative and a stock company. Were the G.L.F. a stock company it would have distributed nothing whatever to patrons, but would have paid the whole $465,000 to its common stockholders as an extra distribution over and above their portion of the $90,000 in regular dividends. At present the amount of stock outstanding consists of about $800,000 in common shares of $5.00 par value bearing 6 percent and owned by some 32,000 persons; and about the same amount of preferred of $100 par bearing 5 percent and owned by some 2,500 persons. Notwithstanding hard times, the G.L.F. has never missed its dividend payments on either class of shares. During the depression it retired about a million dollars of 7 percent preferred and issued the present 5 percent preferred in a somewhat reduced total amount. All in all, its financial record is one of which it may well be proud.

As regards patronage returns, the G.L.F. policy is to relegate cash distributions to a distinctly incidental place in comparison with continuous current returns in the form of fair prices, dependable quality and satisfactory service. Mr. McConnell holds that the two practical functions of cash returns are, first, to enable the cooperative organization, *pending* such cash distributions, to follow "a safe, sound, and intelligent pricing program which takes into consideration the control of volume, the competitive situation, the up and down movement of commodity prices, and the proper balancing of working capital to the needs of the institution"; and, second, to dispose of surplus savings "which are

not needed for good, safe, economical operations" and
the retention of which in the treasury might encourage
over-expansion, "lead into side-lines which are not fundamental, promote inefficiency, and throttle initiative
on the part of management." This is clear thinking
which commercial business, accustomed to piling up
big and often concealed surpluses beyond any reasonable or healthful needs, might well ponder. But Mr.
McConnell is careful to emphasize that cash returns
should be kept within limits which do not impair the
organization's working funds and its satisfactory credit
rating.

In the case of G.L.F. the importance of a high credit
rating comes from the fact that besides needing to borrow funds occasionally to facilitate its operations, it
buys supplies regularly and in large volume from commercial dealers. The things thus purchased include
grain for its feed-processing mills, raw materials for its
fertilizer-mixing plants, seeds, fencing, roofing, farm im-
plements and accessories, paint, motor oil and gasoline.
These things are bought on a specifications basis.
Partly through its own research and laboratory tests but
mainly by availing itself of the more extensive research
and experimentation of state agricultural colleges and
some of the governmental and private laboratories,
G.L.F. works out specifications to which the goods that
it buys must conform, and checks all deliveries carefully to make sure the requirements are met. This not
only insures the quality of its own supplies but has
tended to raise the standards of the dealers. G.L.F. com-

petition with commercial dealers frequently has the same effect, by serving as a spur and a yardstick. But competition is only half of the story. Cooperation between G.L.F and many kinds of commercial business, especially in joint research and improvement of products, has yielded some excellent results.

The present attitude of commercial dealers toward this cooperative organization with its great resources is very interesting, especially when contrasted with what the prevailing attitude was when the G.L.F. was first getting a foothold. Mr. McConnell, in his report at the last annual meeting, made the following comment: "Fourteen years ago it was not uncommon to find a good many commercial concerns with raw materials to sell refusing to deal with G.L.F. at all. In contrast to that I now find one of the most valuable assets of G.L.F. to be these wholesale connections. In the main they are friendly, fully appreciative of G.L.F. ideals and desirous of pouring their materials through this cooperative channel which gives them low distribution costs and the password of which is quality. Manufacturers today actually compete with each other for this cooperative outlet. It is a distinct asset and recommendation for their respective companies to be able to say 'We are one of the big suppliers of the G.L.F.' "

In other words *money talks*. When G.L.F. holds out to commercial dealers several million dollars of that unique commodity which is exchangeable into anything else, these dealers are much more likely to be "fully appreciative" of its ideals than they would be if it had only the ideals without the money. Herein lies one of the most practical lessons of all for cooperatives. Not that each one can attain commanding stature singly, but they can and must do so through federation and conjoined resources. Then they like the G.L.F. will find commercial opposition yielding to competition for their custom.

QUESTION OF ORGANIZATION

There is one respect in which I believe the G.L.F. plan is open to question, and that has to do with the basis of organization and control. I raise this question not with reference to G.L.F. exclusively, but as applying likewise to other cooperative wholesale organizations which follow virtually the same pattern. In order to make this question clear I will outline the organizational scheme briefly. G.L.F. territory comprises New York, New Jersey and the northern part of Pennsylvania: the whole region known as the "New York Milk Shed" from whose dairy farms comes the principal eastern milk supply. Through this territory are distributed about 650 retail outlets for G.L.F. supplies. Of the total about 150 (with 50 branches) are "service stores" which the G.L.F. itself established and owns. About 400 are stores owned by local dealers, who act as agents for the G.L.F. and carry its supplies along with their own. Sometimes these proprietary stores run into adversities and are bought by the G.L.F. and reorganized as service stores. The other outlets, about 50 in number, are stores owned by independent local cooperative associations, some of them

Grange units which have come down from the early days. They likewise serve as agents, and show a similar tendency to be taken over. When that happens the local cooperative group ceases to exist in a fully independent way. It is true that each one of the G.L.F service stores is legally incorporated as a cooperative. But it is also true that the store is owned not by the local group but by the central organization. This being true, the local unit is *not* a cooperative in the full meaning of the term.

Thus it appears that the G.L.F. is not a federation of local cooperative units by whom it as a wholesale is owned and controlled, but is a centralized organization which distributes its goods through stores which it owns and controls. As a cooperative it is composed of the 119,000 individual patron-members who purchase its supplies and some 34,000 shareholders who subscribed its share capital. Thus upwards of 150,000 persons, widely scattered in three states, in the last analysis *own* the wholesale, and in principle, or *nominally,* control it. But one can easily see how such widely dispersed membership leads to highly centralized management. Judged by results in terms of volume, this centralized plan of operation has unquestionably proved efficient and successful. But it involves the vital question of democratic control, and this in turn raises a question of *eventual* results—not after seventeen years only but in fifty or a hundred years, and not from the viewpoint of business success alone, but in terms of constantly strengthening the cooperative foundation upon which the whole enterprise if it is to endure must finally depend.

If in the absence of fully cooperative units to insure responsibility at the base, there are feasible ways in which the great numbers of G.L.F. patron-members scattered over so large an area can still function actively and *responsibly,* and thereby really control the central organization—well and good. But I doubt whether that can be accomplished. It is true that the G.L.F. recognizes the importance of this question and is doing a good deal to promote local initiative and participation, along with centralized efficiency. Its territory is divided into local districts, to which field men are assigned to keep things moving. Local meetings of the patrons in each store district are held at least once a year, with the General Manager or another representative of the central office present to speak and confer. At these annual meetings the local patrons elect a committee of six men, whose function is to keep in close touch with the district store and foster the local well-being of G.L.F. affairs. The local committeemen attend the central Annual Meeting of the G.L.F. which is held at Syracuse, New York, as a conveniently situated city with requisite auditorium and hotel facilities. Those meetings bring together several thousand people. The travel expenses of the local committeemen are paid from the G.L.F. treasury—as a matter of equity, it is explained, so that those living at a distance will not be disadvantaged. The committeemen have one vote each as patron-representatives. Shareholders also attend the meeting and (common) have one vote each in their own right.

As a rule, the only decisive action taken is the election of several members of the board of directors. This usually coincides with a prearranged slate of nominations. A few resolutions are presented for acceptance by vote, and sometimes questions of policy are submitted for advisory opinions. There is not much chance for initiative from the floor, or opportunity for more than very general discussion. Once the meeting is adjourned, everything continues to be handled very expeditiously and efficiently through the compact G.L.F. board of directors; or in matters of property control through the Holding Corporation, whose board of directors is the same as that of the general organization, plus two members of the management. In short the working set-up and procedure of G.L.F. are very much like those of a commercial business corporation.

Mr. Babcock and Mr. McConnell told me of the large measure of member-participation in G.L.F. affairs, and cited examples to show how valuable and helpful it is, and how much the central management relies upon and is guided by such local sentiment and advice. The importance of such participation was stressed at the sessions of the enterprising "G.L.F. University" which was conducted at the Ithaca headquarters last summer for the operating personnel, agents and directors. I am quite ready to agree that much helpful participation can be *generated* and that it is all to the good as far as it goes. But "who holds the purse commands the power." The central organization, by virtue of its ownership of the local units, can and does control them in whatever manner and measure it deems best. Such control as the scattered individual members exert on the central management is very general and remote. In comparing this centralized plan of ownership and control with the alternative plan of fully responsible local cooperative units who own and control the wholesale, I would say that the question at issue is not so much the quantity of participation and its immediate usefulness to the management, but rather its finality and creativeness. We will discuss the matter further in the next chapter.

NEW FAMILY FOOD SERVICE

Now to conclude this sketch by telling of some present pioneering which from the standpoint of consumers' cooperation is more significant and momentous than anything else the G.L.F. has done. There is nothing sensational in the name of this new enterprise. It is called the "Family Food Service." Like many things which become important, it began in a small, casual and unnoticed way. And as so often happens in history, there was a woman in the case from the start.

This woman was the farmer's wife. After the farmer had been getting his supplies for some years from G.L.F. stores she said to him, "Why not bring back a sack or two of flour in the same load?" That was sensible. G.L.F. responded by adding some extra-nutritious flours to its stock. Then it added cornmeal, another household staple. Not long after that the Buffalo mill found that it could easily add the processing of grains into a few simple cereals. These cereals made a hit with the farmers' wives because they had so much substantial food value. About five years ago the national Administration awarded to G.L.F. a year's contract to supply these cereals in quantity for use in federal emergency relief. That put them decidedly on the map. Last year's volume was about half a million dollars. Then Mr. Babcock's fertile mind conceived the idea of making them available not only to G.L.F. patrons but to members of other cooperatives, rural and urban. Most of the cooperative associations whom he approached welcomed the proposal with enthusiasm.

These "Family Foods" are headed by Rolled Wheat, Golden Corn Meal, Self-rising Buckwheat Flour and Wheat Pancake Flour. Their merits, as compared with many of the commercially advertised cereals in fancy packages, are higher quality and lower price. The nutriment value is higher because these cereals retain the vital grain elements instead of having everything squeezed out except starch, which is sweetish and pleasant to taste. They are processed in the Buffalo mill and handled through a subsidiary, "Cooperative G.L.F. Products, Inc." This subsidiary organization, which may eventually be put on a basis of joint ownership by the participating associations, will continue to distribute the cereals to the 119,000 G.L.F. patrons through the present retail outlets. But under the newly projected plan it will also supply the Southern States Cooperative, the Pennsylvania Farm Bureau Cooperative Association, the Ohio Farm Bureau Cooperative Association and the Eastern Cooperative Wholesale. The last is an *urban* wholesale with headquarters in

New York City, serving some two hundred cooperative stores and buying clubs in cities and towns of the Eastern states.

This means that the country's largest farmers' cooperative purchasing association, lineal descendant of the Grange, which first implanted and demonstrated in America the working plan and principles of consumers' cooperation as applied to the distribution of commodities, is now blazing new trails of its own by taking urban cooperators into partnership. Country and city consumers will join forces under the aegis of the G.L.F.

The reason why I have discussed the G.L.F. at some length goes beyond the importance of this organization in itself. I have brought out by means of this concrete example some of the most essential elements of cooperative strength. These requirements apply to all cooperative activity whether rural or urban, though of course in manner and degree suited to the circumstances and objectives in each case. So likewise the question of centralized or decentralized organization has a general bearing. In continuing our review it will be well to keep these considerations in mind.

SOUTHERN STATES COOPERATIVE

The chief cooperative purchasing association in the South is the Southern States Cooperative with headquarters at Richmond, Virginia. Its moving spirit and General Manager is Mr. W. G. Wysor, whose energy and executive ability are reflected in the progress of this organization. It began in 1922 as a seed-supply service, expanded to include feed, fertilizer and other farm supplies, and in its last fiscal year, ended June 30, 1937, did a business of $10,264,000 in serving "more than 100,000 farmers through retail outlets numbering over 700." Its territory comprises Virginia, and parts of Maryland, Delaware and West Virginia. Indirectly, through an affiliated organization, it aids in serving the state of North Carolina.

In general the S.S.C. may be described as a Southern counterpart of the G.L.F., after which it is frankly and successfully modeled. There are some differences of attitude and policy which I think will become more distinct in time, but otherwise the likeness is complete. Mr. Wysor and Mr. Babcock are old friends and have worked in close cooperation. S.S.C. and G.L.F. own jointly a large feed-processing plant at Baltimore, Maryland, called the Southern States Cooperative Mills. G.L.F. supplied most of the capital to build this plant but S.S.C. has gradually acquired major ownership proportionate to the 80 percent of the plant's output which is now distributed in the Southern territory. Eight other producing centers are maintained solely by the S.S.C., and 90 percent of the Association's distributive volume now consists of feed and fertilizer processed in its own plants, and seeds grown to meet its own specifications and tested in its own laboratories. It has never been entirely satisfied with supplies obtained from outside sources, and will gradually extend production into other fields. As mentioned earlier in this chapter, S.S.C.

is now linking up with G.L.F. in the distribution of Family Foods.

Mr. Wysor does not believe that farmers' purchasing cooperatives should restrict their operations to farm supplies. He told me of an important case now pending before the Virginia Supreme Court, whose decision will affect cooperative progress in that State and in other regions. In the town of Harrisonburg, Virginia, there is a couny cooperative association, now affiliated with the S.S.C., which has been built up from its inception by a remarkably competent manager, Mr. C. V. Smith. Although composed of farmers, it handles not only farm supplies, but groceries, clothing, furniture and other consumers' goods. It has been highly successful and its annual business is now around a million dollars. Of course, the local merchants in that county have not watched its growth with enthusiasm. Recently they brought suit against this cooperative, contending that the Virginia law prohibits farmers' associations from dealing in consumers' goods. The decision of the local court was against the cooperative, but with the support of the S.S.C. the case has been appealed to the State Supreme Court, which it is hoped will reverse the judgment. The outcome is certain to have widespread influence in other parts of the country where commercial business interests are making similar attempts to stem the tide of farmers' cooperation consumerward.

S.S.C.'s policy on patronage returns is liberal. It adds one-third of the annual savings to the treasury reserve, and distributes two-thirds to the patron-members in equal parts of cash and 6 percent preferred shares. Last year's patronage distribution of cash and shares amounted to $354,000 which was 3.6 percent of the wholesale volume. Nor is this liberal policy regarded as inimical to expansion. After announcing that larger patronage returns will be paid in the future, the *Southern States Patron* goes on to say that "the farmers who own and use Southern States Cooperative are giving the organization support which, for loyalty and aggressiveness, is without precedent in the South. With continuation of that support we will have, within less than five years, a finished cooperative which will be second in efficiency to none in the world." Let others look to their laurels.

The local service stores are organized like those of G.L.F., with advisory committee elected by the local patrons. Member-participation is furthered by dividing the territory into nine districts and having one member of the central board of directors elected in each district by the local committeemen who represent the patron-members. About forty-five independent local cooperatives which serve as agents are also accorded the right of voting for directors, which gives them a say in S.S.C. affairs. My net impression, when I talked with Mr. Wysor last fall, was that S.S.C. was moving toward a larger measure of localized participation. That impression has been confirmed by the following statement by him which I quote from a recent letter:

We are moving rather rapidly toward becoming a
system of local cooperatives, owning and controlling
the wholesale institution. More than half of our business is already coming from local cooperatives. Some
of these are entirely independent, self-governing units,
and some are Southern States Cooperative service
stores. Legally the latter are subsidiaries of Southern
States Cooperative and, technically, are controlled by
Southern States but, practically, are under the control
of locally elected advisory boards.

I am not sure which plan will ultimately predomi-
nate. [Here he is speaking more generally and not
with reference to his own organization.] The local cooperative with complete autonomy does the best job
if well managed. Comparatively few are fortunate
enough to have really good management, and the
boards of directors are slow to recognize poor management and to change it even when recognized. A
cooperative service store, under centralized control, is
less likely to fail and less likely to do a very poor job.
However, it does not quite get the support usually
enjoyed by a highly efficient independent cooperative.

A strong overtone comes from the concluding paragraph of Mr. Wysor's last annual report:

"Cooperation is working together. It is self-help. It is
economic Christianity. It is the instrumentality through
which all can gain better standards of living. Farmers
and consumers have learned they can pool their few
dollars and their little buying power to build coopera-

tive institutions which can match the giants of private industry. The cooperative method of doing business is gaining acceptance the world over because it is economically sound and morally right."

FARMERS' COOPERATIVE EXCHANGE

The Farmers' Cooperative Exchange is a young but sturdily growing association which has its headquarters at Raleigh, North Carolina. That state was served directly by S.S.C. until 1934, when in a spirit of autonomy the F.C.X. was organized as an independent body with the understanding that it would purchase its feed, fertilizer and some incidental supplies from the S.S.C. Dr. Joseph G. Knapp, whom I quoted in the preceding chapter, was connected with the North Carolina State College of Agriculture before he was called to his present post with the Farm Credit Administration in Washington, and helped to work out a basis of organization which assured F.C.X. of the support of all the agricultural agencies in the state.

This association is headed as General Manager by a former banker, Mr. Manley G. Mann. For a banker to cast his lot with the cooperative movement is as yet something of a phenomenon. F.C.X. has 23 retail service stores of its own, 160 dealer-agents, 10,000 to 12,000 patrons, and its annual business volume in 1937 was upwards of three million dollars. It has already built up a working capital fund of $95,000 of which only $14,000 came from share subscriptions and the rest from operating savings. For the present (and this is a distinctive feature) it is paying its returns to patrons entirely in 6 percent preferred shares. Another innovation is that of issuing a certificate for one share of common stock, one dollar par value, to every new patron as soon as his purchases reach an amount which yield a dollar's savings. The new patron is thereby made a voting member—or, in other words, taken fully into the fold—as soon as possible.

A wise policy which F.C.X. has followed from the outset is to conduct its business on a strictly cash basis and extend no credit. This stand is all the more commendable in face of competition from "time merchants" who with their alluring but enslaving practices are a veritable curse in many sections of the South—and in almost every part of the country, under various names and adornments. Here is a paragraph from the Association's booklet:

"Does the F.C.X. extend credit? No. If it did, wider margins would then have to be taken in the goods handled. It has been learned from experience, over and over again, that business of whatever nature, which extends credit, will incur losses because of certain bad credit risks. These bad debts are reflected in higher prices for the goods handled, which must be taken care of by those who pay for their goods. Operating on a cash basis is the fair way. In this event no patron is paying the bill of somebody else."

I asked Mr. Mann recently if F.C.X. was sticking to this policy. Here is his reply: "We adhere strictly to an all-cash program, both through the wholesale and our retail branches." Bravo.

Although F.C.X. is an organization of the centralized type, it provides for some local financial responsibility. Before a new service store is opened the farmers are expected to raise a fund of $3,000 among themselves —three hundred of them subscribing ten dollars apiece of share capital. These farmers then elect the committee associated with that store, which though advisory and not controlling, has a more substantial backing on account of the local financing. But control is vested in the central organization. "I am 100 percent for central control," Mr. Mann states, "with as much local authority as it is possible to give." He finds that his previous experience as a banker has aided him greatly in his present work.

In the field of cooperative education, F.C.X. is also making a distinct contribution. Jointly with two other organizations it conducts an annual essay contest which is open to all boys and girls in rural high schools throughout the State. Several thousand contestants take part every year. The four whose contributions are adjudged best, present their essays orally at a big gathering in Raleigh, and the winner in that final event is awarded a year's tuition in any of the State's colleges. The 1937 essay subject was "A Well Rounded Cooperative Program for North Carolina" and the winner was a sixteen-year-old lad named Hartwell Dawson from Sampson County. He urged that farmers should stop paying middlemen's profits and avail themselves of cooperative savings. A good topic for this year would be "How Rural and Urban Cooperatives Can Help Each Other." This would be especially timely if F.C.X., through its affiliation with S.S.C., joins (as presumably it will) in the distribution of Family Foods.

EASTERN STATES FARMERS' EXCHANGE

The Eastern States Farmers' Exchange with headquarters in Springfield, Massachusetts, and a territory which now includes all the New England states, most of Delaware and parts of Pennsylvania and Maryland, was incorporated in 1918. In seniority it ranks first among the principal cooperative purchasing associations of America. But that is not its chief claim to eminence. Although it is a farmers' organization dealing mainly in agricultural supplies, it has gone farther than any other cooperative association, either rural or urban, in applying two principles which are fundamental in consumers' cooperation. One of these is the principle of *patron-ownership* of the business. The other is that of patronage returns in *quality* of goods.

In this great enterprise, which in 1937 had 82,500 members and an operating volume of approximately $20,000,000, the status of patrons is extraordinary. They subscribed nothing whatever in the form of share capital. *There is no share capital.* The business was started with capital hired at fair interest. With the funds thus obtained, the first stock of goods was bought from commercial dealers, advantageously in bulk. The farmer patrons then proceeded to buy these goods directly from the Exchange at current market prices. With no mid-dlemen's costs and profits to be covered, savings began to accumulate forthwith in the treasury. From 1926 on-ward two-thirds of these savings were returned to the patrons in cash, thus reducing the net cost to them of their purchases. The remaining one-third was retained in the treasury as working capital, which increased in amount from year to year. During the nineteen years from 1918 through 1936, a total of nearly four million dollars of capital was thus created from savings alone, as compared with somewhat under two millions obtained through loans. In that period the Exchange invested close to three million dollars in its own producing plants and other fixed assets. Its savings were sufficient to cover the entire outlay for productive equipment and leave a million dollars free for liquid use.

This was accomplished, as I have said, without any share subscriptions, such as were made in launching the other cooperative associations which have been re-viewed. At first glance we might exclaim, "Why, the farmers have contributed nothing. What right have they to own the business?" But hold—*they contributed their patronage.* Thereby they paid the hire of initial capital, created additional capital from savings, built the pro-ductive plants and firmly established the Exchange with its present volume of twenty million dollars.

In forthright recognition of this fact the organiza-tion's By-Laws contain the following provision:

"In the event of a dissolution of the Exchange, whether voluntary or involuntary, the net assets after the payment of all just debts of the Exchange and the expenses of liquidation shall be divided among the membership of the Exchange as then constituted and in proportion to their purchases from or through the Exchange in the calendar year in which dissolution takes place, and the calendar year immediately preceding."

Although the Exchange regards itself and is generally regarded as conservative, and although New England farmers certainly cannot be considered radical as that term is commonly employed, I know of nothing in the whole field of cooperation which in the true and constructive sense is more radical than this explicit recognition that the patrons, *by reason of their patronage alone,* are the owners of the business. If some large commercial company, say one of the chain-store organizations, should announce that it had decided to vest ownership of the enterprise in its customers, that would assuredly be hailed as a radical step. In fact it would be such a radical departure from the prevailing business system that its occurrence is inconceivable. But such a commercial concern would be doing only what the Farmers' Exchange has done from its inception.

Mr. Quentin Reynolds, who has been General Manager of the Exchange since 1929 and had a leading part in its progress, touched upon this matter in a talk which he gave last summer at the annual gathering of the American Institute of Cooperation, a forum for the discussion of all forms of cooperation related to agriculture. After stating that the Exchange is a non-stock organization of which farmers become members by virtue of their purchases, and explaining that issuance of certificates of ownership is unnecessary and would involve expense, he went on to say:

"The Exchange system of handling its members' capital seems to us to have proved to be, after nineteen years' experience with it, a mighty effective way for a group of people to conduct for themselves a non-profit cooperative purchasing service. In other words, it seems to us that the instruments required for setting up and maintaining the capital structure of a profit-seeking corporation are not necessary among a group of people cooperating to select and secure their own supplies with their own capital."

There is further significance in the By-law I have quoted. It gives definite expression to the principle of patron-ownership which is implicit in all purchasing or *consumers'* cooperatives. In those which have share capital the members are usually shareholders and patrons simultaneously, and it makes little difference, practically, whether they own the enterprise in one capacity or the other. Laws and regulations which apply to cooperatives differ a good deal from state to state. Evolution of a code of cooperative law, which in another twenty-five years will probably emerge as a new and important field of legal practice, is still inchoate. As yet it is difficult to say how a court would rule on the point of ownership. Doubtless, different courts would have different opinions. But in view of the fact that cooperatives regard patronage as their support and distribute their savings on a patronage basis, inherent logic may in course of time be expected to bring general legal recognition of ownership by patrons. It would appear that the Farmers' Exchange has taken time by the forelock. This highly successful example of a large and powerful organization built up from patronage savings without share capital, and owned by the patrons, is bound to inspire and influence the whole cooperative movement in America. As it is, all true cooperatives subordinate shareholding and dividends to patronage. But getting away from share-capital altogether would differentiate them still more clearly from profit-business, and bring into still stronger relief the fact that they are designed to serve not property but human beings and human needs.

LEADERSHIP IN QUALITY

In serving the needs of its members the Farmers' Exchange puts quality in first place, as more important than either immediate cash savings, or volume and variety of goods and services. In its uncompromising insistence on quality as the cooperative ideal, and in the degree to which it has applied the standard of quality to its own output, this association is out in front. During my field trip last summer I was struck by the fact that representatives of other purchasing associations with whom I talked were generally and heartily disposed to grant such precedence to the Exchange—while hastening to add that their own organizations likewise made quality the prime objective. Some were

inclined to think that the Exchange went to impractical extremes in that direction and was rather super-
superior in its attitude. Be that as it may, Mr. Reynolds
is an uncompromising apostle of quality as measured by
value in use. This high standard is applied also to the
Eastern States Cooperator, which is the best-printed,
illustrated and turned-out monthly magazine in the
American cooperative field.

What I shall now say about the Farmers' Exchange
specifically may be taken as applying broadly and in
varying degree to the other associations. Just as I discussed the G.L.F. as a working example of magnitude
of achievement, I am now taking the Exchange as an
example of achievement in quality. The illustrations
must necessarily be those of staple farm supplies—seed,
fertilizer and livestock feed. But in showing what quality means and how it is attained these illustrations are
equally significant for urban cooperatives which deal
in family foods, clothing and other household supplies.
The test of quality, whatever the goods may be, is value
in use. Goods of superior quality are those which yield
the best results and thereby prove most economical in
actual usage.

In its seed service the Exchange has given special
attention to seed potatoes. It maintains growing and
testing grounds of its own in Maine and Florida and
large areas under contract, and employs a full-time
plant pathologist who controls and tests four generations
of these potatoes before they are distributed to patrons
for use in seeding. The objectives are virtual elimina-

tion of diseases transmissible through seed pieces, and production of the best potato for table use. The pathologist helps growers to care for potato fields and to improve their digging, storage and shipping methods. As a result the planting potatoes thus produced yield much better crops than the general run of "certified" stock. And the extra cost involved is very small—less than six cents per bushel of seed potatoes, which would be covered by one extra potato in every four feet of croprow.

Fertilizers are mixed and cured in the Exchange's new fertilizer plant at Cambridge, Massachusetts, and the branch plant at Wilmington, Delaware. From the outset the Exchange has worked to develop what are known as "high analysis" fertilizers, which combine maximum soil-building and plant-nutrient value with minimum bulk. Reduced bulk means reduced cost of handling and transportation. The formulas are based on extensive research and experimentation by agronomists of the state agricultural colleges and supplementtary tests which the Exchange itself conducts. "In ten years," Mr. Reynolds states, "we have induced our members to double the average concentration of plant nutrients in the fertilizer they purchase through their Exchange. . . . In 1936 Eastern States members saved $120,000 in cash paid for fertilizer, to say nothing of the economies secured by handling 11,500 tons instead of 23,000 tons. . . . Our fertilizer program supplies the cash crop and market garden needs of the membership and is supplying dairymen with the nutrients which must be returned to their meadows and pastures following the decades of depletion when grass was supposed to be a gift of God."

Livestock feeds are processed in the Buffalo mill of the Exchange which, with additions recently completed, is approximately the same size as the G.L.F. mill in that city. When I went through the Exchange mill last summer I was impressed with its cleanness, orderliness and efficiency. The workers engaged in their various tasks looked alert and interested. The plant manager had an easy friendly way of doing whatever was necessary. He was a Cornell man, and there were graduates of half a dozen universities in the laboratory and executive departments.

I saw the whole sequence of feed processing in operation. From each carload of grain as it arrives samples are taken and put through laboratory tests that require several hours. No delivery is accepted until these tests are finished and found satisfactory. Then the grain is thoroughly sifted and cleaned, and elevated into storage compartments. From these compartments the various kinds of grain are brought down through funnels into the grinding and mixing machines, where many varieties of feed for cattle, poultry, pigs and other farm animals are scientifically prepared in accordance with formulas which, like those for fertilizer, are based on data provided by specialized experts. Full advantage is taken of the latest findings of the federal Department of Agriculture, state agricultural colleges not only in the East but throughout the country, and similar institutions in other countries. After the mixing is completed the feeds are put up in sacks, and loaded onto the freight cars for shipment and distribution in the Farmers' Exchange territory.

The feeds thus processed are known as "Open Formula" products. This means that on each sack is printed a full list of the ingredients and their respective amounts. Thus the purchaser knows exactly what he is buying, under the cooperative guarantee. This open formula idea originated in some of the state agricultural colleges, who recommended its adoption as a general trade practice. But commercial dealers with few exceptions have never gone beyond printing the ingredients and omitting the amounts. That leaves the way open to reducing the quantity of ingredients which become too costly and substituting a larger quantity of others which are cheap—which of course alters the feed value of the mixture. About 1921 some of the Eastern and Middlewestern purchasing associations got together and decided to follow the plan completely. Since that time the Open Formula has been fully identified with cooperative production and distribution. It has become a sort of symbol of the general openness of cooperative methods.

STANDARDS OF VALUE IN USE

All of the purchasing associations have accomplished their best results in terms of quality. Those results are the finest credentials they can offer to the American people in behalf of the cooperative way. What has been achieved is in line of cooperative advance according to plan, but has been spurred by practical compulsion. At first, cash returns to patrons were in the foreground. But, as I have noted in the foregoing descriptions, it soon became evident that a goodly portion of the savings should be retained in the treasuries for use as working capital. Then as cooperative distribution of supplies tended to lower the general price level of those commodities—which has almost invariably been the case in areas of active operation—the margin of saving was diminished, and still less could be paid out prudently in cash returns. Furthermore, commercial concerns were always undercutting prices with low-grade products. These developments practically compelled the cooperative groups to concentrate their efforts on superior quality of goods and services. By that time the regional associations were in a strong position by reason of the large capital resources and productive equipment which they had built up, mainly from savings. Thenceforth they devoted themselves to high quality of output, and undertook a sustained campaign to educate their members to a fuller appreciation of quality as measured by economy. Of course some have done better than others. Some have allowed volume and variety to absorb too much of their attention, and in order to meet all levels of demand and attract new patrons have put out second, third and even fourth grades of a given product. But by and large their quality record is one of which they may well be proud.

Of course the farmer in putting seed, fertilizer and

livestock feed to use, can readily check the results. He knows whether his crop-yield per acre is improved and whether his cows give more and better milk. The urban consumer may not be able to check so definitely the things he uses in his home, and for that very reason he needs, even more than the farmer, a cooperative organization which he himself controls and in which he has full confidence.

The rural purchasing associations which have here been presented provide urban consumers with concrete object lessons of cooperative accomplishment in magnitude and quality. The plainest of these lessons is that large resources are required to obtain such results, and that cooperative distribution attains the best standards of quality when it is backed by cooperative production. Rural forces have impressively demonstrated that in union there is strength. Now some of the strongest of those rural forces are taking urban forces into partnership in the new enterprise of Family Foods. That will bring nourishment to the common cause.

In the consumers' cooperative movement the women are always several leaps or laps ahead of the men in seeing commonsense needs and realities. Or, put in a homelier way, the women are always egging the men on to do things that they with their more ponderous minds have not quite got around to doing of their own free will.

The men of the Grange in nothing showed their wisdom more than in giving the women—if giving *is the proper word—an equal place in that great fraternity-sorority. At all Grange meetings the Sisters dispense hospitality with one hand and instigate to action with the other. I have no doubt* they *saw to it that the early Grange stores carried household goods as well as farm machinery. You will recall from the preceding chapter that it was the women who first got the G.L.F. to add family foods to its stock. The same story was told me at the mill of the Eastern States Farmers' Exchange, which is quietly distributing flours and cereals to its own patrons. Throughout the Middle West, except in a few resistant quarters, I heard a similar tale in swelling volume. Women are the scouts and skirmishers, and men consolidate the lines. Now that rural electrification is setting farm women free from household drudgery, what won't they do in the future?*

Here and there I talked with quite a number of women about these things. Space does not permit quoting them all, but the following bit of conversation with a composite of them all, whom we'll call Mrs. Martha Early, will convey to you the general tenor of their talk.

"Mrs. Early, what do you think of this idea of people getting together in cooperatives?"

"What do I think of it? There's only one thing that anybody in his senses can think of it. It's just doing in a larger way what we all do or ought to do in the home. What does home life amount to without cooperation? It's lack of cooperation that's wrecking so many homes today. If we women don't cooperate with our husbands and our husbands with us, and if children and parents don't cooperate—both ways—the home is no home at all. It's just a long and wearing fight-fest. But there's nothing better and happier than a home where everyone pulls together. And it looks simple enough to me that we'll do best and live happiest by pulling together in the community and the whole country. That's what cooperatives are for, isn't it? Well, then, that's what I think of cooperation."

"Well, I won't argue with you about that, because I agree with you, hands down. But here's another question. You're a farmer's wife. What do you think of the idea that farmers' cooperatives ought to stick to the marketing of crops and the buying of farm supplies like cattle-feed and fertilizer? Some people seem to think

that they ought not to go in for buying family food and household goods. What would you say?"

"I'd say those people need educating—or something. Why should a farmer think more of what his cows and pigs eat than of what his family eats? Why should he raise his crops the best he can and not raise his children the best he can? Why should he put everything into the barn and nothing into the house? Did you ever read that story by Mary E. Wilkins called 'Mother'? If you haven't, you ought to. (I hastened to assure her that I had.) All right then. You know that woman got too much of it, and once when her husband was away she moved into the barn, and there she lived comfortably. Lord knows, most of us farm women haven't any right to complain about our husbands. They're forever toiling and doing the best they can. But so are we, and now that the co-operatives have taken care of the crops and the cattle we think it's our turn next.

"We know well enough too why some people want the farmers' cooperatives to stick just to farm supplies. The co-ops are doing such a big job there that they can't be pushed out anyway, and what's more they're buying a lot of things from people who like the farmer's money. But of course the local grocery stores and the chains and the mail order houses and the installment companies, and no end of people that are mixed up with them, don't want to see the cooperatives take that trade away from them—no matter how much the farmers could save. But don't worry. We women are the ones that do the family buying and we know what we're talking *about. Just give us a little more time and we'll take care of that."*

"Bravo! Kipling was right. Let's compare notes again in 1940, say around the Fourth of July. Good-bye, Mrs. Early, and best wishes."

11. MOTOR POWER

AMERICANS are mobile. More than any other people they move by motor power. Amid all the vast variety of things mechanical which marks the present day, the one which best symbolizes America is the automobile. Everywhere, in cities, towns and open country, on highways and byways, it is in perpetual motion, carrying people thither and yon, back and forth, around and around, for pleasure, business or habit. Motor manufacture is now the nation's leading industry. From taxes on the enormous quantities of gas which motors consume, a network of roads to facilitate more motoring has been built from the Atlantic to the Pacific, from Canada to Mexico, till the whole land vibrates to the whir of the engine and the tune of the tires.

The country's farms have been motorized in recent years by trucks, tractors and other gas-propelled machinery. Farmers used to rely on their sturdy teams of horses fed with farm-raised hay, grain and fodder. Now they have to purchase supplies of gasoline, kerosene, oil, tractor fuel, tires and accessories to feed and equip their inanimate mechanical helpers. Motor power has of course aided the farmer tremendously as an agricultural producer. It has also broadened and brightened his life and interests as a consumer, a human being. After the evening chores are finished the young people jump into the car and go to town. Sundays or when work lets up a bit the farmer takes his family for a drive. In an afternoon they cover more ground and see more places and people than they could have done in a week in the old horse-and-buggy days. They visit their city relatives, get the feel of city life, gain a better understanding of city conditions and problems, and come to have closer ties with their urban fellow-Americans. The same things happen in reverse when city folk visit the country. It all makes for reciprocity and cooperation. The motor is now a common denominator of rural and urban life, and motor fuel is a common need.

In meeting that need the American cooperative movement is today making its most striking and promising progress. In this latest and most typically American development of cooperation the farmers have again laid the foundations and built the main structures. But more quickly and widely than any other form of cooperative activity, this kind has spread to the towns and cities. The farmers' cooperative wholesales are beginning to supply urban cooperatives with gas and oil and to admit these urban groups as units of their regional associations. New urban units are springing up everywhere— hundreds of them. Some begin with gas and oil and then add other things, including groceries. They get a better start in that way, because the margin of saving on gas is larger and the handling simpler and less costly in time, energy and money. As someone has aptly said, oil is lubricating the advance of cooperation from the country to the city.

Nearly all the farmers' purchasing associations now include petroleum products in their stock of supplies. In the case of the Eastern organizations described in the preceding chapter, these are still a minor part of the total volume compared to feed and fertilizer. It is in the Middle West, the country's center, that cooperation is advancing most strongly by motor power. There, although other things figure importantly, petroleum sets the pace. That region is now full of gas and oil cooperatives, ranging from little ones to big ones and serving areas of various sizes. The local units are coordinated and massed in great state and regional federations, which own and operate half a dozen processing plants that supply high-grade oil blends for cooperative distribution throughout the land.

American cooperative activity in this field, though it has been under way only fifteen years, already surpasses by far anything which cooperatives have done in the same field in other countries. That is natural in view of the size of this country, its available oil supply and the motor habits of its people. But it is a fact which is going to have momentous consequences.

MIDDLEWESTERN CHARACTERISTICS

Besides running motorwise, the Middlewestern cooperatives have other characteristic features which correspond with salient differences between that section of the country and the older East. Centralized financial and business control is deeply intrenched and accepted in the Eastern states and has imprinted its own image in the public mind. The atmosphere which emanates from it affects people unconsciously. So it was to be expected that when the Farmers' Exchange and the G.L.F. were organized they took, even as cooperatives, a centralized form and had something of a business complexion. Imitation doubtless played its part, in that each of the Eastern associations was modeled more or less after its predecessors. At any rate, the four which I described follow the centralized plan and stick pretty closely to operations which on the surface look much like commercial business. As yet there is only one farmers' regional in the East, the Pennsylvania Farm Bureau Cooperative Association, with headquarters at Harrisburg, which departs from that pattern and which for that reason I shall group with its western confreres.

In contrast, practically all of the Middlewestern organizations are of the decentralized type, in which autonomous local units own and control the central wholesale. Therein they conform more fully with what is generally believed to be the soundest cooperative plan —one which is widely rooted and grows from the bottom up. Such growth may be compared to the natural growth of a tree, whose strength in withstanding the elements is commensurate with the depth and breadth of the roots which hold it fast to the earth. A centralized cooperative is more like a tree which has been set up where it must find a foothold and may need some propping. It may flourish and spread its branches, but can its roots get so strong a grip? In such an organization there is almost always a tendency for a small group at the center to do the thinking and acting. Where only business operations are concerned, this may make for efficiency; but where the objects are more inclusive, it may hamper growth.

Unquestionably the Middlewestern federations are developing in a broader way. Though they derive their support mainly from production and distribution of commodities, they do not confine themselves exclusively to that function or conceive cooperation wholly in those terms. They have added cooperative insurance and cooperative credit, and are giving more and more attention to the humanities—especially education and recreation. Their educational activities are concerned not only with practical problems of management, service and auditing, and the training of their present and prospective working personnel, but with the whole philosophy of cooperation and its social as well as economic potentialities. In that spirit they are exploring the recreational field, and enlisting women and youth.

Furthermore these Middlewestern federations have much more of the consumer viewpoint than has thus far been shown by the Eastern associations, and have gone farther in adding consumers' goods to their stocks. (I am speaking here of general tendencies, and am not forgetting the outstanding enterprise of G.L.F. in its new program of Family Foods.) Many of the local units and some of the smaller wholesales have carried household supplies from the outset. They are now enjoying a brisk trade in home electrical appliances, as an outgrowth of rural electrification. One of the largest regional wholesales has recently begun to deal in groceries on an extensive scale. By and large, the distinction which representatives of the *business* school are wont to draw between cooperative purchasing of farm supplies and what *they* call consumers' cooperation, is in this part of the country dim to the vanishing point. By the same token this is the region where rural and urban cooperators, the leaders and the rank and file, are making most progress in getting together.

So much by way of generalization. Now for something of the concrete story. Space will not permit saying much, except now and then for illustration, about the local cooperative units. Earlier in the book I have gone sufficiently into the way such units are formed and the way they function. Suffice to say here that they are like the living cells which constitute an organism, and that while the wholesale operations which I shall describe are more impressive in size, they are only the collective and coordinated activities of the local units which compose the federations. These local units are *completely* self-governing in their own right.

MIDLAND COOPERATIVE WHOLESALE

It is fitting to begin with the first cooperative oil wholesale in America, which had its origin in the first local unit of this kind.

That original unit was the Cooperative Oil Company of Cottonwood, Minnesota, which was formed in 1921. The local farmers, finding that they had to buy motor fuel in increasing quantities for agricultural uses, decided there was no necessary reason why they should pay the retailers' profits, so they organized the cooperative to buy petroleum products in bulk direct from commercial wholesales. At that time there was a much larger margin between wholesale and retail prices than there is today. These pioneers, following the standard plan of paying current prices over their own cooperative counter, found that after deducting costs of operation, interest on capital shares and working reserves, they could return to themselves as savings as much as 15 to 20 percent of the retail price.

The good news got around, and within a few years a score of similar units sprang up in the district. This growing movement led the commercial dealers to lower their retail prices in that area, which benefited all consumers. For the cooperatives, however, this price reduction resulting from their own activity meant a diminished margin of saving, partly offset by their increased economy and efficiency of operation as they learned from experience. In sixteen years the Cottonwood unit has returned over $70,000 to its members in cash savings. Its 1936 volume amounted to $95,000 on which the savings came to 9 percent. Another early and somewhat larger unit, operating in Freeborn and adjoining counties, has in twelve years had a sales volume of $3,-000,000 and returned over $300,000 in savings to its members. In varying amounts similar figures could be cited for each of the 170 units which are now federated around their wholesale. Instead of taking profits out of their communities and thereby depleting local buying power for the gain of absentee owners, as commercial oil companies do, these 170 cooperatives have constantly increased consumers' purchasing power and thereby built up community and regional resources. In 1936 alone their total savings were $1,250,000. Each local association, composed of several hundred to several thousand persons, maintains at least one station-store-and-warehouse in the local area, and the larger ones have several branches. All of them are centers of community interest and enterprise.

Midland Cooperative Wholesale, which the local units (then only 37 in number) established in 1926, is unique in being the only cooperative wholesale in America that was started without any capital whatever, either shares or loans, and built up wholly from savings. For a time each local unit paid in advance for the supplies which the wholesale bought in bulk directly from commercial producers. During the first year wholesale volume was about $270,000 and $3,500 was returned to the units as savings which they in turn passed on to their individual members. Thereafter by common consent all savings were left in the treasury to provide working capital. Now distribution of savings has been resumed under what is called the five-year revolving plan. This means that each year's savings are retained for five years as working funds and then disbursed. The wholesale's operating capital and surplus is now upwards of $250,000 and its volume for 1937 was $3,696,742. Patrons number about eighty thousand.

This wholesale occupies a five-story building of its

own in the outskirts of Minneapolis. The basement and first story are taken up by an oil-blending plant. There and in a branch plant at Milwaukee all the Midland Co-op oils are compounded, in four grades ranging in price from fifteen cents to thirty cents a quart. The other floors contain offices, workrooms and a good-sized hall for cooperative meetings. In the absence of Mr. E. G. Cort, the General Manager, I talked with Mr. George W. Jacobson, the acting manager, who has been with the wholesale from its inception and contributed much to its development. While he was studying economics in the business school of Minnesota University, the possibilities of cooperation attracted him so strongly that he decided to make this field his life work and has found deep satisfaction in it. He is level-headed, broad-visioned and progressive. Other staff members with whom I talked were up-and-coming. At the Minnesota State Fair—one of the largest of these American medleys of stock-showing, horse-racing, speech-making, circus-barking, church-boosting and victual-eating—I saw the cooperative exhibits and met several of the farmers who are elective officers of the wholesale. From them I got the viewpoint of the people who in the last analysis constitute and control the wholesale. Members from various parts of the state visited the Midland tent to pay their respects and ask the latest news.

The difference between a federation of this kind and a centralized association appears clearly in the Midland plan of government. The territory, which now includes Minnesota and part of Wisconsin, is divided into ten districts. Within each district the local units elect delegates to represent them at an annual district meeting, at which a director is nominated to represent that district on the wholesale board. At the general Annual Meeting in June the ten directors thus nominated are formally elected. They are responsible to the local units. To implement that responsibility the units also elect advisory boards for each district. The respective directors serve as chairmen of these boards, which meet four times a year to consider district and wholesale matters and their inter-relation. Questions or recommendations of the district meetings are taken by the chairmen to meetings of the wholesale board for consideration. "Thus," to quote a statement on this subject, "important decisions are never made without an opportunity being given for all parties concerned to enter into the democratic process . . . The district plan carries with it the possibility of great development in the future . . . Just as the members of the local cooperative associations have learned how to run their cooperative business by running it, so also are the cooperators of the Midland family learning how best to use the democratic process by using it. They are building an economic democracy based upon human values, universal consumer needs and the principle of equal rights and equal responsibility. Their daily acts become part of the structure and function of a new social and economic order having for its principal object the betterment of their homes, families and communities."

Midland regards everything it is doing as consumers'

cooperation and draws no rigid line between rural and urban consumers. Though most of the local units are composed of farmers, a number of urban groups have already been admitted to the federation. Recognizing practical needs, trends and opportunities, Midland began the current year, 1938, by expanding its wholesale service to include distribution of groceries to the retail units.

Early in 1937 this wholesale took the initiative in working out a new enterprise in cooperative gasoline distribution which has attracted wide attention and may have far-reaching results. Like all the other cooperative wholesales thus far, it obtains its supply of gasoline from commercial companies. This plan is not wholly satisfactory. The quality of gasoline may vary or fall off, and difficulties or disagreements may cause more or less trouble. If the cooperative could control production and quality, that would be much better. As a beginning which looks in that direction, Midland and two other large regional groups (Consumers Cooperative Association of Kansas City and Illinois Supply Company of Chicago) have now contracted with a well known oil company to take the entire output of a refinery in Oklahoma, with the stipulation they shall control production and quality under the supervision of a chemist and an auditor who will represent them at the plant. It is further understood that net savings will be divided between the cooperatives and the oil company. Perhaps there are other things in the background. At any rate this is a notable stride toward cooperative refining.

Going beyond the distribution of commodities, Midland has taken part in organizing three mutual insurance companies covering automobile and fire risks, and a cooperative agency through which any desired form of insurance may be taken out. Its affiliated Credit Corporation aids local cooperatives to obtain loans on the most favorable terms, and the Federated Electric Cooperatives serves as an intermediary between the Rural Electrification Administration in Washington and cooperative units in the Midland region formed to construct and operate new rural lines. The wholesale publishes a monthly organ called the *Midland Cooperator,* and in the field of education has successfully developed training courses for the working personnel, and circuit schools for members in cooperation with the local units.

FARMERS' UNION CENTRAL EXCHANGE

Minnesota is sometimes called the Banner State of Cooperation. Several other states have good warrant, I think, to contest that claim, and the decision rests on points. But in the percentage of motor fuel which is cooperatively distributed, Minnesota is in the lead. Cooperative distribution has steadily come up from behind until now, in competition with the commercial oil companies, it holds second place and is going strong. In some counties fully 75 percent of the volume is cooperatively supplied. One reason for this remarkable showing may be that the Twin Cities have twin cooperative oil wholesales, which are engaged in friendly but lively rivalry in the overlapping portion of their zones. In St. Paul, only a few miles away from the Midland headquarters in Minneapolis, stands the four-story oil-blending plant of the Farmers' Union Central Exchange. Built of red brick and set spaciously back from the road with a well kept lawn, it presents a fine appearance. This building, which also contains the offices, was erected in 1935 after the wholesale had found from experience that it could not depend on an assured supply of satisfactory oil-blends from commercial sources. In going over the plant with Mr. Ralph Ingerson and some of his associates I could readily believe that it is "one of the most efficient in the United States."

It is noteworthy that this purchasing wholesale grew out of a grain marketing cooperative, the Farmers' Union Terminal Association, which now has office space in its offspring's edifice. Mr. E. A. Syftestad, now General Manager of the wholesale, was formerly connected with the marketing work. Started in 1927 as a subsidiary of that association and not a cooperative itself, this agency purchased binder twine and saved the association's members large sums of money, forced down the price of twine and raised its quality. Furthermore, with part of the savings it helped farmers to organize a goodly number of local gas and oil cooperatives. As these grew and prospered they tended to add other supplies and felt the need of a federation and wholesale of their own. In response to that demand the subsidiary agency was separated from the marketing association, and reorganized in 1931 as a cooperative wholesale owned and controlled by the local units, whose number has now increased to

235. A comparatively small number of centrally owned service stores have been undergoing change to a cooperative basis. In 1937 the wholesale's volume was above $4,000,000. Its territory overlaps that of Midland in Minnesota and Wisconsin and extends northwest into Montana and the Dakotas. All told there are approximately 129,000 patrons.

The most spectacular achievement of the Central Exchange has been its pioneering part in bringing out the new Co-op Tractor. That event, in which two other regional wholesales joined forces with this one in the business arrangements, took place in the autumn of 1935. It was preceded by long and careful study of the farmer's needs in tractor service, with a view to getting the best possible combination of efficiency and economy. The designing was intrusted to one of the foremost automotive engineers, and a contract for production was made with a company of established reputation in the manufacture of machinery. This is said to be the first tractor in America constructed according to the specifications of the farmers themselves. Its chief features are a high compression motor which gets maximum power from fuel, more effective use of rubber tires, transmission with five forward speeds and reverse, and adaptability for any kind of farm work from the lightest to the heaviest. The fact that it can be driven from place to place or on long road trips at good speed adds much to its convenience.

Over and above its intrinsic merits, it is a striking advertisement for the American cooperative movement.

When it was first introduced numerous demonstrations and tractor contests were staged at fairs and other gatherings, with such impressive results that the "Co-op" soon became "the talk of the country." In traveling through the Middle West last summer I heard many eye-witness tales of its exploits. Evidently it is already setting the pace for commercial tractors, as several of similar type have since appeared and others are reported in prospect. In due course its production may be taken over by the new Cooperative Machinery Company, which has just lately been organized by five regional associations for the "development, manufacture, distribution and sale of farm tractors, farm machinery, other farm equipment and general farm supplies."

Now it might be thought that a wholesale like the Central Exchange, going in for agricultural machinery, would regard itself as being in a different class from those which have to do with consumers' goods—though for that matter the Exchange does carry a full line of electrical household appliances. But at any rate here is what it says about itself: "The Farmers Union Central Exchange is what consumers are rapidly coming to know as a typical consumers' cooperative wholesale association . . . The plan of organization closely conforms to that of the many other consumer wholesale organizations which have grown up in the United States during the past fifteen years."

There speaks the militant spirit of the Farmers Educational and Cooperative Union, with which this wholesale is identified. The Farmers Union, as its name is usually shortened, is a national organization dating from 1902, somewhat similar to though smaller than the Grange, and zealous for cooperation. It has local units in thirty-seven states, and twenty-three state associations. I attended an open session of the Iowa branch in Des Moines last fall and got a sense of the Union's fervor. In between spells of oratory the delegates would stand up and sing the famous Iowa Corn Song:

> "We're in I-o-way, I-o-way
> State of all the land
> Joy on ev'ry hand
> We're in I-o-way, I-o-way
> There's where the tall corn grows."

At that session I met Mr. E. H. Everson of South Dakota, then national President, who said the Union regarded all farmers' cooperative purchasing as consumers' cooperation. The only difference between rural and urban forms of consumers cooperation is a natural difference in the kinds of goods distributed, corresponding to differences in rural and urban needs. In the women's and youth group programs of the Union, which have been most fully developed in the Dakotas, cooperative education is the focus of interest. In various parts of the country cooperative stores composed of Union members include groceries and other household supplies in their stock. This is especially true in Nebraska, where there are now about five hundred stores, gas stations, cream stations and local grain elevators which carry a variety of things. Household goods make up about 25 percent of the wholesale volume of the

Farmers Union State Exchange at Omaha. In fact, that organization has been a pathfinder in this field for many years, and has had far-reaching influence in broadening the vision of other farmers' associations in the Middle West. The national Farmers Union is relaying its elder brother, the Grange, in bearing the torch of consumers' cooperation. In many places I crossed the trail of the Farmers Union and found fine examples of its enterprise. Wherever it appears it is a leavening and dynamic force. In large part it represents the aspiration of tenant-farmers who are struggling to improve their lot, and see in cooperation the most practical and effective means of accomplishing that purpose. Through the medium of the *Farmers Union Herald* which is published monthly at St. Paul, the principles and progress of consumers' cooperation are kept constantly before the organization's members.

As regards future development of the Central Exchange of St. Paul, the wholesale is on record as announcing that "as its capital grows it stands ready to expand into new lines and products on which consumers are still at the mercy of the profit seeker."

CONSUMERS COOPERATIVE ASSOCIATION

In surveying current cooperative progress in America an observer is struck by a certain division of labor among the different organizations in contributing to the wholeness of this progress. Though these organizations are alike in the main and are moving in the same general direction, each one is doing something which differs either in kind or in emphasis from what the others are doing. Thus each brings something of peculiar value to the collective fund of experiment and experience, and forwards cooperative evolution.

The regional federation which will now be presented is outstanding in its entirety. But its most distinctive contribution, I would say, is its present enterprising and vigorous expansion on a large scale into the distribution of groceries, clothing and household supplies, and its increasing inter-relation of these new activities with urban cooperatives in its territory. In its commitment to the policy of dealing in consumers' goods it is doing pioneer work which bids fair to write a new page in the annals of American cooperation.

This organization has its wholesale headquarters in North Kansas City, Missouri. It was formed in 1929 as a farmers' purchasing federation dealing mainly in gas and oil. At that time it had a different name from the one it now bears, but a few years ago it took a bold step in deciding to call itself the Consumers Cooperative Association. "What's in a name?" we sometimes say. Well, in this case I think the name has had a psychological effect on the association's whole outlook.

The founder of the C.C.A. is Mr. Howard A. Cowden. He had started on his own a company which supplied petroleum products to farmers' cooperatives in the Kansas City area. That service led to the development of a regional federation which took over the company and reorganized it as a cooperative wholesale. Mr. Cowden became President and chief executive officer, and has infused this organization with his own spirit of enterprise. He is not one to hang back or sit tight, and is willing to venture something in pushing ahead. The working staff impressed me as having a happy combination of cooperative understanding and efficiency. Somehow that same combination has found expression in the atmosphere of the spacious reception room which one enters in visiting the headquarters. It is bright and colorful, enlivened with growing plants, inviting with comfortable chairs and an attractive library of cooperative literature. In one corner opposite the entrance is a display of C.C.A. products, so pleasingly arranged that one cannot help being drawn to it. After looking it over one can sit down and read the latest Co-op news in a lively semi-monthly publication called the *Cooperative Consumer.*

A turn of events which appears rather fateful enabled the association to acquire in 1935 the modern brick building that contains its offices and processing plants. This building was erected ten years earlier by a commercial oil company at a cost of $245,000. The company's refusal to sell lubricating oil to the cooperative because its business was "not worth bothering about" was a factor in deciding the association to blend its own oils. The commercial company failed, but the cooperative succeeded and bought the building later for $55,-500. The large oil plant has a blending capacity of 55,800 gallons and storage capacity for 492,000 gallons. C.C.A. lays claim to having established in 1929, at its earlier location, the first cooperative oil compounding

plant in the world. It also has the unique distinction
of being the only American cooperative which has thus
far shipped oil to Europe. Shipments have been made
to the cooperative wholesales of Scotland, France, Bel-
gium and Estonia. There is reason to believe they are
precursors of some highly interesting international developments which are now pending, and about which
I shall have something more to say at another point.
C.C.A. also manufactures now its own grease and paint,
and supplies grease to two other cooperative wholesales.
A well equipped laboratory has the double function of
testing for purity and quality the products which are
distributed and aiding in the development of new products, several of which are now in prospect.

This wholesale's territory is more extended than that
of any other single regional association in America.
Some observers feel it is extended too far, especially
where it overlaps areas in which other associations are
operating, and that some of the local units are too distant from the headquarters for close working relationship. There are nine district warehouses, however,
which serve as distributing centers. Altogether 356 units
in ten states are now affiliated with the wholesale, and
some of them are a thousand miles apart. But the area
of concentration is more compact. Two hundred and
nine of the units are located in the single state of
Kansas, 52 in Nebraska, 30 in South Dakota, 26 in
Iowa, 24 in Colorado, 8 in Missouri, 3 in North Dakota,
2 in Illinois, 1 in Utah and 1 in Idaho. I was interested
to learn that some of the units are Grange stores which

have come down from the early days. In the town of Cadmus, Kansas, for example, is a Grange store which was launched in 1876 and is still prospering. All told, the number of individual C.C.A. patrons, who purchase goods from local units throughout its far-flung field of operation, is now around 120,000.

Wholesale volume has grown from about $5000 in 1929 to $3,750,000 in 1936. Owing to a change of fiscal year, figures for the full calendar year 1937 are not available, but volume for the first eight months amounted to $3,090,116, which was an increase of about one-seventh over the same portion of 1936.* Patronage refunds to units have increased steadily and totaled more than a quarter of a million dollars for the period 1929-37. Capital built up chiefly from savings is now upwards of $500,000. C.C.A. recently adopted the five-year revolving fund plan which I explained in describing the Midland wholesale. This is providing larger current resources for expansion.

The most significant line of expansion is that to which I referred at the outset—groceries, clothing and household supplies. It was started in 1936 after careful consideration, and largely in response to demand for groceries from cooperative units in Kansas. Wholesale volume for the first eight months of 1937 was $114,000 and showed an increase of 166 percent over the preceding eight months. The current annual volume rate is about $250,000. At first only a dozen grocery staples were

* 1937 volume, now reported, was $3,894,843. The number of units is now 363.

tried out, then the number was gradually increased till now some 300 to 400 items are being handled. For the present most of these are obtained from commercial sources, in conformity with specifications, tests and quality standards set by the C.C.A. Of the 356 local units affiliated with the wholesale about 50 now include groceries in their stock, and 50 more of the same sort, which are not yet full members of the Federation, will avail themselves of this grocery service and apply their patronage savings to purchase of membership shares. Though most of the stores are rural about 10 percent of them are urban, in large communities like Kansas City itself, St. Louis, Columbus and Springfield, in the State of Missouri; Wichita, Lawrence and Winfield in Kansas; Denver and Boulder in Colorado; and Lincoln, Nebraska. The availability of this wholesale service is encouraging urban consumer groups to open stores. The grocery department of the C.C.A. is headed by men of successful experience in this particular field, who are developing the new work systematically and providing local units with advertising material for store display and circulation among the members. This helps to keep the local inventories moving and to get maximum sales with minimum handling.

Besides groceries, the household supplies of the wholesale include radios, electrical appliances and women's coats. The coats are made by a producers' group, the Worker's Aim Cooperative Association of Hightstown, New Jersey—one of the Federal resettlement communities. The cooperative is self-supporting and is composed

of about a hundred skilled and carefully selected needle-
workers from New York City. The coats are very well
made and of good quality, and sell at prices appreciably
below commercial prices for comparable garments. The
difference between their actual cost and the selling price
is divided between the workers who make them and the
consumers' cooperatives in various parts of the country,
through which they are sold. This is an interesting example of mutually advantageous working relations
between cooperatively organized producers and consumers.

Women in the cooperatives are quite excited about
these garments. In one store along the way I saw a score
or more of them lined up before mirrors, donning and
doffing one coat after another at a furious rate, with so
many criss-cross compliments flying about that a mere
man in the offing was not even noticed.

Since the coats are made for sale in various parts of
the country, extreme styles have been avoided. It is interesting to observe, however, that future fashions, in
response to feminine reactions in other sections, will
have more of a New York air. "Our spring styles in coats
and dresses [a new line] will bear comparison with anything in the Fifth Avenue show-windows," said the
saleslady in the New York City display rooms on Thirty-
fourth Street, near Macy's, "but our prices will still be
kept down. . . . Yes, the women like them and our output is growing all the time."

Until quite recently the C.C.A. was not doing much
in cooperative education beyond some training courses
for its staff, but it now has an educational department

headed by a former college professor who is laying out a broad program for members—men, women and young people.

Women's guilds like those of the Farmers Union in the Dakotas are being formed around the local units and are taking special interest in grocery sampling and quality tests. Here women can take a vital and invaluable part in developing standards on a par with those which the cooperatives have already developed for farm supplies. That is really the most important objective which cooperatives dealing in household supplies must set themselves, and naturally the women members are the ones to take the lead. In the C.C.A. they will have an exceptionally good opportunity, in that Dr. E. J. Petry, who is in charge of the laboratory, is more than willing to cooperate with them and excellently equipped to do so. He is a man of broad education and experience, with an impressive record in *Who's Who,* and he has made distinguished contributions in the field of laboratory experimentation and research. His technical skill and the women's practical everyday familiarity with household and family needs, ought to be a winning combination. In the youth program one of the outstanding aims will be to provide opportunities, through camps, tours and scholarships, for boys and girls from different parts of the country, different farmers' organizations and urban as well as rural communities, to meet one another, get rid of any prejudices they may have, and work together in furthering cooperation throughout the United States. Such a constructive plan well carried out could accomplish wonders.

LOOKING back a moment from this point, we see how American cooperation in growing has learned to mass its resources. First came small local groups, separate and unrelated, each fending for itself. These local groups came together in state and regional federations, and thereby gained collective strength. In due course federations entered into partnerships among themselves. Several undertakings of that sort have already been noted. In one instance, G.L.F. and four other regional wholesales have joined in rural and urban distribution of family foods. In another, three associations have combined to obtain their supply of gasoline more satisfactorily. A similar triple alliance brought out the Co-op Tractor. Five organizations shared in sponsoring the new Cooperative Machinery Company. Just lately the G.L.F. and the Ohio Farm Bureau Cooperative Association have bought out a commercial fertilizer plant in Baltimore and become partners in the new concern, Fertilizer Manufacturing, Incorporated.

But there is more to be told. Within the last few years this movement of inter-relation and integration has attained still larger proportions and produced two results which warrant great expectations. One is the formation of a federation of federations which unites the East and the West and whose prestige and resources are equal to transforming many possibilities into actualities. The other is the establishment of a national whole-sale which will serve as a clearing-house and power-station for urban as well as rural cooperatives and bring national momentum to the whole movement.

These are composite results to which legions of rank and file cooperators and many representative bodies and outstanding leaders have contributed. Credit must be widely apportioned. But again American farmers have been the principal builders, not only through their co-operative associations in the foreground but through three national organizations which stand back of this cooperative activity and give it the benefit of their moral support and man-power. The Grange and the Farmers Union have already come into the picture. Now in accounting for the latest and most promising developments and somewhat discerning "the shape of things to come" we must make the acquaintance of a third organization called the Farm Bureau which, though the youngest of the family, has grown strong and powerful throughout the country and is doing much to mold the future. Here is meant not the future of farmers alone, but the future of American cooperation. This organization now has a leading part in the drama of cooperative progress. Let us see how that has come about and what it imports.

FARM BUREAUS

The term "bureau" suggests something governmental. In origin the Farm Bureau was closely connected with the federal, state and county agricultural extension service which was initiated in 1906 and definitely established in 1914. Under this joint plan the Department of Agriculture, the state agricultural colleges, and farmers throughout the country have worked together for agricultural and rural betterment. Each state college has had an extension leader with assistants assigned to specific functions. Main emphasis has been placed on efficiency in farming, marketing and purchasing, but home economics has been developed among the women and educational club activities among the boys and girls. Extension agents have been stationed in each county, with the task of rallying the local farmers around this service and giving them all possible help along these lines. The work has been maintained chiefly with federal funds and has been of great constructive value, not only to farmers but indirectly to urban consumers through improvement of the quality of farm products which provide urban consumers with food.

Naturally, the county agents tried to get some measure of organization among the farmers to make the local work more effective. As the farmers got used to meeting in groups with the agent, they came to think of permanent organization themselves for purposes growing out of the extension programs. Thus county improvement associations came into being. Linked up as they were with the Agricultural Extension Bureau they naturally thought of their own local units in similar terms. So they formed self-supporting county organizations which they called Farm Bureaus. These in turn soon began to unite in State Federations, which are now forty in number. In 1919 a national body, the American Farm Bureau Federation, was established, with headquarters in Chicago. Total membership is around four hundred thousand. Mr. Edward A. O'Neal, with whom I had a very interesting interview in the summer of 1937, is the national President.

The principal objective of this organization is evidently to shape national policies affecting agriculture, and much of its effort is brought to bear upon influencing Congressional legislation and federal action. As compared with the Grange and the Farmers Union the Farm Bureau Federation has more of a business character and viewpoint, and is more pragmatic and less idealistic. As regards cooperation, the national organization is on record as strongly favoring cooperative marketing, and cooperative purchasing of farm supplies used in production. But it has not yet taken a definite stand on cooperative distribution of consumers' goods. At its annual session in December, 1936, it did recognize this growing movement by recommending that the Board of Directors appoint a committee "to continue the study of this important subject and to make its report to the Board of Directors on a statement of policy, as soon as a comprehensive study may be completed."

That does not sound very exciting, but it is. Especially in those three words, "statement of policy," the drama begins to emerge. It is a drama of conflict—not of arms but of attitudes. Within the national organiza-

tion and among the state federations there are wide
divergences of view. So the matter of deciding on a general policy may have some resemblance to a contest still
popular at country fairs, in which opposing groups lay
hold of opposite ends of a stout rope and try to pull
each other over a dividing line in the middle. But in
this case, it would appear, the group which is pulling
consumerward has on its side the logic of facts and the
force of events. That group is headed by the Farm
Bureau Federations of Indiana and Ohio or, speaking
more strictly, by the cooperative associations which have
grown out of those state federations. Those two associations have been radiating centers of cooperative enterprise. Their progressiveness and the leadership and
initiative of their general managers, Mr. I. H. Hull and
Mr. Murray D. Lincoln, are largely responsible for
recent events which have provided the American cooperative movement with a breadth and strength of
organization, and an equipment for national wholesale
service, that may be said to mark its coming of age. Mr.
Lincoln was out of town during my stay in Columbus,
Ohio; and much to my regret, I have not had the pleasure of meeting him. But nowhere have I met men who
struck me as embodying the whole spirit and philosophy
of consumers' cooperation more completely than Mr.
Hull and Mr. Perry L. Green, who is president of the
Ohio Farm Bureau Federation. Mr. Green is convinced
that farmers can make their largest savings through cooperative buying of food and household goods, and will
do so increasingly.

PENNSYLVANIA PROGRESSIVENESS

Before going on from here we should make the acquaintance of a newcomer in the East whose spirit has more in common with the Ohio and Indiana groups and kindred federations in the Middle West. This is the Pennsylvania Farm Bureau Cooperative Association, headed as president and executive officer by Mr. R. N. Benjamin, who before being called to that post was a dairy and potato farmer in the Keystone State. In a way, as will shortly appear, this new member of the Farm Bureau cooperative family may be called a godchild of the Ohio association. Mr. Benjamin himself stands shoulder to shoulder with Messrs. Lincoln, Green and Hull, shares their breadth and vision and, individually as well as through his organization, has done much to advance the cooperative lines. In the central region he is a valiant recruit to the cause, and in the East he is leaven in the loaf.

This cooperative association was formed late in 1933 as an auxiliary of the Pennsylvania Farm Bureau Federation. That organization had been renewed three years earlier after having suffered disablement at the hands of powers-that-be who were not in accord with its then barely emerging cooperative disposition. Under Mr. Benjamin's dynamic management, the Association got under way as a wholesale owned and controlled by the county Farm Bureau cooperatives, whose needs it was designed to serve. Necessary material resources were first obtained from a cooperative automobile insurance company about whose extraordinary accomplishment I shall say more in the chapter on "Expanding Frontiers." This was the Farm Bureau Mutual Automobile Insurance Company, which had been launched on its brilliant career mainly on the initiative of the Ohio association. The new association became the representative of this company for Pennsylvania, thereby deriving in commissions a steadily growing income which put the wholesale on its feet, helped its constituent county units, and saved its individual policy-holders from 17 percent to 40 percent in their insurance costs. From the outset, moreover, these policy-holders were about evenly divided between farmers and urban people—a potent factor in leading the association quickly consumerward. The county farmers' stores handle food and clothing as well as farm supplies themselves, or join informally with urban groups in doing so. Though the Pennsylvania laws restrict voting membership in farmers' cooperatives to actual farmers, the stores have a good many urban patrons and are now beginning to distribute patronage returns to them in the form of preferred shares which bear interest and are redeemable. Thus urban patrons are brought in under the wings of the farmers, as it were, for these tangible benefits.

Besides linking up with the automobile insurance company and later with one of its offspring, the Cooperative Life Insurance Company of America, the Pennsylvania association went into partnership with the Ohio and Indiana associations in their oil-blending and fertilizer-mixing enterprises, joined hands likewise with

Southern States Cooperative in the Baltimore mills, and became identified with the super-regional and national cooperative organizations which will be described below. It deals chiefly in petroleum products, feed, fertilizer and seed. The remarkably rapid growth of this young association is reflected in the following figures: In its first full year, 1934, volume was about $25,000; the next year, $275,000; the next, more than $500,000; the last, almost a million—$940,090, to be exact. I have had the privilege of reading its audited financial statement for 1937, and must say in admiration that I have never seen a more complete one. It fills fifteen pages, and breaks down all the income, expenditure and operations in exhaustive detail.

One of the most valuable assets of this association, I would say, is the fact that being new, and having one foot in the East and the other in the Middle West, it can look about and take full advantage of the comparative and combined experience of cooperatives in these two regions. It has speedily learned one lesson, namely, that the interests of farmer and townsman as *consumers* are essentially one. The evolution of the association's attitude in this regard is shown by the wording on the editorial masthead of its monthly *Pennsylvania Co-op Review*. At first this read: "A magazine to stimulate the farmer consciousness in his struggle upward toward economic independence." Since March, 1936, this has been changed to read: "A magazine to stimulate CONSUMER consciousness in its struggle toward economic independence."

That points the way. Let us resume our journey.

Within present space I shall have to abridge the story and omit details. Important as the Indiana and Ohio associations are in themselves, I shall say only enough about their inner workings to bring out their character. Both have evolved from purchasing departments of the respective Farm Bureau Federations. The Indiana association was organized on a cooperative basis in 1927 and proceeded to help the local farmers set up county cooperative units, which now own and control the wholesale to which they owe their existence. This reversed the usual order but arrived at the same destination. In Ohio, where cooperative marketing was tried first and found wanting, a somewhat similar evolution was completed in 1934, and that association is likewise owned and controlled by county units. Both organizations distribute gas, oil, motor accessories and farm supplies and have recently added radios and household electric appliances. The Ohio association has linked up with G.L.F. in distribution of Family Foods. Total wholesale volume for 1937 was stated as $6,644,623 in Indiana and reached $8,457,697 in Ohio. The Ohio association has about seventy thousand members, the Indiana association about fifty thousand. They have cultivated their state fields in an intensive way. Between the two, when all is said, there is little to choose. But I would say that the Ohio organization is second to none the country over in its broad and well knit program, and the ability and enthusiasm of its working staff. At later points I shall cite its remarkable development of insurance as a means of furthering cooperative enterprise, and its excellent work in cooperative education and recreation. Visually the most striking exhibit is its eight-story headquarters building in the central business section of Columbus. The Indiana association occupies leased quarters in Indianapolis at present but has plans for a similar home of its own. Its organ is the *Hoosier Farmer* and that of the Ohio organization is the *Ohio Farm Bureau News*.

A successful fight against exploitation of farmers by fertilizer companies marked the beginning of joint action between these neighboring associations, who started the teamplay that has been getting bigger and better from year to year. After trying various expedients and finding it was impossible to get an adequate supply of fertilizer of high quality at fair prices, the Farm Bureau cooperative organizations of Ohio, Indiana and Michigan succeeded in working out a novel solution of this problem. They found a copper smelting company in Tennessee which had a nasty problem of its own—how to get rid of the sulphur fumes generated in its plant, which polluted the surrounding air and were a nuisance to the countryside. One way of disposing of these fumes—given an incentive—would be to convert them into sulphuric acid which when applied to sulphate rock yields superphosphate, the main bulk ingredient of fertilizer. The cooperatives proposed that the copper company build a fertilizer plant at Lockland, Ohio, and said they would take its entire output of fertilizer made according to their specifications. They would pay the company current market prices but at the close of each year the difference between manufacturing cost and sales proceeds would be divided 50-50 between the company and the associations. This proposal was accepted. A large plant was built at Lockland and a smaller one at New Albany, Indiana. Two other state cooperative associations joined up later. The arrangement has worked out satisfactorily, and has also served as a practical demonstration of a mutually advantageous relationship between a commercial producer and cooperative distributors. I understand that some of the business interests are watching this enterprise rather closely, and that several other similar tie-ups have taken this one as a precedent.

UNITED COOPERATIVES

It was the Indiana association's initiative in oil blending, however, which was destined to bring the major results in massing resources. The decisive first step was preceded by four years of unsatisfactory but enlightening experience in dealing with commercial oil companies. Meanwhile a study was undertaken of the effect of high quality oils in prolonging the life of internal combustion engines used in motorized farm machinery. On the basis of information obtained it appeared that the use of superior oils would save Indiana farmers about six millions dollars a year in replacement costs. The association concluded that the only adequate course was to build its own compounding plant and thereby fully control the quality of its oils under the supervision of its own chemist. This plant was built in Indianapolis and began production in the spring of 1930.

As the joint fertilizer program which originated in Ohio was working out so well, the Indiana organization invited the Ohio and Michigan associations to become its partners in oil processing. A tri-state Farm Bureau Oil Company was accordingly launched and the plant was enlarged. Later the new Pennsylvania association joined the partnership. The fame of this Co-op oil was spreading and events were shaping for still larger union of cooperative forces.

A federation of federations, called United Cooperatives, was formed in 1936 by re-naming the Farm Bureau Oil Company, itself composed of the state associations of Indiana, Ohio, Michigan and Pennsylvania. This new federation included also the Southern States Cooperative of Richmond, serving Virginia, West Virginia, Maryland and part of Delaware; and the Farmers Cooperative Exchange of Raleigh serving North Carolina. To cap the climax the Cooperative Grange League Federation Exchange of Ithaca, with its forty million dollar volume of operations in New York, New Jersey and northern Pennsylvania, joined this great combination at that time and made it greater still. A new and thoroughly up-to-date central oil blending plant with adequate laboratory facilities was built last summer at Indianapolis, and the plant of the Farmers Oil Company there was taken over and moved to Warren, Pennsylvania, as a branch to serve that region and save transportation costs.

United Cooperatives oils are now being distributed throughout the entire region over which this federation of federations extends. They are available to urban cooperative patrons as well as to farmers. United Cooperatives is triply well named. It unites in one cooperative enterprise of imposing magnitude the state and regional associations of which it is composed, with aggregate resources which approach one hundred million dollars. It unites the Middle West, the East and a goodly portion of the South. In fact it takes in all of the farmers' cooperative purchasing associations east of the Mississippi with only two exceptions—the Eastern States Farmers' Exchange of Springfield, Massachusetts, which in the New England tradition is disposed to stay by itself; and the Illinois Supply Company of Chicago which is the purchasing department of the Illinois Agricultural Association (a state Farm Bureau organization with a different name) and appears to represent an extreme of resistance to the present consumerward trend.

United Cooperatives goes along with that trend, takes the broad view that all cooperative purchasing is essentially consumers' cooperation, and proposes to serve consumers in constantly increasing measure. Without question—and this is the third reason why it is so aptly named—it will be a powerful constructive force in uniting rural and urban consumers in common cause. It will bring something of the freer and more democratic spirit and character of the Middle West into the East, and help to check and modify the tendency of Eastern cooperatives to become highly centralized and controlled from above. Reciprocally, it will give the Middlewestern cooperatives the benefit of the larger business experience, resources and experience of the Eastern associations—especially G.L.F. In due course it may bring momentous results in the way of coordination between farmers' marketing organizations and cooperatively organized consumers. If directly or indirectly through the good offices of this new medium the grain crops of Middlewestern farmers can be bought by Eastern cooperatives and processed into feed for livestock and nourishing food for human beings, what a boon that will be for all concerned, and for really constructive solution of the agricultural and interrelated economic problems of production and distribution which are harassing and perplexing the nation.

NATIONAL COOPERATIVES

But however far-reaching United Cooperatives may be, it is not the terminus. Concurrently with the developments which led to its formation, other events closely related but still more inclusive were shaping toward the creation of a national cooperative wholesale. That enterprise took definite form in the autumn of 1936 when National Cooperatives was established with headquarters in Chicago. It had been incorporated in February, 1933, but was in a formative stage for several years until the Chicago office was opened.

The purpose in view from the outset was to have a national wholesale which should serve urban as well as rural consumers. That purpose was shown by the fact that the Central Cooperative Wholesale with headquarters at Superior, Wisconsin, had a co-equal part in organizing National Cooperatives. I have not heretofore mentioned the Central Cooperative Wholesale, because it is in a somewhat different category from the others which have thus far been described. It is by far the largest and best developed of the regional cooperative wholesales in America, as yet only three in number, which deal primarily and mainly in consumers' goods—food, clothing, household supplies and incidentals. In that field—to which the term consumers' cooperation is applied too narrowly—this wholesale has set the pace, and provided the outstanding example of progress, efficiency and quality output. I shall say more about it in the next chapter which discusses cooperatives in towns and cities. Suffice to note here, as showing its stature and importance, that it serves about one hundred and fifty local and district consumers' cooperative groups situated chiefly in northern Wisconsin, Minnesota and Michigan, and sparsely in outlying areas which extend west into the Dakotas and south through lower Minnesota and Wisconsin into Iowa. Its annual wholesale volume is around three million dollars. Mr. Ivan Lanto, who had been the head buyer of that organization for many years and is familiar with consumer needs and commodities, was elected Manager of National Cooperatives and took up his new work on October 1, 1936.

The other American associations which National Cooperatives represents are United Cooperatives, including its seven constituent organizations; Consumers Cooperative Association of North Kansas City, which started with oil but has now added groceries; Midland Cooperative Wholesale of Minneapolis; Farmers Union Central Exchange of St. Paul; Consumers Cooperatives Associated of Amarillo, Texas, and Pacific Supply Cooperative of Walla Walla, Washington, both of which deal mainly in petroleum products; Eastern Cooperative Wholesale of New York and the Cooperative Wholesale of Chicago, which serve urban cooperatives. From this list several things are evident. First of all, National Cooperatives is truly *national* and countrywide in scope. It already includes most of the regional associations from the Atlantic to the Pacific. Second, it is composed mainly of associations whose major dealings are in gas, oil and motor accessories. This is reflected in the fact that the Executive Committee consists of Mr. I. H. Hull, Mr. Howard A. Cowden and Mr. E. G. Cort, who have been closely identified with cooperative oil operations. Third, it includes the three regional wholesales which serve urban consumers primarily, and other wholesales which are steadily expanding into the urban field. Thus it is very well equipped to do an all-round job in the United States. What is more, its range has already extended over the invisible frontier into Canada. Election to membership early in 1937 of the United Farmers Company, Limited, of Toronto, Ontario, forged the first cooperative business tie between the sister nations who are virtually one in their way of life.

National Cooperatives, though only a few years old,

has speedily demonstrated its practical value. It made a timely beginning with radios and household electrical appliances, to meet the new demand for such things that rural electrification created. It studied the relative merits of commercial products of this kind, selected those which best combined economy and quality, and then entered into contracts with manufacturers to make these things for National Cooperatives on a specifications basis under the Co-op trademark which the national office now controls. It has served as the medium for distributing these Co-op products to the constituent regional wholesales, which in turn distribute them to their local units. Volume has grown from month to month and so have the savings, all along the cooperative line. Without investing any capital for the present, but operating on a brokerage basis, National Cooperatives has been able to finance itself thus far mainly through its operations in this kind of consumers' goods.

How soon a national wholesale grocery service will be initiated is a matter still under discussion. The need and opportunity for such service are growing fast, as regional purchasing associations tend to add groceries to their stock and urban stores increase in number throughout the country. National Cooperatives does not intend to undertake this task, however, until it is prepared to do a thorough job. That involves adequate laboratory arrangements for a wide range of quality tests. It calls for a staff of buying specialists. It needs additional regional wholesales to serve as connecting links between the national wholesale and the local units. So it is a complex problem which will take time, thought and working capital for its solution. But research is now being conducted and much useful data are being disseminated. When the time is ripe National Cooperatives will probably organize a department of wholesale grocery distribution.

With regard to dealings in gas, oil, motor accessories and farm supplies, this national wholesale is rendering good service as an intermediary, in bringing representatives of various regional associations together to discuss and agree on joint undertakings of one sort or another. The engaging personality of Mr. Lanto is a distinct asset in such mediation. In some overlapping areas where a little friction has arisen, the national office has helped to smooth out the differences. It has represented groups of associations in working out details of important contracts. Some large operations in gas, oil and farm machinery have been facilitated in that way.

These are preliminary and experimental steps toward ambitious plans in prospect. On September 4, 1937, at a meeting in Paris of the International Cooperative Wholesale Society which federates the cooperative wholesales of twenty-seven nations, Mr. Howard A. Cowden, in behalf of National Cooperatives, presented a proposal to organize an International Cooperative Petroleum Society, to be owned and controlled by American and European cooperative wholesales and to undertake its own processing, refining, transportation and distribution. He advocated this plan on the ground that it would provide cooperatives throughout Europe and

America with assured oil supply of high quality, give millions of cooperators the benefit of the resulting savings, would carry out the "good neighbor" policy of the United States and bind the worldwide cooperative movement more closely together.

This proposal was referred to the Executive Committee of the International Society and is now under consideration. "Undoubtedly," Mr. Cowden has stated since his return to America, "an international petroleum society in some form, participated in by cooperatives of the world's major powers, will be established."

13 . TOWN AND CITY STORES

IN following the rise of American cooperation we have now reached its summit. Not the last peak of the mountain, which as an ideal will always lead on, but a summit of achievement on the way. Standing there we can see two upward trails. One starts from the nation's farms and the other from its towns and cities. As they near the top they converge, and finally meet on the common ground of National Cooperatives. Up the wider trail have journeyed the cooperating farmers of America in ever growing numbers. The other trail we are now going to explore.

What have urban cooperators accomplished in their own right, and what do they bring to this union of forces?

Measured in physical dimensions their contributions are comparatively small, notwithstanding the fact that the country's total population is nearly four times that of its farms. Though there are some notable exceptions, urban cooperatives in general are still unimpressive in stature. Nor has their history shown the sturdy and steady growth of the farmers' cooperatives, by and large. It has been fitful, up-and-down, beset with trials, errors and failures. The towns have done better than the cities, where repeated failures might seem to signify some inherent unfitness of the cooperatives to cope with urban conditions. But when this record of failures is compared with that of commercial ventures of corresponding size and resources, it is at least doubtful whether the cooperatives have fared any worse than the average. Such a comparison has to be rough and based on commonsense observation, because no conclusive figures are available. But we know that business failures are far from uncommon, owing to such practical factors as incompetent management, inadequate resources, over-extension of credit, acute competition and economic depression. Contingencies of that kind, rather than anything intrinsic, probably accounted for most of the cooperative failures as well. The constructive side of that painful experience is its teaching of what to avoid. Today, as we shall see, urban cooperatives are getting on much better. They are on a firmer footing and failures are rare. In the field of commercial business, on the other hand, we need only turn to the financial pages of the newspapers to find that profit concerns are failing at the rate of several hundred a week.

What urban cooperatives lack in comparative size, for the time being, they make up in the range of their social and economic pioneering and in their challenging potentialities, especially now that they are connected with the central power plants which the rural movement in its cityward advance has provided. There is good reason to believe that the next ten years will be marked by progress in the urban field as decisive as that which in the last decade rural cooperation has accomplished. We shall therefore view these town and city enterprises from the standpoint mainly of their present character and promise, and confine our retrospect to a brief resumé of false starts in the past and the well rooted growth which began about twenty years ago.

BEGINNINGS AND RECESSIONS

By a striking coincidence, the first urban consumers' cooperative society in America was launched in the same year (1844) that the Rochdale Pioneers opened their little shop in England. There were further likenesses between the two undertakings. The cooperators of Rochdale were weavers, and the man who initiated the American venture was a tailor, John Kaulback by name, of Boston, Massachusetts. The Rochdale shop's first stock of goods consisted of a few simple household provisions. The Boston group started even more simply, as a buying club whose first purchases were a box of soap and half a box of tea. It did not open a store till the following year. The weavers regarded their shop at the outset as a means primarily of improving their situation as industrial workers, by reducing their living costs and thereby augmenting their resources. They were thinking of themselves as producers and wanted to establish cooperative factories with the savings obtained through cooperative purchasing. Kaulback gathered his fellow-cooperators from the ranks of his own craft union, apparently with somewhat similar motives.

But there the resemblance ended. The weavers of Rochdale builded better than they knew. As soon became evident and as time has amply proved, they in their practical commonsense, which amounted to wisdom, had laid down the rudiments of principles and policies that were destined to become the main foundation stones on which the consumers' cooperative movement throughout the world has since been reared. It is true, they did not expect or foresee that course of development; they originally looked upon cooperative buying as incidental, simply a means to the end of cooperative production. It is true that in the light of subsequent cooperative experience and requirements their simple rules have been expanded, modified and supplemented, in much the same way that the Constitution of the United States has been interpreted to grant broad "implied powers" that were not definitely specified and were probably not in the minds of its framers. In the case of consumers' cooperation, for example, the simple Rochdale rule of "honest weight and measure" has gradually evolved (and nowhere I believe more fully than in the farmers' cooperative purchasing associations of America) into what is now the constructive principle of quality measured in terms of value-in-usage. Likewise, there have been later developments in the form of cooperative organization and its capital structure. Here again the American movement has contributed variations of great importance, especially in building up capital without recourse to share subscriptions.

I believe the time has come when the cooperative movement as it stands today can be adequately understood and advanced only by taking due account of such creative modifications or expansions of the original Rochdale rules, and of differences in national traditions, characteristics and conditions, which call for certain differences in cooperative methods. But when all is said, the fact remains that the Rochdale Pioneers did bring the rudiments together in just the right combination to insure the success of *consumers'* cooperation, with the result that their original expectations were reversed and production was subordinated to consumption as the determining goal.

The Boston enterprise was not so well grounded. Instead of selling goods to the members at current market prices and returning savings to them in proportion to their patronage, it sold as near cost as possible and its only distributions were dividends on capital shares. It grew rapidly and looked very promising. So-called "divisions," each with a retail store, were formed in many localities and bound together in a Workingmen's Protective Union. In seven years over four hundred such divisions were in operation, mostly in New England but extending to New York, Ohio, Illinois, Oregon and even Canada. That was the peak of success. Subsequently the movement suffered a division within its own ranks and split into two parts, both of which did well for a time but failed under the stress of conditions at the onset of the Civil War.

Not long thereafter, when American farmers organized the Grange as Patrons of Husbandry, a group of wage-workers, not to be outdone, launched an organization called the Sovereigns of Industry and went in for cooperation on an ambitious scale. They began right in one respect at least, by adopting the Rochdale plan of distributing savings to members in proportion to patronage. They also grew rapidly—in fact, too rapidly. Within a year they had over three hundred councils and forty thousand members. But the depression of 1873-78 was too much for them, and as an organization they had to dissolve. Some of the stores survived much longer, and by no means all of them were failures financially. On the contrary, many became so prosperous that a few insiders contrived to get control of their shares and turned them into ordinary stock companies.

Another period of speedy but unstable and unsuccessful expansion commenced with the outbreak of the World War and continued up to the depression of 1921-23. Again labor organizations took hold eagerly. The American Federation of Labor at its convention in 1917 endorsed consumers' cooperation, appropriated $50,000 "for advancing the cause of cooperation throughout the United States," and appointed a lecturer and a field worker to interest its constituent craft unions. The miners' unions espoused this cause and, building on some beginnings they had earlier made in Illinois, they opened many cooperative stores in that state and in Pennsylvania, Indiana and Ohio. The Brotherhood of Locomotive Engineers set up stores in railroad centers, and tried especially to bring farmers and laborers together and thus bridge the gap between the principal producers and consumers of food.

Many local cooperative stores sprang up independently in towns and cities, chiefly in New England, the Middle West and California. Their members were drawn largely from the so-called middle class, with an admixture of idealistic zealots who had overflowing enthusiasm but lacked commonsense and practical experience. As a rule these local cooperatives were poorly prepared for and conducted, remained isolated from one another, and paddled their own canoes as best they could.

Under these conditions there was urgent need for regional and national federation of urban cooperatives in wholesales which would bring them the same practical advantages of mass resources and create the momentum that the farmers cooperatives have so successfully achieved. To meet this need a number of organizations were formed. Most of them, though well-intentioned, failed because they were not soundly conceived and developed. Two were solidly grounded, and have grown steadily and strongly. One of these is the Cooperative Central Exchange of Superior, Wisconsin, which figured prominently in the preceding chapter and which I shall soon discuss further. The other is the Grange Cooperative Wholesale of Seattle (first called the Associated Grange Warehouse Company) which although primarily representing cooperative groups of farmers in that region has from the outset included household supplies and had considerable urban patronage.

The other half-dozen are accounted for in the following obituaries. The names of some of them are so similar to names of going organizations today that I must warn against confusion. Those whose roll will now be called are utterly extinct—some of them for reasons too instructive to be omitted from the annals:

The Central States Cooperative Wholesale of Chicago, controlled by the United Mine Workers of Illinois; departed radically from the Rochdale plan and proceeded to substitute what it called the "American Plan." Under this scheme the wholesale, instead of limiting its functions to supplying local autonomous units with goods and aiding other groups to organize on a similar self-governing basis, undertook to control everything from its own office. It selected all the local store managers itself and handled all the ordering and bookkeeping. The argument was that self-governing local groups moved too slowly and did not conduct their stores and accounts efficiently, and that a new and more expeditious plan was required in this country to promote the movement "rapidly and safely." But this plan proved to be too rapid and not at all safe. The wholesale went into receivership, and though it was reorganized and continued for a while it had lost its grip, and it passed out of the picture.

Meanwhile, the Pacific Cooperative League at San Francisco had been following a similar highly centralized plan, working from the top down instead of from the bottom up. It ended in bankruptcy. The Tri-State Cooperative Association at Pittsburgh, the Cooperative Wholesale Society at St. Paul, and the New

England Cooperative Wholesale at Boston, made their respective exits under circumstances unnecessary to detail. Fifth on the list was the National Cooperative Wholesale, which began to have trouble as soon as it started in 1919 at Chicago and opened branch warehouses on the Atlantic and Pacific coasts. It was too keen for quick results—took the bit in its teeth and set up retail stores which were run from its headquarters. The quick results were that it had to close its Seattle branch in four months after the opening, its Hoboken branch four months later, and in another month shut up its central office and passed away.

All those fiascos should have been more than enough, but the most flamboyant of all is yet to be chronicled. That was the Cooperative Society of America, a fraudulent non-cooperative launched in Chicago at the same time as the wholesale just mentioned. In the next few years it enticed over ten million dollars from working people with its grandiose projects, opened over two hundred stores, went into various lines of business and got so entangled in a web of financial confusion that it ended in bankruptcy.

Of course, the depression of 1921-23 played its part in these major calamities. Prices fell rapidly and found the stores loaded with goods bought at much higher prices. Purchasing power of members was reduced by unemployment. So most of the stores connected with the half-dozen unsuccessful wholesales, and many isolated ones which had no cooperative wholesale connections at all, were caught between the upper and nether millstones and ground out of existence. Nevertheless, amid the general wreckage, remnants here and there survived; indeed, a good number altogether. And some fundamental lessons had been taught so plainly that the educational results could be entered on the credit side of the ledger.

NEW AMERICANS JOIN IN BUILDING

Over against the foregoing record, which is mostly one of failures, can be set another record which is almost wholly one of successes. This record has been made by new Americans.

I have told a good deal in previous chapters about what old-line Americans have achieved through cooperation, from the early years of the Republic down to the present. But those are not the only Americans. The first child in a large family is not, by virtue of that fact alone, the best. Each of the children may excel in some distinctive individual way, and a family which has children of varied gifts and abilities is richly endowed. The American nation is a family of that kind, whose sons and daughters have come to this new land from nearly every race and country of the world. Even the original colonists were of varied strains—English, Scottish, Scotch-Irish, Welsh, Dutch, Scandinavian, French, Spanish, German, and doubtless others. And down through the years from that time to this, what element has not been added and compounded in the American whole—*e pluribus unum*. These racial components have made their own distinctive contributions to the nation's common wealth. I do not mean its material wealth only, but its wealth of inner resources, appreciations, potentialities. For the most part these contributions have been so woven by time into the very warp and woof of our national life that now we take them for granted as wholly American. That is as it should be.

Some of these new Americans have had a notable part in the up-building of cooperation in the United States, and those who have come here from Finland have made the most distinctive contribution of all. Others have given in goodly measure. In the Middle West and Northwest one finds many Americans of Swedish, Danish and Norwegian blood in the ranks and among the leaders of cooperative enterprise. Americans of Bohemian origin have developed one of the outstanding cooperative stores in this country, and others of Jewish extraction have established the largest and most complete group of cooperative apartment houses. At length the Negroes, who were brought to these shores almost as soon as the white colonists landed and who have made such rich gifts of joyousness, gentleness and faith, have begun to form cooperatives which reflect those qualities. Who knows—perhaps they will make their chief contribution in creating new forms of cooperative recreation, which is thus far taking itself rather too seriously.

Finland is a little country with a great spirit. As I write these lines the Helsinki Chorus of young men from that country's capital is touring America and expressing this spirit in song. Finland has won a place of special honor and respect in the United States by its prompt and unquestioning payment of its war debt. That respect is heightened in any American who visits Finland, as I did two years ago, and sees on the one hand what hard-working folk the Finns are—sturdy women loading and unloading cargo ships at the docks along with men—and, on the other hand, what a beautiful clean white city they have created. Helsinki, with its thoroughly modern buildings in the functional style of architecture, stands as a symbol of the commingled efficiency and aspiration of the Finnish people—of a strength of character which has made their native cooperative movement one of the strongest in the world.

Soon after the turn of the century in 1900, latter-day colonists from Finland began coming to the United States. They planted colonies in eastern Massachusetts, in Brooklyn and New York City. But the region which they colonized in largest numbers was northern Wisconsin, Michigan and Minnesota. There was something about that region which reminded them of the Old Country and made them feel at home. The young unmarried men found work in lumber camps, mines and mills. The families bought little farms. In due course these colonists became naturalized Americans. As born-and-bred cooperators they proceeded to organize cooperative associations on American soil—lodging houses, restaurants, bakeries, and stores which carried mainly food, clothing and other household supplies. Year by year these units grew in number, and formed partnerships with one another for cooperative objects that called for joint resources. In 1917 delegates representing nineteen local stores met in Superior, Wisconsin, at the head of the Lakes, and organized the Cooperative Central Exchange, which later was named Central Cooperative Wholesale. Its function was to supply the local stores with goods at wholesale rates, and from the outset it was owned and controlled by the autonomous units which subscribed for shares to provide the working capital.

CENTRAL COOPERATIVE WHOLESALE

The story of this wholesale federation's growth during the subsequent twenty years is one of the brightest and most interesting pages of American cooperative history. The organization has had its problems and adversities, internal and external. It has had to weather economic storms and depressions. But it has come through all these trials not only successfully but with such truly remarkable success that its example has inspired and spurred the whole American movement. Nothing is more convincing than a concrete visual demonstration. Directly and indirectly, this particular demonstration has been a dynamic force in the advancement of urban cooperation in America. Its intangible influence has been unconsciously absorbed and expressed through innumerable channels. Although the federation itself is really more rural than urban in composition, as fully three-quarters of the individual members are farmers, it deals predominantly in consumers' goods as distinguished from farm supplies, and follows methods which are equally applicable under urban conditions. Its largest stores are located in cities or good-sized towns. Its viewpoint is shown by the following excerpt from its log-book for September, 1918, when the wholesale was one year old: "Keenly interested in the development of a national consumers' cooperative movement, the C.C.E. board sends three delegates to the first congress of the Cooperative League of America, held at Springfield, Illinois." Since that time the federation has been represented at every biennial congress and has contributed much to the progress of this national Cooperative League, which will presently be introduced.

Growth of the Superior organization is remarkable not only on the business side but in point of the broader educational and recreational activities that have been developed from the beginning, in pace with its resources. We will note a few of the landmarks. Wholesale volume in the first full year, 1918, was only $130,000 but yielded savings of 15 percent. That year the wholesale purchased a three-story brick building for use as headquarters, though it had only two full-time employees and depended largely on members' voluntary or part-time assistance. In the next year volume nearly tripled, and a bakery was established. A four-weeks cooperative training school was conducted with forty students enrolled. These schools have been continued ever since and have helped to make the wholesale's working staff second to none in fitness. Shortly afterwards a full-time educational director was engaged. By

1920 the number of constituent units had increased from nineteen to forty-four, employees from two to seventeen, and the volume topped $400,000.

Then came the depression. Three local units went under. Wholesale volume dropped off about one-quarter in 1921, but it came back and passed the half-million mark in 1923. Meanwhile, the educational department, then headed by Mr. V. S. Alanne who has become a leader in this field, took the initiative in bringing about the formation of the Northern States Cooperative League, for the purpose of fostering the movement's general progress in that part of the country. By 1926 member-units were sixty, and volume above a million dollars. That year a new building was bought for the bakery and publication of a magazine now called the *Cooperative Builder* was begun. Two years later member-units were eighty-four and volume a million and a half.

1929—"The October stock market crash is a harbinger of another serious depression," said the log. But did the federation run to cover? It kept right on. Though volume fell to $1,300,000 in 1932, that was the low point, from which it has since grown steadily to nearly $3,000,000 in 1936. The Northern States Women's Guild was organized in 1930 as a regional federation of local guilds. A Cooperative Youth League soon followed. In 1931 the present manager of the wholesale, Mr. H. V. Nurmi, was elected to that post. A clothing department was started and soon developed a quarter-million-dollars business. In 1934 the Coopera-

tive Publishing Association was incorporated and has
become an important factor in the field. In 1935 the
present much larger headquarters building was bought
and occupied. An up-to-date coffee roasting and blending plant was installed, and the new Co-op Coffee was
an immediate success. "Widespread interest in consumers' cooperation general throughout the country
with increasing organizational activities in CCW area,"
said the log. Here follows the concluding entry for
1936:

"The number of member societies has increased to
107 and the CCW serves over 160 cooperatives, member and non-member. Sales jump to $2,845,741 and
efficiency of the Wholesale is reflected in an all-time
low total expense ratio of 4.98 percent. Employees number 71. Six new stores opened in the area. Twelfth
Cooperative Training School held. The *Cooperative
Builder* becomes a weekly and subscription lists increase
sharply." Nineteen thirty-seven volume was three and
a third millions. There are now thirty-five thousand
individual members of the retail units.

This is a record of which all American cooperators
may well be proud. I spent some time in and about
Superior last summer and can testify that nowhere else
in the country is there so much cooperation to the
square mile, so to speak, as in this region. On every
hand you see it, hear it, feel it. The CCW headquarters
and warehouse are A-No. I exhibits of efficiency in
their orderliness, airiness, lightness, facilities for convenience and saving of labor. Efficiency is accompanied

by humanity. This wholesale has gone farther than any other in America either commercial or cooperative, I would say, in collaborating with labor unions and maintaining mutually satisfactory wage scales and working conditions. Practically all the employees are unionized; they are also cooperative members who receive patronage returns from savings. Thus they feel that they are working for and bargaining with an institution of their own, and the directors feel that they are dealing with fellow-members as well as employees. Such an inter-relationship of interests, equal-sided and free from paternalism no matter how benevolent, would appear to contain the way out of the problem of labor relations which bedevils capitalistic business, and which by no means all cooperative organizations have as yet satisfactorily solved.

As regards quality of output, CCW sets the pace in the field of *consumers'* goods. Dealing as it does in several hundred items, it cannot at present duplicate what the farmers' cooperative wholesales have accomplished with their staple farm supplies—feed, seed, fertilizer, oil—which they produce in their own plants and thereby fully control. CCW does that in its own bakery and its coffee plant and in a recently added flour and grain-grinding mill. Its radios and electrical appliances come through National Cooperatives with the Co-op trade-mark. It can obtain tires, oil, paint and a few miscellaneous items from cooperative sources. Everything else, for the present, it is compelled to buy from commercial manufacturers. In doing so it takes full advantage of research and laboratory findings of federal and state departments and private agencies. It makes frequent use of what are called "blind tests," in which unidentified samples are sent to commercial laboratories for analysis. The results are sometimes considerably different from those of identified tests. When CCW has by these means satisfied itself of the satisfactory quality of goods it contracts with the manufacturers to supply them under quality specifications. They are then distributed with the Co-op imprint, first-grade goods indicated by a red label and second-grade by a blue. Further tests are made of all deliveries, and if the quality falls off the contract is ended.

All this is excellent as far as it goes, and it cannot go much farther with present resources and equipment. Mr. A. J. Hayes, who fills an important place in the CCW personnel and is an unusually clear and intellectually honest thinker, sums the matter up very fairly in the following statement:

"The Co-op line rightly enjoys the reputation of a high average of dependable quality. Without any question, investigation would easily bring to light that some of the Co-op goods are not all that they should be, let alone the best that money can buy. Nor does that embarrass either us, our affiliated store societies or their members. What would embarrass us would be proof that we cannot continue improving the line, or that our aim of a higher level of achievement attendant upon a more extensive cooperative movement in the future is unrealizable, for of those things we are confident. . . . If one expects present-day cooperatives to give perfect protection to consumers in the matter of quality and price of all things entering into commerce, then we certainly are 'on the spot.' But if we are tried upon the demonstrable possibilities and achievements in relation to resources, then we are certain cooperatives would come through with flying colors."

The feasibility of installing an extensive laboratory is now under consideration. I think it is more likely that joint laboratory arrangements will be worked out under the auspices of National Cooperatives, which the Central Cooperative Wholesale, as previously mentioned, had a leading part in establishing. If the combined resources of all the rural and urban cooperative associations now represented in National Cooperatives were utilized, a central laboratory could be set up adequately to serve them all and make an invaluable contribution to the whole movement in quality standards.

OUTSTANDING STORE-GROUPS

This is an appropriate point to become acquainted with the four largest co-op store-groups in the United States, because three of them have been built up by Americans of Finnish origin and the other by newcomers from Bohemia. They are a good deal alike and go well together. Each of them may best be described as a sort of town department store, which has grown by accretion till it now carries about everything that the cooperative members need from day to day.

First in stature is the five-divisioned enterprise of

the Cloquet Cooperative Society. It consists of two large stores and a combined garage, filling station and automobile sales department in Cloquet, Minnesota, an attractive town of sixty-five hundred people, about fifteen miles west of Superior; and two branch stores in smaller places not far away. The original store was opened in 1910 and the latest in 1936. These two carry a variety of goods which includes groceries, meat, clothing, hardware, coal, household electrical appliances, furniture, paint, building materials, livestock feed, farm machinery and numerous incidentals. The branch stores have a little of everything. All the buildings are owned by the society. When I visited the Cloquet stores, both of them were doing a brisk business. The automobile department sells about a dozen cars a month. Total operating volume in 1936 was $1,125,713, and patronage returns were 5 percent. The society now has two thousand seven hundred members and is still growing fast. About a third of the members are of Finnish stock, another third Scandinavian, and the rest mostly Polish and French-Canadian. The majority are employed in local mills and are unionized.

Besides Mr. Tuohino, the manager, I met the society's secretary Mr. A. W. Heino, a young man who was graduated from Minnesota University and has an engineering job in a wood-conversion factory. He was full of enthusiasm and said that cooperative meetings took most of his evenings. In driving me about in his car he pointed out half a dozen cooperatives of different kinds. There is the Tri-Co Oil Association, composed of the store cooperative and two others, which specializes in gas and oil and pays patronage returns of 10 percent. There are two farmers' cooperative dairies from which the stores buy milk, butter and cheese, taking nearly the whole output of one of them and thus effecting a good producer-consumer relationship. As showing what a difference the spirit of cooperation makes, Mr. Heino told me the society bought its second Cloquet store from a couple of men who were not doing any too well, and in a short time had almost as much trade there as in the main store.

Next in size comes the Cooperative Trading Company of Waukegan, Illinois, a community north of Chicago which may be called either a large town or a small city. Here we have a central store, five branch stores, a dairy, bakery, filling station and warehouse. It all began in 1910 with the refusal of a group of housewives to put up with an increase in milk prices by retail distributors. These women formed a buying club and got their milk directly from neighboring farmers. The following year men and women joined in organizing the Cooperative Dairy—not a producers' group to sell milk to the public but a consumers' group to purchase milk from the farmers, and then pasteurize and bottle it in their own plant for themselves. This original core of the whole enterprise has grown and prospered. Milk is delivered to patrons in the surrounding district. Besides paying the farmers a fair price the cooperative divides with them whatever annual savings are made in the dairy.

In 1916 the group broadened out, adopted its present name and added groceries and meats. Branches were opened as membership and resources grew. A bakery was acquired, and in 1936 a filling station and gasoline bulk plant were built. This is one of the best-looking stations I have seen anywhere—done in white and well designed, with a central tower bearing the motto "CO-OP" and flying the Stars and Stripes. Mr. Jacob Liukku, the manager, with whom I talked in August, told me they expected to open a new branch the following month in Zion about seven miles away. One of the present branches is in Highwood, eighteen miles distant, but all the others are in Waukegan. Early addition of clothing and hardware departments is now in prospect. The membership has increased to two thousand five hundred, of which not over 20 percent is of Finnish stock, the rest representing practically every racial element in this variegated industrial community. Several directors are "old-line" Americans. The employees are unionized and labor relations are mutually satisfactory. Patronage returns of 5 percent were made in 1936 on a sales volume of $709,735.

The United Cooperative Society of Maynard, Massachusetts, a town not far from historic Concord, has developed in much the same way as the Waukegan society, but in a different order. Here a grocery store came first in 1907, then bakery, meats, milk, coal and wood, paint and hardware, feed, and a filling station. The milk is bought from individual farmers and processed in the society's dairy for its own members; such substantial savings are effected that the cooperative wants to lower the price to consumers below what the state authorities will permit. Of the 1,050 members, fully two-thirds are of non-Finnish stock and generally "American." Mr. Arno N. Rivers is the present manager. The volume of business in 1936 was about half a million dollars.

The fourth store-group is that of the New Cooperative Company of Dillonvale, in the southeastern corner of Ohio. It goes back to 1908, and the word "new" in its name refers, I think, to a reorganization which took place at the outset, when a group of thirty-five miners from Bohemia took the original business over from a miners' union. The union had let members buy as many shares as they wished, and then found that all the savings were required to pay dividends on the shares, with nothing left for working capital or patronage returns. The group which took it over when the union lost interest was fully familiar with sound cooperative principles and followed the plan of limiting the number of shares a member could own, paying only a low fixed interest, reserving part of the savings for operating use, and paying out the balance in proportion to patronage. This sounder plan succeeded so well that now there are, besides a large store at Dillonville, seven branch stores in nearby towns, a newly built sausage plant and a warehouse. The main store is much like the one at Cloquet in its variety of household goods and farm supplies. With a little rearrangement it would blossom into a department store. I imagine that something of that sort, and perhaps the rendering of whole-sale service to smaller cooperatives in the district, is in the minds of the directors. There are now a thousand members of half a dozen or more racial elements. Most of the men work in mines and railway yards and are unionized, but some are farmers. Altogether, it is an interesting combination. The veteran manager is Mr. Joseph Blaha, and Mr. John J. Azallion heads the field department. The total sales volume in 1936 was $639,-476. In the years since those thirty-five miners started the ball of cooperation rolling, the society has returned to its members in cash savings about a quarter of a million dollars.

ESSENTIAL ASSETS

Not only these four largest cooperative merchandis-ing enterprises in our towns and cities, but most of the others which have stood up under the test of time and attained substantial size, have been founded and devel-oped by groups of new Americans. What accounts for this fact? Assuredly there is no lack of cooperative capacity in Americans of native descent, because Ameri-can farmers who can trace their lineage back to colo-nial days have created great cooperative associations, surpassing, in some respects, those of any other country in the world. Can it be that the farmers and the immi-grant groups possess certain assets for cooperative suc-cess which urban Americans in general have not, here-tofore at any rate, possessed in adequate measure? There I think lies the answer.

These assets are two, which go together and reinforce each other. The first is *rootedness* and the second is *sense of community*. The farmer is locally rooted in his farm, township and county. He has lived on his farm all his life, grown up with it, cared for it, and year after year brought forth crops from its soil. He does not have to do much thinking to realize that his interests are bound up with the welfare of the local farming community. His recognition of that plain and simple fact was what first led him into organized cooperation with his neighbors. Gradually this sense of community among farmers grew statewide, regionwide, countrywide—and now it is becoming still broader in its growing recognition of an identity of interests between the farmers and their fellow-Americans of the nation's towns and cities. The immigrants from other lands go through a similar process. While they are taking root in their adopted country, they form colonies to help one another in getting a foothold. For the same reason they tend to stick to these colonies at least for the first generation, and become somewhat rooted in the neighborhood. Having a sense of community among themselves they naturally form cooperatives to further their progress. Gradually they and their cooperative societies become inter-related with the new environment, and their sense of community expands.

That is the main reason, I believe, why the cooperatives of the farmers and the immigrants have shown so much stability and vigor. On the other hand, the great mass of Americans who live in the cities have either lost whatever rootedness and sense of community they may once have had, or they have been born and reared under conditions in which they have failed to acquire these essential fixed assets. Neighborhood disintegration under the stress of city and industrial conditions was noted in my opening chapter as the cause of some of our most serious social and civic problems. Tenancy and transiency, insecurity of employment, livelihood and residence, are poor equipment for sustained and successful cooperative activity. But the glaring prevalence of these conditions points to the necessity of overcoming their deteriorative effects by bringing into the situation something which will replace the lost unit of the neighborhood and impart rootedness, stability and a sense of community to American city life.

Now at last it begins to look as though the people who live in towns and cities are getting a new sense of community based on the growing realization of their common interests as consumers, and are forming consumers' cooperative units which provide them with a local focus of activity and link them up with a national movement. This widespread urban development of cooperation during the last five years has grown up out of the depression. Under stress of the grievous aftermath of the last big business boom, the very foundations of people's thinking have been shaken. Their minds have been opened to new perceptions. They have revised their scale of values. They see now that whatever other monopolies big business may have, it most certainly does not possess any monopoly of understanding and commonsense. Confidence in the ability and willingness of capitalistic profit-business to serve the common good has been badly impaired. There is a growing feeling that new viewpoints and bases are needed. Consumers' cooperation offers a viewpoint and a basis of organization which are new to the great majority of Americans who live in cities. So, as one result of their thinking, these urban Americans are now turning in constantly increasing numbers to the cooperative way of bettering their own lot and that of their fellow-consumers.

RECENT PROGRESS

So widespread and rapid is the present rise of these urban cooperatives that even the approximate total number will not be known until the Bureau of Labor Statistics at Washington completes a census of them which it is now conducting. If they continue to increase at their present rate, that count will soon be out of date. But it will show the present geographical distribution and the general size and character of the existing cooperatives. In the meantime we can get a fairly good line on them by taking account of two other regional groups, besides the one centered in Superior, which are federated around their own wholesales.

The larger of these groups is the Eastern Cooperative Wholesale with headquarters in New York City and a branch office in Boston. Its territory includes all the Atlantic States from Maine to Maryland and extends west to Buffalo, New York, and Pittsburgh, Pennsylvania. Mr. L. E. Woodcock is the manager. It began in

1929 as a central buying agency for ten units, but did not become a distributing wholesale with its own warehouse until the spring of 1936. By the autumn of that year it was serving seventy-eight units. Today it serves about two hundred. Its operating volume doubled between September, 1936, and April, 1937, and is now going at the rate of about $650,000 a year. That is rapid progress. So rapid in fact that it is straining the wholesale's working capital to keep pace with it, and giving its inventory men a stiff problem to keep a sufficient stock of goods in the warehouse to fill promptly all orders from the retail units, whose combined membership is now about 15,000 persons.

Of the two hundred units about fifty are full-fledged stores dealing in groceries, meats and miscellaneous household goods. By "full-fledged" I mean that they carry a fairly complete variety and are open during the usual store hours every day. Somewhere around one hundred are as yet in an earlier stage of development, and in order to keep down expenses are open only on certain days or during certain hours and have a smaller stocks of things that the members especially want. The remaining fifty are still in the buying club stage and make use of some member's house or office as a place where pooled orders are delivered and apportioned. The monthly *E.C.W. Cooperator,* as a medium of publicity and serviceable information, is helping to build up the movement in this wholesale area.

Buying clubs are the protoplasm from which stores evolve. They get the members accustomed to doing things together, give them some practical experience in cooperative buying, and allow for preliminary study of cooperative principles and methods before the running of a store is undertaken. One of the commonest reasons why many stores peter out or do not get very far is that they are started without adequate preparation, with insufficient working funds and inexperienced or incompetent management. It is best in the end to take ample time and make a good beginning. In this connection it is interesting to note that there is an organization in New York City called Cooperative Distributors, which serves buying clubs and individual purchasers on the mail-order plan and now has a store at its headquarters for the convenience of local patrons. It specializes in things of light weight which can be sent readily by mail, and does a business of about $150,000 a year.

A rather typical example of the modest and slowly growing store in a small community is that of the Hanover (New Hampshire) Consumers' Cooperative Society, which had its beginning in January, 1936, as a buying club of only sixteen members, most of whom were faculty members of Dartmouth College and their wives. The executive committee "started to work amateurishly but resolutely to educate itself in the principles of cooperation, and to procure and disseminate information which would enable club members to purchase more intelligently the ordinary commodities of daily life. In this work the United States Bureau of Standards and the Consumers' Division of the Department of Labor were of great assistance. They reported on specifications submitted to them, and furnished the club with standards of quality. . . . Local testing groups were organized. . . . The emphasis was gradually shifted from rosy dreams to unsentimental facts and figures."

The informal club was incorporated as a cooperative association and opened its first "store" in the basement of a member's home. That soon proved inadequate for the growing membership and volume of business, and in January, 1937, the society rented larger basement space on the main street and proceeded to expand its operations under the management of Mr. R. P. Bristol. Now there are about two hundred members drawn from Hanover and nearby towns. For the fifteen months ended January 1, 1938, the net savings were $450, of which $300 was distributed to members as patronage returns at the rate of 3 percent on their purchases. The remaining $150 was added to working capital. Membership continues to grow, and there is good reason to expect that more of the townspeople who are not connected with the college and more farmers from the countryside will share in the development and benefits of this sturdy enterprise.

One of the most promising store-groups in the Eastern Wholesale district is the New Jersey Consumers' Cooperative, which grew out of discussion and buying clubs and now comprises four stores in as many towns, with delivery routes ramifying out from them. All of the present stores have been opened within the last year or so. In October, 1937, the organization took over the largest store on the main street of Madison and is now using that as its center. The combined volume is already running at the rate of above one hundred thousand dollars a year and there is no reason why this enterprise, which has been soundly developed from the beginning, should not in due course attain much larger proportions. The manager, Mr. George S. Meakin, is a man of exceptional competence and cooperative spirit. As compared with 134 member-families at the outset, there are now 1035, drawn principally from the native middle class. The store centers (besides Madison to which the original store at Chatham has been transferred) are Caldwell, Fairlawn and East Orange.

The evolution of this successful undertaking is not only interesting but instructive as regards methods which yield durable results. For this story I am indebted to Mr. Prentice C. Ford of the board of directors and to a written account by Mr. Frank Eakin.

Two buying clubs got together several years ago and rented at fifteen dollars a month a rather dingy place which "seen through sufficiently imaginative eyes was a building of much promise." The joint group began coal, fuel oil and groceries operations with share capital of only four hundred dollars. As its member-families were scattered through a dozen towns, it bought an old 1935-model Ford truck and provided a delivery service. Depending largely on volunteer service for a while, the association engaged as manager a young college graduate who had no store experience and gave his time in order to learn. They "wanted a manager whose idea would be to help members to purchase to their advantage, not one trained to assume that success meant accumulating profits for others than customers."

This group was especially fortunate in having among its members "a number of men whose interest in cooperation at the start was practical rather than idealistic. They were technicians and engineers who were annoyed by their dependence, as consumers of goods, on advertising ballyhoo. . . . Studying results of scientific tests by federal and other research agencies, and making laboratory tests of their own as far as practicable, these zealous technicians have contributed in large measure to the cooperative's success. They discovered soap, for example, of a brand quite unknown to the country at large, which was in every way as good as the best of the nationally advertised brands and could be bought at considerably less. The same is true of various other products."

Furthermore, goods are sold for cash only. Some members who have been used to monthly charge accounts find this inconvenient, but they usually adjust themselves without difficulty to the cash basis. Deviation from it, as experience has abundantly shown, is one of the surest ways to wreck a cooperative enterprise. Savings to members on groceries have averaged about 5 percent, and on coal and fuel oil up to 15 percent. The business in coal, which more than anything else has given impetus to the whole enterprise, has continued to loom large. Coal and fuel oil sales together now constitute 60 percent or more of the total volume, which in 1937 was $108,700. The Madison headquarters store has a complete market handling meats and vegetables as well as groceries. The others carry groceries only. All the build-ings are rented. Each store has a regional committee with considerable local autonomy but tied in with both the board of directors and the headquarters manage-ment.

Expansion into non-grocery lines is in view. This asso-ciation, from its own experience, advises others in urban communities not to start with groceries alone, but to include other things in which the margin of saving is larger. It regards its own expansion "as an absolute es-sential, awaiting only the discovery of the best lines and of practical ways of adding them." It expects to develop credit unions and cooperative medical service among its members.

"The problem of all problems is that of member edu-cation, and therewith member assimilation. Growth in membership has been rapid and education has not kept up. . . . Educational activities have been alternately promoted aggressively and allowed to lapse. At this time some regions, notably Caldwell and Fairlawn, are carry-ing through a strong educational program, but the cen-tral organization is limited to the publication of a house organ, *Co-op News,* and to monthly meetings of a rep-resentative assembly."

There is a marked tendency at present for urban cooperatives in large cities to form citywide federations in order to work more closely together and mass their resources. In New York City this may go further and result in some sort of combined business organization on the part of all the local associations. As these include not only grocery stores and buying clubs but apartment houses, restaurants, laundries, et cetera, with a collective operating volume of roughly $1,500,000, the question of just what kind of a partnership would be practicable is an interesting one. Chicago has a city federation which is still in its infancy but has already worked out some joint services. For example, the dozen grocery stores buy their fresh vegetables and fruits together. They have a truck which goes to the markets every morning and deliver to each store its portion of the order.

Two of the best single grocery stores which I saw on my field trip are located in Hyde Park, near the University of Chicago, and in Evanston, the seat of Northwestern University. The former, dating from 1935, is operated by a group of five hundred people composed almost wholly of university professors, public school teachers, social workers and clergymen, and is managed by Mr. Robert Overstreet, a young graduate of Antioch College. It is very well set up and efficient, and remarkably superior to the general run of commercial stores in its appointments and facilities. Volume is over $100,000 a year. In educational and recreational activities this society, called Consumers' Cooperative Services, has so much going on or projected that an outline fills five typewritten pages. The Evanston Consumers' Cooperative started less than three years ago as a buying club and now has four hundred members and a store which is running nip-and-tuck with the other in volume. Mr. Hugh E. Bogardus is the manager. It has a nucleus of educators but is reaching out among other elements of the community. Both of these stores are good examples of successful results accomplished by people who have approached cooperation from the intellectual side.

The Cooperative Wholesale, with headquarters in Chicago, serves about one hundred and sixty stores and buying clubs in Illinois, Michigan, Indiana and Ohio. As it was launched only in the autumn of 1936 its volume is still small, but it is growing rapidly as new stores appear on the scene. That central region, which ought to be one of the most fertile fields, affords plenty of opportunity for team play between rural and urban cooperative associations which head up in Chicago. Mr. A. W. Warinner is the executive officer of this enterprising wholesale. Mr. and Mrs. Warinner kindly conducted me through the new warehouse last summer and showed me some products of exceptional quality which are being distributed. Combined membership of the units in this wholesale district is about twelve thousand five hundred.

This rounds the circle of federated urban cooperatives which deal in household supplies. Besides the wholesales centering in Superior, New York and Chicago, there are a few other organizations which call themselves wholesales but which for the present at any rate are too small to justify that designation. They are more like jobbers. Elsewhere, local units are still compelled to make out as best they can by dealing with commercial wholesales.

After visiting a good many such stores myself I have

one general comment, which is not exactly a criticism: these stores are monotonous in their similarity to one another. At least nine out of every ten, probably nineteen out of twenty, are grocery stores—some larger or neater or brighter than others, but still, when all is said, just grocery stores. Why not have a bit of variety? Now and then one is refreshed by discovering something different. Out there in Chicago, for instance, there is a little enterprise called the Consumers Cooperative Clothiers, which deals in men's tailormade suits, coats, underwear, socks and ties. There are practical reasons for trying something else besides groceries. If a grocery store is to be fairly complete in its stock it needs considerable working capital. It necessarily has a lot of stuff to handle and has hard going to maintain high standards of quality. But if it specialized in a few things it could do with less capital, save a lot of handling expense, and establish a reputation for exceptional quality. Suppose it carried a dozen "Co-op" products, such as G.L.F. Family Foods, Superior coffee, Columbia soups, Hightstown women's coats, and others equally good. I am inclined to think that such a store by its combination of novelty and quality would soon make a place for itself. Or a store might specialize in dairy products, especially milk. As a result of recent agitation against high retail milk prices in New York City, the state authorities have now granted a milk-selling license to a newly formed organization called the Consumer-Farmer Milk Cooperative, which will buy its milk from up-state dairy farmers' cooperatives, have it pasteurized and bottled by a company in the city, and distribute it through stores. Of course, this will be resisted to the utmost by the commercial distributors, and it is going to be a lively experiment to watch, if it is actually carried out—which is not yet certain.

LUBRICATING THE ADVANCE

At earlier points I have mentioned the fact that urban gas and oil cooperatives are springing up in towns and cities, and that while they tend to add groceries after a time, the grocery stores tend to add filling stations. It is tit for tat and all for the best. Nobody knows yet how many urban cooperative gas stations there are—that is another thing the government count will show—but I found them in nearly all the cities I visited. Without exception they were coming along successfully and returning good savings to their members from the margin of about five cents a gallon between the wholesale and retail price of gasoline. One of the most valiant of them is Konsum, Incorporated, at Washington, D. C. It started in a modest way late in 1936 with one leased pump in a commercial station, and even so paid patronage returns of 8 percent. Now it has a well located station of its own and is going strong. Besides succeeding itself, it is helping other local groups through the medium of the District of Columbia Cooperative League (of which Mr. Ernest H. Collins, who had a leading part in organizing Konsum, is the president). Mr. Collins is connected with the Rural Electrification Administration, where he has a good deal to do with the new rural cooperatives formed to carry out the local projects. He may be said to see those rural groups from the top down, or from the administrative point of view. But as a member and officer of Konsum and the local League, he is looking from the bottom up, not as an administrator but as a consumer. I cannot help thinking that every government official who has to deal with cooperatives could understand them more adequately if he were likewise a member of one himself.

The largest unit I saw is the four-year-old Cooperative Oil Association in Minneapolis, which is linked up with the Midland Wholesale, operates four stations, has some 3,500 patrons and has already returned savings of $15,000 in four years. I think it leads the gas cooperatives in large cities, which have to face stiff competition from the commercial companies. But the volume record is still held by the Consumers' Oil Company of Greeley, Colorado, which is considerably older. It sold two million gallons of gasoline in 1936, and in that year alone distributed over $111,000 in savings to its two thousand members. These few examples are sufficient to show what a good job the oil co-ops are doing in "lubricating" the urban cooperative movement.

Now to conclude this part of our survey I will tell a little about the lustiest city cooperative that I encountered. This lusty youngster is the Racine Consumers' Cooperative of Racine, Wisconsin, which was launched in February, 1935. It has been chock full of humanity, breadth and vision from the outset, and has also been a thumping success on the business side. The man who took the initiative in founding it and who heads it as Manager is a labor leader and something of a radical, Mr. Herbert Katt. In the depth of the depression he had got a lot of the unemployed men together in a self-help cooperative, through which they were enabled to exchange their labor at odd jobs for pieces of furniture, clothing, et cetera, which were given them as pay in lieu of money. After that temporary expedient had served its purpose this enterprising leader stirred up interest in the idea of a cooperative which would represent all elements. That meant factory workers chiefly, because Racine is an industrial and strongly unionized community. But farmers of the surrounding district were asked to join hands with labor, and likewise teachers, professional people and a few business men of liberal outlook. All responded heartily. Today the society has three thousand members, of whom about half are labor union people. The president is a farmer.

They began with a gas station, soon added another, then a third, a fourth, and a garage. Meanwhile they undertook distribution of coal, and before long bought a coal-yard of their own. A grocery store came next, and after that a double store which carries paints and household electrical appliances. Thus this cooperative quickly developed a well selected group of services to meet the practical needs of its members. Gas, oil and motor accessories are still 80 percent of its total volume, which for the year just ended was close to a quarter-million dollars. Savings have grown to more than a thousand dollars a month.

But the best thing about this cooperative is its inclusiveness, its fine spirit of fellowship and the good time its members are having as they take things in their stride. For the last year or so they have had an educational director on full time—another young Antioch College man, Mr. William B. Lloyd, Jr. He is right on the job, but not too heavily. He doesn't let education weigh them down. I had the good luck of being present at a party they gave in their hall one evening for their former president, Mr. P. W. Voltz, and Mrs. Voltz, who were reluctantly leaving Racine to take up residence in Washington. It was a jolly affair, with Co-op cigars to smoke and Co-op beer to drink, and ended in a singfest of Co-op songs. Here's one that goes to the tune of "Marching Through Georgia."

> "Open wide your Co-op hearts
>   We'll sing another song
>   Sing it with a spirit
>   that will start the world along
>   Sing it as we hope to sing it
>   many millions strong
> *Forward with co-op-er--a--tion.*"

WE have had a rather long pull of cooperative stores, but not too long for their importance as the usual foundation upon which consumers' cooperation is built up and provided with resources for other kinds of cooperative activity. A broad groundwork has now been laid in the United States, and the next stage of cooperative progress will probably be one of varied and interesting developments in new fields. Such diversification is already under way. The present chapter will tell about these beginnings. Most of them are small as yet, but others are large. Some, such as cooperative housing and restaurants, are almost necessarily identified with urban conditions. But the majority are so broad in character and scope that they relate to the whole cooperative movement in America and hold out opportunities of growing achievement for either urban or rural cooperators or both in unison throughout the country.

By way of newsiness I will commence with the latest addition to the family—the Cooperative Book Club with national headquarters in New York City. This has been brewing since last spring, was definitely set up in November, and forthwith announced itself in No. I, Vol. I, of the CBC *Reader's Observer*. It may be suitably introduced by quoting from an opening article by Professor Harry A. Overstreet:

317

"I hail with delight this new venture in cooperation. So far as I know, it is the first of its kind. If it succeeds, as I have every reason to expect, it will have an effect upon our individual and national life that will be deeply important. Books are the heart and soul of our civilization. They are essential to intelligent living. But books are confoundedly expensive. The formation of the Cooperative Book Club will give us consumers a chance to stretch our book dollars. It will give us an opportunity to expand our personal libraries and thus have at our command the books we care about. Thus the Club should have a powerful effect in enriching the intellectual life and increasing the book-reading pleasure of thousands of our people.

"This new cooperative applies the principle of open membership. To become a permanent member one need only subscribe for one two-dollar share. Members have one vote each in controlling the organization, which is independent of any private financial interests and has no political or sectarian affiliations. The headquarters will buy for members any books they wish, and mail the books to them anywhere in the United States postage prepaid, at the going retail price. By pooling orders and buying books in large quantities, substantial savings will be effected, and net savings above operating reserves will be returned to members periodically in proportion to their patronage. The club's bulletin listing new books will be mailed regularly to the members, and in due course cooperative reading circles will be formed in local communities."

In such reading circles, linked up with rural as well as urban cooperative groups, I can see great possibilities of furthering the whole cooperative movement on the intellectual side, and making the adult education movement in this country more self-propelling than it is today. This club will render another signal service by bringing into the cooperative family such outstanding educators and writers as those who have already agreed to act on an advisory board. For the present, until there is time to carry out the usual cooperative procedure of elections and create an initial working fund, the central organization is provisional and all services are being contributed as voluntary offerings. The club concludes its first announcement with these words: "If you believe in Cooperation as an effective defense against high prices, as millions of Americans are finding it to be in other great fields of consumer wants, we believe you will want to take part in building the larger service toward which the Cooperative Book Club looks through the association of thinking people."

COOPERATIVE HOMES

From books to homes is a natural transition. Cooperative housing is making headway in America, but as yet only in a few places and chiefly in New York City. Be it said first that a considerable number of apartment houses in the expensive living districts which call themselves cooperative are not such in any full sense of the term. Most of them were neither built nor bought by cooperative groups organized for the purpose, but were erected by private contractors or real estate companies for reasons of profit. These builders then proceeded to sell the suites separately on a so-called "cooperative" plan to people who happened to be looking for apartments in that district. A considerably larger sum could often be obtained for a building by selling it in that parceled-out way than by making a single turnover. When the suites were occupied, certain quasi-cooperative features were put into operation, especially some measure of joint management. But even this is farmed out as a rule to firms which make a busines of managing apartments. In fact, I have never observed anything about these apartment houses that was essentially different from the ordinary run, or noticed that the occupants had anything more to do with one another than is generally the case.

A true cooperative housing group is not composed of people who have been assembled by a real estate dealer, but of people who want to live together and definitely plan for it. At least, that applies to the original nucleus of cooperators, who either have a building constructed or purchase one already standing. After that, the members of the first group may invite friends to participate, but always subject to the group's approval. The purpose, in short, is to bring together people of congenial interests who are likely to derive pleasure from this close association. The parallel economic object is to effect savings through this cooperative arrangement. As in merchandising, these savings may take the form either of periodical returns in cash, or better value-in-usage, for a given money outlay. Usually a cooperative apartment yields both kinds of savings, their relative proportions depending on whether the particular group is more desirous of obtaining living quarters at low money-cost or of securing a larger measure of satisfaction in home surroundings. And, of course, that in turn depends considerably on the group's income level.

An excellent example of the sort of cooperative apartment house which is suited to the interests and needs of people of moderate income, in such fields as teaching, writing, social work and public service, is presented by Our Cooperative House which is situated in a quiet part of the lower West Side of New York City, near the Hudson River. It is an exceptionally good-looking twelve-story apartment which was planned and built in 1930 by the original group of cooperators, who from the very beginning followed the standard cooperative plan of organization and development. They subscribed a certain amount among themselves in capital shares and borrowed the rest of the money required for construction. Monthly payments by the residents cover their proportionate shares of all upkeep costs, depreciation allowance, interest on mortgages and capital shares, amortization of mortgages over a term of years, and a safe margin for contingencies. Whatever remains free and clear at the end of each year, after these reserves have been provided for the ensuing year, may be paid back to the residents as savings. The monthly payments range from $45 for one room and kitchenette up to

$115 for terrace suites on the upper floors overlooking the river. Any apartments come high in New York.

There is an attractive cafeteria with very good food and no tipping. Other common facilities include reception and lounging rooms, library, and a hall for meetings. The residents run the house themselves, electing their own management committee and sub-committees for specific purposes. There are various social, educational and recreational activities in which residents may join or not, as they prefer. The individual suites are light and airy and the appointments are thoroughly up to date. All in all, it is a homey and welcoming place, where people enjoy living together in a truly neighborly way.

This apartment house is one part of a larger cooperative enterprise called Consumers' Cooperative Services, which had its beginning in 1921, and now includes a dozen cafeterias, a bakery, and two stores which carry the baked foods and a selective stock of groceries. Altogether there are about five thousand members, and the total budget is roughly half a million dollars. As a well integrated urban cooperative enterprise it is one of the most interesting and successful that America has to offer. Miss Mary Ellicott Arnold, as Treasurer and General Manager, has had a leading part in its advancement. The organization has always been liberal in its relations with labor unions. Last spring, following upon some incident or difficulty connected with cafeteria employees, the members at a special meeting requested the directors to negotiate an agreement with the Cafeteria

Workers Union under which the rate of wages would be fixed at 10 percent above the average rate paid by the ten best agreements among other cafeterias. This conforms with what some regard as the ideal cooperative policy regarding wages. No doubt, the example will have wide influence. In the year ended March 31, 1937, Consumers' Cooperative Services expended nearly $10,000 toward education and publicity in forwarding consumers' cooperation in the Metropolitan area. Mrs. Cedric Long is serving as general manager in the absence of Miss Arnold on leave. This organization publishes a lively and meaty monthly bulletin called *The Cooperative Crier*.

One of the largest groups of cooperative apartments in the world is that of the Amalgamated Housing Corporation. This group of buildings is located in the outlying Van Cortlandt Park section of New York City. The nucleus was formed in 1926 by a group of members of the Amalgamated Clothing Workers. They were aided individually when necessary by ten-year loans on the part of this strong labor union. Share capital was supplemented with construction funds borrowed from an insurance company. This enterprise has steadily grown until today it embodies a total outlay of $3,500,000 and provides for more than six hundred families. Participation is not confined to members of the one union but is open to other industrial workers. The plan of organization and operation is about the same as that previously outlined, but owing to the magnitude of this undertaking there is a larger measure of centralized management on the administrative and business side. There are many group activities, however, to which the residents are closely related. This compact little community has its own library, play rooms and day-camp for children, food shops, milk distribution, transportation service to and from schools and transit lines, and various other facilities. It also has a farm up-state from which it gets part of its fresh food supply. Until recently it bought electric light and power from the metropolitan utility company at wholesale rates and gave residents the benefit of net savings between those and the retail rates. When the company tried to abrogate this contract the community installed a Diesel plant of its own and is now saving from $10,000 to $15,000 a year in that way.

Mr. Abraham E. Kazan, the President and executive head of Amalgamated Housing Corporation, is not only an able administrator but a man of insight and vision, who sees cooperative housing as a practical means of re-building neighborhood life. In a recent article on this subject he put the matter so succinctly that I will quote the paragraph: "The cooperators have learned to take pride in their community and its accomplishments. The general indifference of the ordinary city dweller toward his neighbor has been almost eliminated. Here one member of the community meets another member as a co-partner. Their common interests bring about a finer and more intimate relationship, which is reflected on the community at large. Indirectly and unconsciously the influence of the community is carried over to the individual. Each cooperator feels that he is one of the owners of the development and responsible to the others for the condition of the community." Turn back, if you please, to the second chapter where I quoted de Tocqueville's fine characterization of the New England township as a unit of democracy, and I think you will agree that such a cooperative community as the one Mr. Kazan describes comes nearer than anything else to fulfilling under present urban conditions the same integrating function, non-politically, that the township and town meeting served in village days.

There are at least thirty-five cooperative housing associations within the New York City limits, which have erected or purchased buildings that accommodate some 2,200 families and represent an original cost of about $13,000,000. Most of the apartment houses are of modest proportions. A majority are situated in the borough of Brooklyn and have been developed by groups of Finnish immigrants. I went through some of the earliest of those houses back in 1919, and recalling how much interest they aroused I am inclined to think they gave the original impetus to this metropolitan movement. Here and everywhere it is a form of cooperation which must necessarily grow much more slowly than merchandising because of the large initial capital required. At a later point, however, I will touch on some interesting possibilities of making cooperative insurance resources count for housing projects.

The only other part of the country which shows any similar development as yet is the state of Wisconsin, where two projects are pending or in process. One in Milwaukee is growing out of a self-help association of workers, such as I mentioned in describing the Racine cooperative. The other at Madison will consist mainly of individual homes costing from $3,500 to $6,500 each, on beautifully situated land in the city's suburbs beyond the University of Wisconsin. When I visited Madison last summer Mr. John S. Bordner, who is largely responsible for the idea and the very sound and careful way in which it is being worked out, showed me various plans and drew such an alluring word picture of the prospective community that I looked wistfully in its direction. As the tract is seventy-five acres in extent there will be plenty of open space and wooded ground, with ample provision for children and outdoor recreation. Most of the residents will be university professors and public officials. They will be given opportunity to select sites and architectural designs to suit their taste and purse—in the same way that residents of a cooperative apartment house select particular suites. But the land will be bought and the houses built with funds raised through share subscriptions and loans. Several apartments may be erected later, but the distinctive character of this community will be one of separate cottages. There will be community control of design, to fit harmoniously into the physical environment. "Rugged individualism" has not been entirely absent, but has adjusted itself to other considerations—or perhaps better said, to consideration of others. "We have had assurance," Mr. Bordner writes, "that our first fifty-seven lots may be built upon this spring, and bids will soon be let."

GREENBELT

There is another enterprise now under way which is difficult to classify, but which I will bring in here because it is superimposed on community housing. This is the operation by the Consumer Distribution Corporation of a group of semi-cooperative activities in the newly created community of Greenbelt, Maryland, a few miles from the nation's Capital. Greenbelt itself is a creation of the federal department known till recently as the Resettlement Administration but now called the Farm Security Administration. This governmental department cleared and landscaped the tract of land (whose natural border of trees suggested the appropriate name) and erected the dwellings, which in structure and appearance are halfway between apartment houses and cottages. They are set up in units of various sizes and colors, each unit centrally heated and accommodating a number of families in small but conveniently equipped and comfortable suites. These suites are rented to people of modest means, including some who work on the experiment-land of the Department of Agriculture and others who are employed in local industries and offices. Selections have been made on the basis of income primarily, from a host of applicants, and now Greenbelt is a going human community. When my good friend Mr. R. H. Elsworth took me out there one Sunday afternoon last September, the place was thronged with people who were going through sample apartments and, in many cases, deciding to apply for residence.

The Consumer Distribution Corporation, whose headquarters are in New York City, was established in 1935 by the late Edward A. Filene of Boston and the world at large, and endowed by him with a fund of a million dollars. Its specific purpose was to help consumers to organize their own cooperative department stores. The procedure in view was that this corporation should first arouse local interest in such a project, and assist people to form cooperative groups which would go through a preliminary period of education and preparation. Then a department store would be set up in that locality under the combined auspices of the corporation and the cooperating group. The corporation would serve as its wholesale source of supply and would finance and largely manage the undertaking during the first five years. But this overhead financing and managing would be reduced from year to year, while simultaneously the financial and administrative responsibility of the cooperative group would be increased. At the end of the five year period the store would be fully turned over to the group, which would then proceed to run it on an independent basis.

Of course, this would be just the reverse of the natural and usual form of cooperative evolution, in which the impulse and initiative begin with the people themselves. But from the experimental viewpoint it was very interesting and held possibilities of large scale urban development of cooperative merchandising. I understand that the corporation considered quite a number of places for the initial location, but for one reason or another did not find any where the essentials of success appeared to be assured. Then it was invited to come into the Greenbelt community and apply this plan not to a department store exactly, but to the operation of a number of departmentalized services which include a general store, a self-service food and meat market, a drug store, a motion picture theater, a beauty parlor, a barber shop and, of course, a filling station and garage. This invitation was accepted and the plan is now being applied under the direction of Mr. Flint Garrison, who is Executive Vice-President of the Consumer Distribution Corporation.

This strikes me as an ideal or at least made-to-order setting for the experiment. Here is a completely new community, which must have services of this sort and which can organize them on a cooperative basis from the outset. The conditions are favorable for success, and if successful results are accomplished the experience and prestige thus acquired can then be turned to good account in other places without the present governmental underpinning. Greenbelt contains nine hundred families, numbering presumably about three thousand persons. That is a fair-sized base—not so large as to be unwieldy and not too small to be somewhat representative. These people elect the board of directors of Greenbelt Consumer Services and, so to speak, ask the corporation to serve as their operating agent temporarily. It is in view, I believe, that savings will be reserved for the present to build up working capital, against the day when the services will be turned over to the community to operate on its own. The undertaking will be watched with lively interest, and on the part of cooperatives, at any rate, with the best of good wishes.

COOPERATIVE HEALTH SERVICE

Potentially allied with housing, and in fact with all other forms of cooperation, and now beginning to take shape and go along with them, is cooperative health or medical service. The new Bureau of Cooperative Medicine was established in New York City in 1936 by the Cooperative League of the U. S. A.; and Dr. James P. Warbasse, President of the League and himself a surgeon, is now devoting his energies especially to the development of this new field. He has written a book on the subject entitled *The Doctor and the Public*. The new Bureau is headed by Dr. Warbasse as president, Dr. Kingsley Roberts as medical director, and Mr. Martin W. Brown as secretary. It was created, according to the announcement, "because the interest in cooperative health protection has recently become so great, and because of the highly specialized nature of medical service." It "is prepared to give instruction and advice on the organization of health associations by groups of people who wish to obtain medical service on a cooperative basis." It will soon begin publication of a monthly journal to be called *Cooperative Health*.

To avoid confusion and indicate some of the reasons

why this particular cooperative movement is encountering bitter and determined opposition on the part of professional medical organizations, it is necessary to understand clearly what a cooperative health association is. It is not a governmental affair, either federal, state or municipal. In other words it is quite distinct from so-called "state medicine," which means medical service administered by public authorities, such as departments of health, clinics and hospitals. At present such public service is supposedly confined to the "indigent," and any extension of it beyond those limits is frowned upon by the medical profession. I think that one reason why they are now opposing cooperative health associations is because they have thus far failed to distinguish them from medical service under state control. Against that, sound arguments can be advanced on the score of perfunctoriness, politics and poor quality. But these arguments are irrelevant with regard to cooperative medical service, which keeps clear of political entanglement.

In the next place, these cooperative associations are not organizations of physicians or hospitals but are composed of the consumers of medical service—the people who are commonly known as the patients and who at last are beginning to lose their patience. In face of the ever increasing tendency toward medical specialization and higher and higher fees for such specialized doctoring, the consumers, unless they are abundantly supplied with money, are up against a tough problem. In the old days of family doctors a person might hope to find out simply and quickly what if anything was wrong with him. Today, if you think you have a sore throat and go to a throat specialist, he will probably tell you that you should have your eyes examined, the eye man will pass you along to a liver man, he to a heart man without a heart, and by the time you get to the end of the line you'll need an orthopedist and an emergency loan. If a person is downright indigent he can avail himself of public medical care. If he is a millionaire he can run the gamut. But if he is just an ordinary person of moderate means, it behooves him to keep himself well.

These are the people who are forming voluntary health associations to keep well with the aid of medical advice, and also in case of illness or accident to have what is actually medical *service*. A secondary but practically important object is to obtain competent advice and service as economically as possible within bounds of adequacy. "Economically" is, of course, a relative term, which measured in money would differ from one income-group to another. But naturally the movement is beginning with low-income groups.

In traveling over a considerable part of the country last summer I made a point of looking up any developments of this kind. I found that in all but a few instances they had not yet got beyond the hoping and planning stage, but that almost everywhere such local movements were in view. Likewise, almost everywhere, the chief problem was how to overcome the resistance of medical organizations. I say organizations rather than medical men, because there are plenty of individual physicians who are in hearty sympathy with the idea and want to do anything they can for it which professional etiquette and conventions will permit. But most of the medical bodies—local, county, state and national—are still dead against it. I cannot help feeling they would be much wiser to accept this middle course and lend it a helping hand, if only as a dam to stem the tide running toward state medicine which they oppose even more bitterly. If they remain fixed and unyielding, that rising tide is liable to get beyond their control.

Without specifying names and places or going into medical details, I will say just a little about several groups which are actually under way. One is in a rural village of the Middle West. It is composed mainly of farmers, several hundred of them, who deliberated long and carefully before they got to the point of forming an association. Fortunately—or so it seemed at the time—they found a family doctor who had practiced in that village some years earlier and was very well liked. They engaged him on a full-time basis as their physician and compensated him with a collective fund made up from small individual monthly contributions. It was sufficient in amount to do very nicely for a country doctor. In return he conducted regular examinations, gave whatever routine treatments were necessary, and supplied ordinary medicines without further charge. For special treatments and medicines, extra allowances were made. Patients requiring hospital care were taken to a larger town not far away. This arrangement worked out very satisfactorily and there was a marked diminution of illness in the community. But then certain difficulties arose, not at all of a medical character, which necessitated a change. I believe this group is now making ready to resume activities.

In a large city there is another association which now includes some four hundred wage-workers, though it was formed less than two years ago by only twenty. They have an arrangement not with one doctor on full time but with a selected group who retain their general practice but give regular preventive and curative service to the members of this group on a similar basis of periodic collective payments. Local professional hostility is now putting serious obstacles in the way of this cooperative, and the outcome remains to be seen.

These two instances, as it happens, illustrate the kinds of cooperative medical service which are needed, respectively, in rural and urban communities. In the former, that is, in villages or small towns, a good, friendly, reliable family doctor is the primary need. But in cities, as Dr. Roberts explained to me, people of small means can make out passably well on their own for routine or minor ailments which may require attention. What they have not the means to obtain and what they are very badly in need of is specialized examination, diagnosis and treatment. In cities, therefore, the practical necessity is to form cooperative groups of consumers who will make arrangements with *cooperating* groups of medical and surgical specialists to provide them on a fair and reasonable basis with such specialized service. That is the objective toward which the Bureau of Cooperative

Medicine is now moving in New York City. Consumer groups are already taking shape in the boroughs, and I understand that a well equipped group of specialists are holding themselves ready to cooperate when a sufficient period of education and preparation has been completed.

Exhibit A of cooperative medicine in America is the Cooperative Hospital of Elk City, Oklahoma, of which Dr. Michael Shadid is the originator and director. He was a practicing physician in that small rural community. In the autumn of 1929 he got a representative group of citizens together to discuss the idea. As the result, a community health association was organized with authorized capital of $100,000 divided into 2,000 shares of $50.00 each. Dr. Shadid himself sold the first three hundred shares to some of his patients. Then others—not the local doctors however—took hold and helped him. A hospital of size suited to local needs was built and well equipped. Now this pioneer undertaking has grown to the proportions of 2,400 member-families. The yearly dues are $12 for one person, $18 for two, $22 for three and $24 for a family of four or more. These dues entitle the members to free examination, treatment, surgical operations and nursing care. Certain modest supplementary fees are paid for use of operating room and anesthetics, occupancy of bedrooms and medicines to take home. The fame of this cooperative hospital has spread far and wide, and by the same token the opposition of organized medicine has become more intense. At present the issue is being fought out on technical grounds in the Oklahoma courts. One of the most significant facts about this Cooperative Hospital is that it is sponsored by the Farmers Union of Oklahoma in another demonstration of that group's character and vision. The national organization of the Farmers Union, at its national convention last November, ringingly endorsed the cooperative health movement and the Bureau of Cooperative Medicine.

I am inclined to think that for reasons of practicality, economy and good social strategy, it may be better for a while at least to utilize groups already existing instead of creating new ones for this special purpose. The members of existing groups, as for example labor unions, know one another. There they are, without having to be brought together, which takes time and expense. It would be a comparatively simple and quiet matter to form an association for health purposes composed of these same people. The new organization would be an *alter ego* of the one already in operation. Sometimes even the *form* of having two organizations would not be necessary. As a matter of fact, some of the labor unions have provided their members with medical service for many years, and so have fraternal societies and various other bodies. If there is an active and intelligent participation on the part of the members, and democratic means of insuring satisfactory service, that is moving in the same general direction as cooperative health service and might with mutual advantage be connected up with it.

Both directly and indirectly, the movement progresses

with growing recognition that under present conditions "many person do not receive service which is adequate either in quantity or quality, and the costs of services are inequitably distributed. The result is a tremendous amount of preventable physical pain and mental anguish, needless deaths, economic inefficiency and social waste." This blunt statement is quoted from the majority report in 1932 of the Committee on the Costs of Medical Care after five years' study under the auspices and with the support of several large foundations. There is no getting away from the facts except to change them, and that is what cooperative health service proposes to do.

There are some cooperative burial associations, mainly as yet among rural and new American groups. I found more of them in Iowa than anywhere else, and a few in Wisconsin and Minnesota. There are two ways of organization. In a district where store or other cooperative societies already exist, a number of these societies join forces in forming a cooperative burial association, for which they as units subscribe the necessary capital. The services of the burial association are then available to the members of all the societies. One such in the Superior district serves five thousand families. The other plan is that of direct individual membership. This apparently prevails in Iowa, where there are ten associations, united in a state federation. One of them, for example, started out with 350 members, grew much larger as its friendly and uncommercial services were appreciated, and now has a beautiful funeral home. As regards economy, these associations have usually reduced the cost of funerals to about one-half of the prices charged by commercial undertakers. This has almost invariably forced the latter to lower their rates somewhat. At the same time it has caused them to do everything they could to cripple the cooperatives. Commercial undertakers have state organizations which bring political lobbying to bear, and by that means especially they have been able to impede the cooperatives more or less. But this movement expresses human rebellion against the inhumanity of exploiting people at a time when their defense is weakest, and like cooperative health service it is bound to advance.

CREDIT UNIONS

Credit unions are groups of people who by pooling individual savings create a fund from which any of them can in case of need obtain loans at low interest. The method of saving is to invest in capital shares of the union which have a standard par value and purchase price of five dollars, and are transferable only from one member to another under specified regulations. The number of shares that a member may own is not rigidly fixed but is subject to action from time to time by the board of directors, which depends on the union's financial condition and needs. Each member, irrespective of the number of shares he holds, has only one vote. Loans are made only to members. The union's savings, over and above operating costs and reserves, are returned to members in the form of dividends on their shares.

It is evident from this summary description that credit unions are identical with cooperatives in structure and methods except at two points. The first one is that the number of shares a member may buy is not permanently fixed, as it usually is in the case of cooperatives. This is more of a difference in by-laws, however, than it is in practice. A cooperative may change the maximum number if it so desires, and credit unions usually hold to a certain limit. The second difference is that the credit union's net savings are distributed entirely as dividends on shares, which of course means that the dividend rate is somewhat variable; while cooperatives pay only fixed interest on shares and distribute savings in proportion to patronage. This looks like a more important difference at first glance. But the question arises—what constitutes the patronage of a credit union? Is it the borrowing, or the putting in of individual savings as capital? That question might be argued somewhat, in view of the difference in function between a credit union and a cooperative store. In any event, the practical reason why the union returns all savings as dividends and none on borrowing-patronage, is that this is the simplest and most inexpensive course to follow from the viewpoint of bookkeeping and clerical detail and is generally satisfactory to the members. In effect, moreover, the unions do return savings to borrowers by constantly lowering the rate of interest as their reserves increase and they can do so without impairing the union's solvency. The maximum interest rate is 12 percent, but the general average is about 6 percent; and some unions with a large surplus have rates considerably lower. The usual dividend rate is from 4 percent to 5 percent.

Apart from these inner differences, however, it is a fact that credit unions have had an origin and course of development somewhat different from those of cooperatives. The idea originated with the mayor of a small town in Germany back in 1848, whose name was Friedrich Wilhelm Raiffeisen. He saw that this was the only means by which poor people without influence could help themselves and each other. His unions paid no dividends whatever, charged only 4 percent interest on loans, and divided the small savings between reserves and educational work. The first credit unions on the American continent were established by French-Canadian priests.

The late Edward A. Filene, to whose large endowment of the Consumer Distribution Corporation I referred earlier in this chapter, became interested in the idea while traveling abroad, and was largely instrumental in securing the enactment by Massachusetts in 1909 of the first state law in this country authorizing the formation of credit unions. In 1921 Mr. Filene and Mr. Roy F. Bergengren combined in organizing the Credit Union National Extension Bureau, with headquarters in Boston, for the triple purpose of securing the enactment of similar laws throughout the country, helping to organize credit unions widely, and putting them on a nationally federated basis. For this pioneer work he endowed the Bureau with a million dollars.

All those results were accomplished with remarkable rapidity and success by 1934, and in that year the Extension Bureau was discontinued and the Credit Union National Association was organized, with headquarters in Madison, Wisconsin, and Mr. Bergengren as Managing Director. Today there are credit unions in every state without exception, numbering altogether about 6,700 with a total membership close to 1,500,000 people. Wisconsin leads with upwards of 500 unions, New York and Illinois are close behind, and then come Massachusetts, Pennsylvania and California. A general federal law was enacted in 1934, authorizing formation of credit unions under federal charters, and vesting jurisdiction of them in a newly created Federal Credit Union Section of the Farm Credit Administration. This special Section of the FCA is headed by Mr. Claude R. Orchard, who for many years was personnel officer of Armour and Company at Omaha, Nebraska, where he had a good deal to do with the formation of fully a hundred credit unions among the employees of that company.

The fact just noted brings out one of the most striking differences between the development of credit unions in this country and that of cooperatives. The first, and still the main development, of the credit unions has been in connection with industrial plants, not only with the approval but with active encouragement and assistance of the plant management. I am not going to discuss the various reasons which may enter into the rather pronounced contrast between the favorable attitude of industrialists toward credit unions and their prevailingly unfavorable attitude toward consumers' cooperatives. I will simply point out one obvious reason for their approval of credit unions and relate a little human incident by way of illustration. In a plant down in Texas one of the workers had worried a long time about some bills that he owed. Finally he spoke to several of his friends to see if they would lend him $150. They sat down and went over his accounts and found that he owed $500 altogether. Then they helped him to join the plant credit union of which they were members, and endorsed his note for a loan of that amount. Next they settled with his creditors for $420, and asked him to use the remainder in ways that would give his wife and himself some enjoyment. At closing time next day this man told the head of the plant that it was the first day for two years that he had been easy in his mind and able to give the company a full measure of service.

Similar cases could be duplicated by thousands. Of course a worker who has debts on his mind, especially if the creditors are loan sharks or installment agents, is not at his best. Troubles on this score are a big factor in labor turnover, and that is costly. So it is wholly natural that from this point of view employers should be well disposed toward credit unions, and there can be no reasonable doubt that the thousands of credit unions in industrial plants have in this way alone made a great contribution to their efficiency and output.

But of course credit unions are not identified with industrial plants exclusively. Far from it. They are all-pervasive, and are a godsend to all kinds of people of small means under all sorts of conditions. First, they are a simple and convenient means of saving, and pay dividends considerably in excess of what savings banks would pay in interest. Although most of them are very modestly conducted, without any fuss and feathers, they have an extraordinary record of solvency and security, and the percentage of failures among them even during the depression has been microscopic. They are an ever present help in time of trouble, emergencies or ordinary needs in course of living. They are a haven of refuge and protection against the wiles and extortions of the loan sharks and of many alluring loan companies that are little better. Possibly some conception of the suffering they have prevented and the individual and social betterment they have effected may be gained from the statement that some 750,000 people are at present being aided with loans which total $65,000,000. For the foregoing figures I am indebted to Mr. Bergengren and to Mr. R. C. Christie, of the national organization.

Although the national organization, called CUNA for short, is not affiliated in an official way with the cooperative movement, and holds itself somewhat apart, a great many of the local credit unions grow out of local cooperatives and are inseparably bound up with them. Not infrequently these particular local unions, while belonging to their state and national CU associations, enter into federations among themselves which keep them closely related with the regional cooperative groups. Furthermore, every credit union, no matter where it is or what its affiliations are, is a training school for other forms of cooperation, and its members are thereby better prepared to take part in organizing cooperative stores, apartment houses or what not. Though there are now coming to be more credit unions in the rural areas, this is still on the whole an urban movement, and I would say that it tends to generate cooperation in the cities in somewhat the same way that the farmers' mutual fire insurance companies generate more highly developed forms of rural cooperation. One of the greatest sources of strength which the credit unions and the farmers' insurance groups have in common is that both, in order to function safely, must *know their individual members intimately;* and in order to do that, must remain small in membership. Just as the farmers' groups have almost eliminated the moral hazard by knowing their policy-holders at close range, so the credit unions have reduced losses to an almost negligible percentage by knowing at close range their member-borrowers. This necessity of remaining small and compact will safeguard the credit unions, I believe, against a tendency toward centralization and impersonality which is apparent in some of the cooperative wholesales. The wholesales will do well to study the credit unions and also to ponder the results obtained by the farmers' fire insurance groups, where total achievement surpasses that of any other cooperatives in America.

Credit unions are especially adaptable for cooperative health service, and I rather expect to see some interesting developments along that line in the near future. CUNA has already worked out several forms of insurance for its constituency, and is giving a good deal of thought, I surmise, to some way of establishing a central credit union bank. It would be an unfortunate division of forces if the credit union and consumers' cooperative movements should fail to work closely together in any such major undertakings.

COOPERATIVE INSURANCE

The rise of cooperative insurance in the last few years, in more highly developed forms and wider variety than that of the farmers' mutual companies which bulks so large in total volume, holds great promise for advancing the whole cooperative movement. It will do so in several ways. In the first place, the cooperative automobile, fire, general casualty and life insurance companies, of which there are now about a score of large size, are drawing thousands of newcomers into the movement and acquainting them with its economies and broad social objectives. In the second place, these cooperative insurance companies are demonstrating that they can achieve success in one of the most tightly held strongholds of commercial business. But the most constructive service of all will be that of saving vast sums of money from being diverted by the commercial companies to the bottle-necked financial centers for use in profit-business financial schemes; and making these funds available for the up-building of cooperative undertakings in many parts of the country.

Without describing the leading cooperative companies or citing general figures, I will simply illustrate by what has already been done in one quarter the way in which the last objective named above will gradually be attained. This illustration will be drawn from the experience in the insurance field of the Ohio Farm Bureau Cooperative Association and Mr. Murray D. Lincoln, its General Manager. In 1926, following a study of excessive rates for automobile insurance, that Association with the assured support of other cooperative bodies, launched the Farm Bureau Mutual Auto Insurance Company. The Ohio Farm Bureau Federation appropriated $10,000 as the initial capital. The first year's volume of insurance was $114,100. Present volume exceeds $5,550,000. This is now the seventh largest mutual casualty company in the country, and its operations already extend into ten states.

As a magnified return of the original $10,000 from the Ohio Farm Bureau Federation, the Auto Insurance Company has aided the Federation and affiliated cooperative activities to the extent of more than three-quarters of a million dollars, in the form of investment of its funds in their shares. The largest block of these funds was used to assist the Cooperative Life Insurance Company of America, and another portion to start still another member of the family on its way—the

Farm Bureau Mutual Fire Insurance Company. An additional half-million dollars has been expended constructively by the auto insurance company and its offspring on educational work which has benefited the whole cooperative movement, and almost another half-million has been paid as commissions to sponsoring cooperative associations in other states. "Thus," Mr. Lincoln states, "cooperators are finally doing for themselves, with more economy and effectiveness, things which private business has previously done for its own profit, and these activities are made possible only by the capital which consumers have furnished."

That is the way in which from year to year, decade to decade, cooperative insurance can and will work wonders in building up and diversifying the whole cooperative movement in America, especially cooperative housing; rearing upon economic foundations high towers of attainment in the educational, recreational and cultural fields of human activity.

IN Chapter 2 I said that although the life of a nation forms an organic whole it has three aspects—political, economic and cultural. That chapter dealt with the political life of the American nation. Those which followed have dealt with the consumers' cooperative movement in relation to the nation's economic life. The present chapter will consider this movement in its relation to American culture in the broad and inclusive sense of that term. This means not merely that sometimes superficial polish or adornment which is implied when we speak of some people as being more "cultured" than others, but refers to the underlying tenor, color and content of our life as a nation. Thus broadly conceived, our American culture, of course, comprises everything which makes up the nation's being and character, including the political and economic, which are by no means insulated departments but simply nominal and more or less specialized divisions between which and the rest of our national life there is a continuous flow of action and reaction, a constant reciprocity of influence and effect. This will be kept in view, and some of the things which we shall now discuss will be drawn from or extend into the political and economic divisions of the cultural field. But they will be considered from the viewpoint of their integration with the whole.

Integrating forces in the consumers' cooperative are those forces which are integrating, or are responsible for integrating, the movement itself and the relationship between this movement and other activities and forces with which it is necessarily concerned. Here again I want to keep clear of any implication that the particular cooperative forces which will figure in the present chapter are the only ones which are responsible for or measurably rendering such constructive service. In fact, we have already seen how National Cooperatives is doing so on a nationwide scale, United Cooperatives in the great area east of the Mississippi, the various regional wholesale federations within their respective districts, and the local units in their own communities. We have also seen that their activities are by no means confined, in most cases, to strictly business operations, and that with comparatively few exceptions they include education in cooperative principles as an essential part of their work and keep the broader character and objects of the movement constantly within their field of vision.

But with regard to the organizations which will now be presented, two things may be said which put them in a still broader and somewhat different category from all the others. First, they are charged with the task of integration more *expressly* and *primarily* as regards its inclusively *cultural* character. And second, they are *representative* of all the other cooperative organizations, or of a typical cross-section of them, within their regional or national areas of jurisdiction. This means that the culturally integrating activities and influence of those other organizations are, or by all means ought to be, represented and magnified in the constructive service of these organizations which are more definitely charged with broad cultural advancement of the movement as a whole.

Chief and most widely representative of these latter organizations is the Cooperative League of the United States of America, to which we will hereafter refer more familiarly as the Cooperative League. It came into being twenty-two years ago, at the very time when (as we can now see in retrospect) those enduring and successful American cooperatives were arising which were destined to constitute the makings of the consumers' cooperative movement in this country. Nothing is more striking in history than the way in which new forces appear upon the scene, sometimes coming apparently from nowhere, when need and opportunity provide the psychological moment. In this instance such a combination of circumstances brought forth an organization and a man. The man was Dr. James Peter Warbasse, then a practicing surgeon who had become deeply interested in the field of consumers' cooperation at home and abroad. His original commitment to this movement was brought about very largely through the influence of his friend, the late Albert Sonnichsen of New York who, after adventurous years as a sailor and espoused cooperation writer, became editor of a magazine, *Consumers' Cooperation,* which the League took over; served as the League's first Secretary; and in 1919 wrote his book, *Consumers' Co-*

operation, which was "an outstanding contribution to cooperative philosophy."

Dr. Warbasse, a native of New Jersey, is a descendant of Peter Worbasse who migrated from Denmark to America. He took his M.D. at the Columbia University Medical School and did post-graduate work in the universities of Göttingen and Vienna. After serving as chief surgeon of a well known hospital in Brooklyn, one of the five boroughs of New York City, he became editor of the *New York State Journal of Medicine* and special editor of the *American Journal of Surgery,* and wrote books dealing with medical sociology and the conquest of disease. There is something fateful, it seems to me, in the fact that a man of this particular kind of preparation and outlook should have been called to the cause of American cooperation at that timely juncture. Physicians are equipped to diagnose ailments of individuals, and by analogy, it would appear, should be better fitted to diagnose and prescribe for social ills. In any event this doctor has done a job of that sort which will go down in history. His book *Cooperative Democracy,* a new edition of which was published in 1936, is one of the standard works on the history, principles and practice of consumers' cooperation.

The Cooperative League was formed at a meeting of people engaged or interested in cooperation, which was held at the home of Dr. Warbasse in Brooklyn in March, 1916. Dr. Warbasse was elected president and has been continued as the League's head ever since. Within a few years after the League's inception he retired from surgical practice and has devoted himself, and in generous measure his own private means, to advancing the cooperative movement. For the first few years the League was not a body which represented cooperative associations in an organic way. It was created by a few people of vision in much the same way that the National Grange, as related in an earlier chapter, was first invented for the farmers and soon took root among them. As the National Grange had to enlist the farmers, so the Cooperative League had to tackle first the task of discovering and rounding up, by correspondence and visitation, as many cooperative groups as it could find throughout the country. In the autumn of 1918 at Springfield, Illinois (home of the Great Emancipator who stood for "government of the people, by the people and for the people") it held its first national Congress, which was attended by some three hundred persons representing about four hundred cooperative units. That gathering has gone down in the annals as the "First American Cooperative Convention." Since then these Congresses have been held biennially in different regions, with a view to widely distributed interest and participation. Cooperative problems and results are discussed by leaders and the rank and file, and the series of published proceedings presents a lively and human picture of the movement's progress.

At the second Congress, held at Cincinnati in 1920, the League was established as an organically representative organization and has taken on more and more of that character and responsibility as its constituent member-organizations have increased in number, resources, influence and assertiveness. Its growth in representativeness has been especially notable in the last five years. Theretofore its active support had come mainly from urban groups and those of New Americans (of Finnish stock especially), and in its financing dependence was placed largely on the personal contributions which Dr. Warbasse made. But then the large and well financed farmers' purchasing associations, having become more or less imbued with consumer consciousness, began to join the League. A potent factor in bringing in such accessions of strength has been the dynamic character and activity of Mr. E. R. Bowen, who became general secretary of the League in 1934 after long experience and study in the fields of agricultural and cooperative economics, and is now one of the outstanding leaders of the American cooperative movement.

At present the League is composed of and organically represents twenty-one consumers' cooperative business organizations, most of them regional wholesale associations, and five regional or district leagues, with a combined non-duplicating membership of eight hundred thousand persons. It has no direct membership of individuals. These eight hundred thousand persons are members of local cooperative units in their own communities. The local units are members of district, state and regional cooperative federations, and these in turn are members of the Cooperative League of the U.S.A., which is thus a representative body built up on lines analogous to those of our American democratic political system of townships, counties, states, and nation. Of the twenty-one affiliated business organizations, eleven are farmers' purchasing associations, all of which have been mentioned or described in earlier chapters, but should be named again here to show just which associations are giving the League their moral and financial support. They are as follows: Consumers' Cooperatives Associated, Amarillo, Texas; Consumers' Cooperative Association, North Kansas City, Missouri; Farmers' Union Central Exchange, St. Paul, Minnesota; Grange Cooperative Wholesale, Seattle, Washington; Indiana Farm Bureau Cooperative Association, Indianapolis; Midland Cooperative Wholesale, Minneapolis, Minnesota; Ohio Farm Bureau Cooperative Association, Columbus; Pacific Supply Cooperative, Walla Walla, Washington; Pennsylvania Farm Bureau Cooperative Association, Harrisburg; and United Cooperatives, Indianapolis. There is one other which I am taking out of its alphabetical order for special mention—Farm Bureau Services, with headquarters at Lansing, Michigan. Mr. C. L. Brodie, the General Manager, is an influential cooperative leader in the Middle West, who in his general viewpoint is somewhere between the Indiana-Ohio men (with whom he has had working relations for some time through the Farm Bureau Oil Company and its successor, United Cooperatives) and the extreme represented, say, by the Illinois Supply Company, to which the very words "consumers' cooperation" are anathema, at least as regards any possible bearing those words may have upon its own extremely businesslike operations.

This attitude of Illinois Supply Company is difficult to understand on any grounds of reasoning and consistency, inasmuch as gas and oil, which are consumed in enormous quantities by urban as well as rural consumers, and which farmers consume in motoring for pleasure as well as in working on their farms, bulk large in the company's brokerage volume.

The remaining ten business cooperatives which make up the League are of semi-urban and urban character: Central Cooperative Wholesale, Superior, Wisconsin; Cooperative Wholesale, Chicago; Eastern Cooperative Wholesale, New York; National Cooperatives, the new national wholesale which serves both rural and urban regionals; Farm Bureau Mutual Auto Insurance Company, Columbus; Workmen's Mutual Fire Insurance Society, New York; Consumers' Cooperative Services, and Cooperative Distributors, both of New York; Franklin Cooperative Creamery Association, St. Paul (a very interesting cooperative which is controlled by the employees as consumers and is taking other consumers into partnership) ; and finally Cooperative Recreation Service of Delaware, Ohio, which is now on a semi-cooperative basis.

The five regional or district leagues are the Northern States Cooperative League, Minneapolis; Eastern Cooperative League, New York; Central States Cooperative League, Chicago; California Co-op Education Association, Pasadena; and Northern California Co-op Council, Oakland. The first three are regional.

The names of all these member-organizations in themselves tell quite a story. They show first of all that the national League has done a fine piece of work in bringing farmers' cooperatives and urban cooperatives together on common ground as consumers. This, I would say, has thus far been its greatest accomplishment as an integrating force and its most valuable service to the American movement as a whole. Though some large and important farmers' cooperative associations do not yet appear on the roll, the majority are there and others will doubtles follow in due course. Of course these farm groups in the League now provide the bulk of its membership and support. That is as it should be, by virtue of the fact that the country's farmers founded and have mainly built up the whole American movement. If the steadily growing liberal elements in the farmers' cooperative ranks can now still further, through the medium of this national League and in collaboration with urban forces, take their due share in leading the movement forward on the broadly cultural and human side, such liberal but sane and practical leadership will go far, I am sure, to enlist in this movement a constantly increasing proportion of the American people.

Now with reference to the three regional leagues which are named above, I am going to say little in detail, although they are highly important; because everything I would say about them is implied and comprehended in what I shall say about the national league's activities, and would be redundant and boring if it were said about each of the regional leagues in turn. Suffice it to say, in general terms, that each commensurately with its numbers, resources and abilities, is doing in its own area what the national body is doing in the large; and that each has contributed to, is represented by, and can extend its constructive influence through, the national organization. The oldest, and largest and most active of these leagues is the Northern, which was formed in 1922 at Superior, Wisconsin, where as earlier related the new Americans in that region, hailing from Finland, have written one of the most successful chapters of American cooperative history. They, and Americans of native descent working with them, made as notable a success of the regional league as they did of the regional business federation and wholesale. That league's first Secretary, Mr. V. S. Alanne, is himself a new American of Finnish stock. He was one of its chief builders and continued to serve as its executive until last year, when he resigned to devote himself to close-range cooperative education in the wholesale organization at Superior. Mr. Cecil R. Crews, formerly assistant secretary, then became the general executive and is vigorously carrying on. In 1925 the headquarters were removed from Superior to Minneapolis, which meant less intimate association with the business wholesale and more distinctness as a league.

That league in a way grew out of the wholesale. In the case of the Eastern and Central leagues, however, the reverse has been true, in that the present wholesales in New York and Chicago have grown out of the respective leagues. In fact each wholesale is the *alter ego* of its league, or *vice versa*, as you please. Mr. L. E. Woodcock is executive of both the wholesale and the league in New York, which share the same headquarters, and Mr. A. W. Warinner is executive of both the wholesale and the league in Chicago, which likewise share the same headquarters. Which plan is better on the whole is a debatable and debated question. The *alter ego* plan is doubtless more economical in overhead expense. But when the same man is trying to do at one and the same time two jobs which are supposed to be rather distinct in character and purpose, and each of which is supposed to exercise some check and balance on the other, it must be quite a task to keep them both going forward adequately, or otherwise not to let one encroach upon the other. Mr. Crews appears to have this question in mind when at the end of his report in the last Cooperative League Year Book he says that the continued existence of a regional league "calls for a redefining of its place in the movement, a readjustment of its policies and aim, and a rechecking of the most necessary types of work it can do efficiently." This is an organizational problem which needs study and recommendation by the national body.

For the last sixteen years the national organization has been comfortably established (but with no room to spare) in its substantial four-story brick abode, the Co-operative League House, at 167 West 12th Street, New York. I would like to call the roll of every member of its capable and friendly working staff (besides Dr. Warbasse and Mr. Bowen who have already been introduced), but as space does not permit, I shall have to let two persons represent the whole. One of these persons is Mrs. J. N. Perkins, who always greets the visitor with a rare and delightful blend of individualism and cooperativeness that strikes me as just the right combination for all true cooperators. Her official title is Financial Secretary—which may have something to do with the strategic position of her office near the door. The other person is Mr. Wallace J. Campbell, whose activities as Assistant Secretary are so varied and comprehensive as to baffle description. He can pull out of his head without a moment's hesitation the answer to any factual question as a magician pulls rabbits out of a hat, and he somehow manages to keep his liveliness and sparkle. I am in debt to Mr. Campbell for many items of information along the way and especially at the finish, in my final check-up of details.

I have earlier described the League's new Bureau of Cooperative Medicine and shall speak later of its still newer Cooperative College. It has also an Auditing Bureau, and a Design Service headed by Mrs. Esther Greenleaf, an architect-artist, who is adding color to the cooperative movement by her designs for posters and displays and package labels.

Though, of course, the Cooperative League has accomplished much as a nationally integrating and constructive force in the American cooperative field during the quarter-century nearly of its life, its potential usefulness in the future looms so much larger than I am going to let its past speak for itself, in the main, and focus the rest of this chapter upon some of the problems or opportunities of integration which now face the League and call for cooperative statesmanship. We have had enough detail, in course of the present account, and the time has come to emerge from the factual forest and get a clear and sweeping view of the open expanse, the hills and horizon.

POLITICAL INTEGRATION

One of the most vital responsibilities of the cooperative movement is that of maintaining its standard policy of political non-partisanship. In this regard I believe the present completely non-partisan position of the American movement is one of the strongest in the world. In several European countries political dictators dominate coperatives as they do everything else. In several others the cooperatives of their own volition or under stress of circumstances have more or less cast in their lot with one political party or another. An observer from this distance cannot justly judge them; they feel that they are right, and perhaps under the conditions which exist in their countries they are. But with a shifting of the political scene their party alignment may prove to be injurious. At any rate, the non-partisan policy of the American cooperatives, combined with unremitting endeavor to get all the parties, and all the state governments as well as the federal government, to give consumers' cooperation a fair and equal opportunity to prove its merit, is *in this country* the soundest and best policy, and is at length bringing some real likelihood of practical results. Here and there in a growing number of states results have been obtained in the last few years which are highly encouraging. One of the most notable gains is the enlistment in this cause, evidently as an outcome of his own thought, experience and·conviction, of the Governor of the great State of New York, the Hon. Herbert H. Lehman. In his annual report to the Legislature on January 5, 1938, he recommended State encouragement of consumers' cooperatives as "yardsticks for the measurement of fair and just distribution costs." What he said on that occasion applied particularly to the distribution of milk. "Properly operated consumers' cooperatives," he said, "can supply milk at better retail prices and yet not impair a fair return to the producer." In addressing a Farm and Home Week gathering at Ithaca, New York, on February 18th, he developed the idea more broadly, declaring that the problem of reducing the cost of distributing farm products to the ultimate consumer was "the most important of all those problems confronting us at the present time; one that neither the State alone nor farmers alone can solve; a problem of equal importance to farmer, consumer and business groups."

In simple equity, as I said in another chapter, the federal government should extend to urban cooperatives the same credit facilities that it has for some time extended to farmers' cooperatives, and that it has always, in one way or another (not to mention outright grants of land or money), extended to commercial business. On February 18th, the same day that Governor Lehman was speaking at Ithaca, Mr. Jesse H. Jones announced that the Reconstruction Finance Commission was now prepared to lend up to $1,500,000,000 to "all types of business, little and big." This announcement was made in response to President Roosevelt's request to Mr. Jones to "make credit available to all deserving borrowers to which you are authorized to lend, especially loans that will maintain or increase employment." Whether consumers' cooperatives can obtain loans from this huge fund remains to be seen. At this writing a delegation representing consumers and consumers' cooperatives, led by the Consumers National Federation, is getting ready to call upon President Roosevelt and urge the establishment of a Consumer Bureau in the proposed new Department of Welfare which is included in the President's plan of administrative reorganization.

INTEGRATION WITH LABOR

Another problem in integration concerns the reciprocal relations between cooperatives and labor unions. As yet in the United States the cooperatives, by and large, have not come to close grips with this problem and worked out any generally accepted policy. In the main the actual practice is to drift, although here and there labor receives unusually generous treatment.

So far as the white-collar workers go, I can testify from my own observation, as well as common report, that they are generally allowed (but not forced) to put in far too much overtime work, which, whether paid or unpaid, is bad for efficiency in the end. I also observed that in some of the wholesales and productive plants, where workers were employed in considerable numbers, these employees were not unionized or encouraged to unionize. Nowhere, as I recall, did I find any outspoken hostility to organized labor, but neither did I find, generally speaking, much disposition to help the workers to organize. This observation applies especially to some of the farmers' purchasing associations, and points to the need of better and more mutually sympathetic understanding between farmers and industrial workers.

Notable exceptions, which I have already cited, are the Central Cooperative Wholesale at Superior, and Consumers' Cooperative Services in New York City. In the cafeterias run by the latter organization, wages are 10 percent higher than the best prevailing commercial wages in the same line of employment. Of course, this raises the question whether, if wages continue generally to rise (as naturally organized labor hopes they will), the cooperatives are going to find themselves caught on a rising floor that will eventually squeeze them up against the ceiling. Perhaps the Scottish cooperative plan of *reducing the hours of work* by 10 percent is more practical and humane in the end. In so far as the cooperatives recognize and deal fairly with unionized employees, and the employees *as consumers* become members of the cooperatives and share their responsibilities, control and benefits, it is likely that integration will work itself out in a natural and almost unconscious way.

Reversely, organized labor in America has no very specific policy toward the enlistment of industrial work-

ers in consumers' cooperation; though as far back as
1917 the American Federation of Labor at its Annual
Convention endorsed and sponsored the movement
strongly in general terms.

"We believe," this Resolution declared, "that the
American Federation of Labor should assist in establishing, building up and strengthening in every way possible a legitimate organization of bona fide workers in
our country and Canada as part of the great world cooperative movement; so that after the trade union
movement has secured for the workers the wages that
they are entitled to for the labor they perform, they may
be assured in spending those wages that they will get
for them full value. . . . The cooperative movement is
the organization that is designed to protect the workers
in their relations with the merchants and the business
men in the same sense that the trade union movement
protects them from the employers. The two movements
are twin remedies."

At the same time the Federation appropriated $5,000
to engage a lecturer and an organizer in the field. Nothing much came of it. "Most of our efforts," said Mr.
William Green, the Federation's president, to the 1936
Congress of the Cooperative League, "met with little
permanent success. Cooperative stores were short-lived
and after a few years hundreds of them failed and went
out of business."

At the 1936 Convention of the A. F. of L. another
strong resolution was adopted. At the 1937 Convention
the Executive Council submitted an extensive report on

this subject, which, after calling attention to the marked success of the American cooperative movement in recent years, strongly advised the labor unions to participate more actively in this movement and establish or join cooperatives in their local communities, *provided* these cooperatives recognize trade unions, bargain collectively with them and, as far as possible, carry goods which bear the union label. The report went on to state that unions should profit from past experiences and failures by studying the principles of consumers' cooperation, on the one hand, and the methods of sound business management on the other. It commended, as successful working examples, the cooperative stores at Racine, Wisconsin, and at Dillonvale, Ohio, in which union labor has had a leading part; the Franklin Cooperative Creamery in Minneapolis; and similar, though as yet smaller enterprises in half a dozen other places. It also endorsed credit unions "as a form of consumers' cooperation particularly adaptable for trade unions" in enabling their members to protect themselves from loan sharks and installment houses and get "a bit of comfort and enjoyment."

Last spring the A. F. of L. printed in its organ, the *American Federationist* (issues of March, April and May) a message to union members called "An Idea Worth Hundreds of Dollars." Part 1 dealt with the practical results of cooperation, part 2 with the Rochdale principles for cooperative stores, and part 3 with credit unions. These articles were later distributed as a compact booklet. Some of the craft unions and State labor

federations in this organization—most recently, the
Utah Federation, last November—have likewise gone on
record. So, all in all, the A. F. of L. is fully committed
to consumers' cooperation in principle.

On the other hand, the Committee for Industrial Organization, headed by Mr. John L. Lewis, which is still
engaged in a bitter conflict with the A. F. of L., has as
yet no general policy either for or against the consumers'
cooperative movement. In an interesting talk last summer with Mr. Jacob Baker, at C.I.O. national headquarters in Washington, I got the impression that the C.I.O.
feels it has a full-time job of labor organization on its
hands for the present, but that it certainly is not opposed to the movement and is fully aware that some of
its national and local leaders, on their own responsibility, are doing a good deal to encourage and assist it. Of
course the United Mine Workers of America, which Mr.
Lewis has long headed, went in for cooperatives rather
vigorously some years ago, as I noted earlier, but did not
have much success with them. Last summer the United
Rubber Workers of America, and a few months later
the Steel Workers Organizing Committee, both affiliated with the C.I.O., unanimously endorsed consumers'
cooperation and urged their members to join local cooperatives in order, as the S.W.O.C. put it, "to protect
the workers and their families, as consumers of goods,
in terms of lower prices and higher quality of goods."
These *official* pronouncements by C.I.O. groups are significant of the trend. Early this year Mr. Homer Martin,

president of the United Auto Workers of America, in an exclusive interview with representatives of the Cooperative League, said that he was *"for* the consumers cooperative movement 100 percent." Producers' actual costs and the prices which consumers pay must be brought nearer together, he continued, and "consumers' cooperatives, working jointly with the labor movement, would control that spread. In South Bend, Indiana, I understand, the merchants and real estate dealers and other distributors got together and decided exactly how a raise in wages to the workers would be divided among *themselves* in increased prices. *Nothing was left for the workers."* Especially important were Mr. Martin's words anent the relation between farmers and industrial workers: "I see in consumers' cooperation the common denominator of consumer interest, which can be a tremendous factor in bringing together American farmers and labor."

Here, then, is a four-cornered job of integration waiting to be done, which is worthy of the League's best efforts. The four corners are cooperatives, farmers, A.F. of L. and C. I. O. At the League's 1936 Congress the following resolution was adopted: "Be it resolved that a commission be created to study the relation between the Cooperative Movement and the Labor Movement in the United States." In pursuance of this action a committee of three persons was appointed but has not yet presented a report. It would be very timely and desirable, I should think, to have that report in hand as the basis of further consideration and more constructive action as soon as possible by the Cooperative League, and the cooperating labor groups. Organized labor has a tremendous responsibility to the individual union members and their families, and all cooperatives, but especially the national League, has an equal or even greater responsibility to all laborers whether organized or unorganized, in their capacity as *consumers,* to see that this essential integration between the cooperative and the labor movements is effectuated.

INTEGRATION WITH THE CHURCHES

The churches of America—Catholic, Protestant and Jewish—have become increasingly active in their endorsement and encouragement of consumers' cooperation in the last few years. Catholic interest appears to run more especially toward credit unions. The first credit unions on this continent were formed by Catholic priests in Canada and New England, and that fact may have given rise to a natural pride in fostering this particular form of cooperation. But the Social Action Department of the National Catholic Welfare Conference is taking a broad interest in the cooperative movement as a whole. As representing the Jewish faith, the Central Conference of American Rabbis, at a meeting in June, 1936, adopted the following declaration: "We believe that the cooperative enterprise when socially motivated and administered, is one means of establishing a social motive of service in the production, distribution and consumption of commodities." A joint conference of

Catholics, Jews and Protestants, on the subject of consumers' cooperatives and credit unions, was held at Washington in February. Its keynote was sounded at the opening session by Mr. E. R. Bowen, when he said that "cooperation in economics is synonymous with brotherhood in religion."

Protestant advocacy of cooperation has had expression in many quarters, but in the most widely representative way through the Federal Council of Churches of Christ in America, which in furtherance of resolutions adopted at its gatherings has instituted in its Industrial Division a Committee on the Church and Cooperatives. Two years ago it conducted a National Sight-Seeing Seminar on Consumers' Cooperatives, which was "attended by leaders of all denominations from all sections of the country." It shared in sponsoring the joint conference at Washington, and held regional circulating seminars this winter at Columbus and Boston. In fact, the Federal Council is becoming so active and enthusiastic in the cooperative field, and is reflecting and generating so much interest and enthusiasm in church circles, that an observer wonders hopefully what may not result.

Because consumers' cooperation does imply brotherhood of man, and because it has proved itself to be a practicable and successful way of actually putting the conception of human brotherhood into effect, one would think that *all* churches, by virtue of their professed belief in brotherhood, would on grounds of consistency be inescapably committed to the furtherance of this movement. But as everybody knows or eventually discovers, human affairs are not governed altogether by consistency. Some churches are composed of and controlled by people whose circumstances and conditions of life are such as to predispose them toward consumers' cooperation. That is well and good. Others are very largely composed *of* such people but are very largely supported and controlled *by* other people who are not thus predisposed. Still other churches are *composed of,* as well as *controlled by,* people of the second kind—who by and large are committed to maintain the profit system and are opposed to consumers' cooperation which is working to replace a system of *profits for some* by a system of *savings for all.* It is of course possible that pastors and laymen who believe in cooperation may succeed in converting those who do not. That is a consummation devoutly to be wished, but not one to be expected momentarily. Until such conversion takes place on a scale sufficient to overcome resistance, there will continue to be—in churches and church bodies thus controlled—a good many resolutions passed, gestures made, and discourses delivered. But there will be very little action. The other churches and church bodies, however, which are not thus controlled, may and probably will do a good deal to forward the cooperative movement. To aid them in practical ways, help them to keep religious zeal and idealistic enthusiasm from getting the better of their commonsense, persuade them to take time to understand cooperative principles and to make sure of competent operating management before they embark on cooperative undertakings—is another responsibility of integration which rests jointly upon church leaders and the Cooperative League. May good preparation wait on evangelization.

COOPERATIVE EDUCATION AND RECREATION

Cooperative education, as was explained at an earlier point in passing, is not proposing to replace our present public or non-profit schools, colleges and other educational institutions by others which are organized and conducted on the cooperative plan. It would replace educational enterprises that are run for profit, which it classes with other forms of profit-business. But that is not its immediate objective. Its present purpose is to educate people in cooperative principles and methods. The people whom it aims to educate are, in order of urgency, as follows: first, the cooperatives' present employees, up to and including the managers; second, the present members, up to and including the directors and officers who are chosen from the members; third, the prospective employees, some of whom are recruited from among members or the sons and daughters of members; and fourth, the public still at large, which is a great reservoir of potential members and workers.

Let us reverse this order, and begin with education of the public. In the main that job is taking care of itself. By this I mean that the remarkable progress of cooperation in recent years is attracting more and more public attention, arousing quite a bit of curiosity, stimulating an increasing measure of genuine interest, and helping to produce a small but growing kernel of understanding.

Almost every day the newspapers contain items about some cooperative activity. Magazine articles have been coming out lately at a high rate of speed. Less often—fortunately, no doubt!—someone is impelled to write a book. But most of the cooperative education which the proverbial "man in the street" acquires is absorbed unconsciously and impalpably. It must be freely admitted that if you were to stop a hundred men in the street at random, and ask them, "What is cooperation?" or still worse, "What is consumers' cooperation?"—well, you would be forced to conclude that they had failed to keep their pores more than a wee bit open. But last year three states—Wisconsin, Minnesota and North Dakota—passed laws providing for teaching of cooperation in the public schools.

As regards the education of present employees, that partly takes care of itself by virtue of their daily work and cumulative experience, and the rest of it is on the whole being done pretty well by courses which are conducted by nearly all the regional leagues and wholesales and by many of the local units. The easier and simpler part of this employee education is that which deals with the brass tacks of the day's work—in short, with *cooperative* business standards, methods and efficiency. But though this is "simpler" it is far from simple, because the manager and patron-serving employees must come to have a very different attitude and scale of values from those of a commercial profit-serving enterprise. That takes time and seasoning, and some employees brought from commercial to cooperative jobs can never get over

the sense of perpetual drive to batter down sales resistance and sell something or other at all costs. On the
other hand, one of the things which impressed me most,
when I talked with young men now working in the cooperatives who were formerly employed in profit-business, was the uanimity and warmth of appreciation with
which they testified to the democratic fellowship, teamplay, service and quality motives of the cooperatives as
contrasted with high-hattedness, the ofttimes invidious
rivalry, self-interest and subordination of value to profit,
in their former places of employment.

Now when we come to the education of members—ah,
there's the rub. You may be thinking, "Naturally the
members know all about cooperation." But wait a minute. Take any society, club or what-not to which you
personally belong. What percentage of the members (ex-
cepting yourself, of course) know very much about the
real objects, activities and operation of that organization, whatever it is? Not many and not much. Well,
that's the way it is in a cooperative association too. Not
quite so bad, on the average. There is a larger nucleus
of members who do understand what it is about. But not
yet large enough for boasting. You see, new members are
always coming in, some from intelligent study and conviction, but many as a by-product of their patronage
when their savings become sufficient to pay for a share
and thereby make them members. So it's a sort of endless
educational problem of catch-as-catch-can and no rest for
the weary. But the cooperatives, especially their Education Committees (and educational directors when there

are such) must be credited with a tremendous amount of intermittent industry, in the total, and with a dogged determination. That may, alas, stand in their way. For there is this fundamental truth to be kept in mind—that if a person gets to feeling that he is a sort of target for education, and that he is in danger of being educated against his will, he balks, ducks and takes to cover. It is the same old story, that you can lead a horse to water but you can't make him drink. After all, people must educate themselves. You can cram them with information, but that's not education. But if without their being aware of just what you are doing, and perhaps best without your being fully aware of it yourself, you say or do something that strikes a spark in them and gets their starter going, then some actual education may ensue. By and large, cooperative educational endeavor is in need of more indirectness and unawareness, of less doing-for and more leaving-to.

On paper, and as measured externally by the number, wide distribution and interesting variety of classes, camps, seminars, institutes, schools or what-you-will, a great deal of cooperative education is going on in most sections of the country most of the time. The rise of cooperative education in the last few years is shown by this fact; in 1934 there was only one full-time educational director in the wholesales (i.e., in the Central Cooperative Wholesale at Superior) but today there are nine such full-time directors in regional wholesales and leagues, others on part time, and still others who are working for local units or small district federations. In a generally promotive way, and also more specifically in helping to locate educational directors of the requisite ability, the Cooperative League has been of much assistance to the regional organizations.

For a well planned and sustained educational campaign covering a good-sized area, the program which is carried out from year to year through the Education Department of the Ohio Farm Bureau Cooperative Association, headed by Mr. William Winemiller and associates, struck me as on the whole the best of those with which I came in contact. Mr. Winemiller is in love with his work, has a sound foundation of study, a quick mind, and an engaging personality that elicits confidence. The program which he has developed revolves around study and discussion groups for members (in practice, mainly officers and leaders, I think) and also for present employees and for youth groups. I had the privilege of being present at one session of this sort, which was held at Antioch College. It would not be safe to draw any general conclusions from a single instance. It was an interesting session and I can appreciate the value of such discussion, even though it may appear somewhat too formulated and methodical. Mr. E. R. Bowen of the Cooperative League was telling me recently about the informal and spontaneous way in which Study Circles have developed in Sweden, and I am inclined to think we might allow for more of such freedom ourselves.

There is one weak link in the chain of cooperative education, and that is education organized specifically for prospective employees and especially adapted to their needs. In the main they are still left to shift for themselves, or rather to appear on the scene out of thin air, as it were, and announce that they not only desire a cooperative job but are well equipped to fill it. Some, as I have said, are drawn from the ranks of business. Some are sons or daughters of members or present employees, who are taken on and grow up in the business. That is probably the best way of training them, but it ought to be supplemented by more orderly study of cooperative principles than is now provided. Last fall the Cooperative League, with a view (primarily but not exclusively) to meeting that particular need, initiated what it first called the Cooperative Institute. This comprised an eight-weeks' course of lectures, seminars and study at this Institute in New York, followed by a substantial period of actual cooperative experience with various regional or local associations. On rather short notice, eighteen students from fifteen states and one foreign country enrolled. They came from as far afield as California, Idaho, Utah, Minnesota, Kansas, Alabama and Virginia. They were a sturdy and likely group, and had the advantage or disadvantage of a high *per capita* of lecturers, whose number, indeed, considerably exceeded that of the students themselves. During their stay in New York they went the rounds of all the leading cooperatives in this city and had plenty of opportunity to ask questions. I understand that their subsequent service with cooperatives in various parts of the country worked out favorably in most instances, and that somewhat over a half of them are already assured of permanent employment. Now this institute has been renamed the Cooperative College and is having its second session with about the same number of students drawn mostly from the Eastern area. The success of this new educational enterprise is due in goodly measure to the personality and capability of Mr. Lionel Perkins, who serves as Registrar.

While cooperative education is growing, cooperative recreation is still inchoate. It is like a chrysalis which will eventually unfold a butterfly. Some of the educational and recreational directors think that it has already unfolded and that the butterfly is already fluttering about, but although I tried hard and used strong field glasses, I was not able to detect it. I saw some folk-dancing, some "quadrilles" (as they call the old-fashioned square dances in the Middle West), and some grand-marching, heard some group-singing, watched some floor games—but they were all things that I had seen and heard many times many places long before I ever heard of cooperation. It seemed to me that some of the cooperative enthusiasts were simply putting Co-op labels on wine of old vintage. They are grasping at this and that, but have not yet discovered, evolved or invented something truly new to symbolize cooperation, bring lilt to the movement, and capture the imagination.

Cooperative recreation—or re-creation as its votaries like to call it—has an inspiring vision. It aims to replace the motive of playing *against* the other fellow by that of playing *with* one's fellows, and to infuse man's economic relations as well with this same spirit. It wants to help man to rise above *things*. "Things are in the saddle, and ride mankind," said Emerson more than half a century ago. Cooperative recreation wants to sing with the poet—

> "We are the music makers,
>   And we are the dreamers of dreams,"

and play the prelude to a new day—

> "For each age is a dream that is dying,
>   Or one that is coming to birth."

AT the end of our journey along the cooperative road, looking back and looking forward, what conclusions shall we draw, what expectations entertain?

We have seen evolution in process, and in broad outline have traced the gradual development of American cooperation from the early years of the Republic to the present day. We have learned that it derived its inspiration from the Declaration of Independence and the American Constitution, that it sprang from native roots and has been created in the main by old Americans and enriched by contributions from new Americans. We have found that the rudiments which inhere in the Rochdale Principles have been expanded, modified and applied in characteristically American ways, and that this American movement has molded new forms and brought new values and objectives to the worldwide cooperative movement.

We have observed that even the definition and interpretation of consumers' cooperation have undergone a gradual broadening, through the influence of practical considerations and events. The shadowy borderland between cooperative purchasing of farm supplies and cooperative purchasing of household goods has been illuminated by the light of understanding, and by steadily

379

growing recognition of community of interests between consumers on the farms and in the cities. To argue any longer for essential difference between these two kinds of purchasing is a waste of energy, better put to more constructive use. Both are consumers' cooperation, one rural and the other urban. Farmers and city dwellers have joined forces and will henceforth advance together. In union they have built a countrywide groundwork and cooperative structure, and have achieved results and massed resources which equip them for the greater tasks and potentialities of the future.

"Can cooperation succeed in America?" is a question which can now be answered positively. *It is succeeding.* What the rate and scope and measure of its future growth will be time alone can tell. It has barely attained young manhood, and is still slender of body alongside the bulky giant of capitalistic business. What we may reasonably expect is that it will grow as a young man grows, in body, spirit and estate, and that it will bring the vigor of youth to the working out, through cooperative means and methods, of some of the vital economic and social problems which have followed in the wake of the Industrial Revolution and the profit system.

The abuses which have sprung up under the capitalistic profit system and are rife in America today, are simply the *occasion* for cooperative action. Its *warrant* lies in the profit system itself, even though that system could be stripped bare of all abuses. Consumers' cooperation has no quarrel with capital, which it uses as an instrument; but it challenges capitalism and the profit system on grounds of social economy—the greatest good of the greatest number. It indicts them as wasteful of material goods and human lives and values, and therefore inefficient in the true and ultimate sense of the term; however "efficient" they may boast themselves to be for strictly business objects and the distribution of stipends, profits and power. Over against such largesse in the enrichment of *some* people who, though their number is large and their visibility high, are after all only a small proportion of the country's total population, consumers' cooperation sets the profit system's exploitation of consumers, who are *all* the people.

It does not charge that our profit system of production and distribution is malevolent, but does contend that it is bungling and extravagant because it has no way, other than guessing, to measure in advance of production the kind, quantity and quality of goods which consumers want. So it has to produce more or less in the dark and then try to dispose of the products by acute competition, enormously expensive advertising, high pressure salesmanship and the battering down of consumers' sales-resistance. Over-production and recessions *necessarily* occur, in cycles. And consumers pay all the bills—all the costs and all the profits. Society pays the wreckage.

Consumers' cooperation proposes to replace this profit system of exploitation, not all at once or by any revolutionary methods, but gradually, piecemeal and at points of greatest need, with another system which I have called a *mutation* of capitalism. This cooperative system calls for reorientation—substitution of production for the service and benefit primarily of consumers, in place of production for the benefit primarily of the producers and distributors. In other words, capital and industry are to be made the servants of the people and not their masters. With cooperative organizations through which the wants and demand of consumers can be known and approximately measured in advance, and through which consumers can express their wishes, needs and tastes, production will be much better adjusted to demand than it is or can be under the profit system. Over-production, waste, recession and recurring crises and unsettlements will be measurably lessened at least. The savings thereby effected will be equitably distributed to the consumers who provide the market and impart the values. Security of assured compensation for service will replace competitive risks and precarious profits. Material resources will not be bottled up in a few financial centers and diverted to grandiose speculations, but will be used for building up the communities which create them. And the greatest good of the greatest number, in *human* and *spiritual* as well as material terms, will be advanced.

There is no enmity or animosity on the part of cooperators against their fellow-Americans who are now engaged in profit business, and there should be none on the part of those Americans against the cooperators. It is not a question of business *men* but of business *systems*. We have read in the present account of many examples of cordial and mutually advantageous teamplay and inter-relationship between cooperatives and commercial companies. In fact, American cooperatives in the large are now purchasing supplies from these companies in such great and constantly growing volume that the cessation of their custom would result in very considerable losses to commercial business. The two systems will and must go along together for the present, and no doubt for a long time in the future. If we assume that both are truly trying to serve the common good, and find the best solutions for our common problems, then surely the only reasonable course for both is to work heartily together, make experiments and compare experience, and aim through mutual understanding and the growth of common interests to reach eventually a common goal and "a more perfect union."

APPENDIX: A FEW FIGURES

COMPLETE figures regarding the number of consumers' cooperatives in the United States will not be available until various bureaus of the federal government, including particularly the Bureau of Labor Statistics, furnish their current studies, assemble the data, eliminate duplications and present the net results. That is going to be quite a job—especially the elimination of duplications in figures gathered by different bureaus and applying to different categories of cooperatives.

In the meantime, however, some of the major figures are definitely known, and have been utilized in the present account. By way of summary and classification I will bring them together here, and will then append some general observations about other cooperatives which still remain to be counted.

Largest by far in total membership are the Farmers' Mutual Fire Insurance groups, which were described in chapter 6. Their number is about 2,000, their combined membership approximately 3,000,000 and their volume of outstanding insurance $11,000,000,000. Nearly all of these groups are units confined to a single county or several contiguous counties. Only a very few extend over a whole state. The figures here given, moreover, do not include any of the cooperative fire insurance companies of broader geographical scope, which are in a different category and will be mentioned below.

Next in total membership, and first in number of units, come the credit unions, of which there are now about

6,700 with a combined membership of 1,500,000 and an outstanding loan volume of $65,000,000.

Third place is occupied by the farmers' cooperative purchasing associations, which at the close of the calendar year 1937 numbered about 2,500 with combined membership of about 1,000,000 and an operating volume for 1937 of approximately $400,000,000. The statistical job of keeping current count of these associations is excellently done by the Cooperative Division of the Farm Credit Administration, which eliminates duplications as it goes along. If a given farmer is counted in the local purchasing association of his community, he is not counted again in the district or regional bodies which include that local unit. All but a small percentage of these 2,500 associations are such local units; but this figure includes some district federations covering areas not very large, and also the big regional associations, most of which have been described or named in the chapters dealing with farmers' cooperative purchasing organizations. Therefore the summary figures here given take in all the separate membership and volume figures which I have cited along the way for specific regional associations. Furthermore, these figures cover (1) all the stores dealing in household goods and (2) all the gas and oil stations affiliated with *farmers'* regional purchasing associations. I note this fact especially because I have seen some loose figures which list such stores and stations separately, and then add them into the general total without eliminating the duplication.

Town and city cooperative store associations, affiliated with the three regional wholesales which deal *primarily in groceries and household goods,* number about 375 with a combined membership of 62,500.

We can now get a definite total. Adding the foregoing figures for these four groups of cooperatives, we have 11,575 associations with inclusive membership of 5,562,500.

It would be quite inadequate, in trying to measure the *proportionate* importance of consumers' cooperation in America, to take as such measurement the percentage which these 5,562,500 individual members constitute in the country's total population, which includes babies, minors and the very aged, or in other words a large number of people who do not figure in membership of any kind of organization. To arrive at a true measurement it is necessary to get the percentage which these individual members of cooperatives constitute in that part of the population from which they are drawn—which means the nation's *families*.

The individual cooperative members represent families. If one person in a family belongs to a given cooperative, that enables the family to avail itself of the cooperative's benefits in terms of insurance, credit, or purchase of commodities. As a rule, therefore, only one person in a family, presumably the father or the mother, joins the same cooperative. But sometimes, for reasons of interest or convenience—especially in the case of urban stores—several members of a family may join the same local unit, or different units for different objects. The father, for example, may belong to a credit union from which he can obtain loans for family use; and the mother may join the local cooperative store where she does most of the household-buying. Thus it appears that while the total of 5,562,500 individual cooperative members represent families, the number of families thus represented is, by reason of such duplications, somewhat smaller than this inclusive figure. What percentage the duplications would form is something I do not know and will not attempt to guess. That is the government's job which is now under way. All that can be said for the time being is that this figure of 5,562,500 may be accepted as the *maximum* number of *families* (without allowing for duplications) which make up the constituency of these *four major categories* of consumers' cooperatives.

Two other sets of figures, which are quite definite in themselves, apply to cooperatives that are still subject to more or less government tutelage and cannot yet be called full-fledged. There are about 285 rural electrification cooperatives with 150,000 members; and 550 production credit associations with membership of 250,000. No doubt these two membership totals somewhat overlap each other, as well as the preceding totals for farmers' insurance groups and purchasing associations.

Now what cooperatives as yet lie beyond the borders of definite figures, and are still to be counted? Most numerous, probably, are the rural telephone service associations, which in a small way are comparable to the rural electrification groups. There are cooperative burial associations, especially in the Middle West; and here, there and everywhere cooperative health associations are beginning to take shape. Scattered about in an isolated way, and unaffiliated with any of the present regional wholesales, are more cooperative stores; and in the last few years many similarly unaffiliated gas and oil stations have sprung up in various parts of the country. There are some consumers' cooperative bakeries, dairies, restaurants, lodging houses, laundries, printing plants, et cetera. College student cooperatives include eating clubs, dormitories and miscellaneous services.

Finally, at the base of the cooperative pyramid, are two groups which are vitally important as further foundation and fresh reinforcement for the consumers' cooperative movement as a whole. One of these groups consists of innumerable consumers' buying clubs, which until they emerge from the chrysalis stage are so quiet and inconspicuous that even the government bureaus, I imagine, would find it impossible to make a comprehensive count of them. They are, as I have said earlier, the germ plasm out of which new cooperative enterprises are continually evolving.

The other underlying group already large in number of policy-holders and strong in material resources, consists of about a score of cooperative insurance companies which insure against automobile casualties, fire, death and other contingencies. The example cited in the chapter on "Frontiers" is sufficient to show the great potentialities which are now opening up, in the way of making the financial resources of these companies available for the development of cooperative enterprise as distinguished from capitalistic profit-business, of which the large insurance stock companies and some of the largest *so-called* mutual companies are a formidable bulwark. The truly cooperative companies, by supporting cooperative enterprise, will render a constructive social-economic service far surpassing the importance of their insurance operations in themselves.

ACKNOWLEDGMENTS
AND REFERENCES

THIS is not a complete bibliography but simply a list of books and other printed material of which the author made use and which he desires gratefully to acknowledge.

Baker, Jacob: *Cooperative Enterprise.* (Mr. Baker was chairman of the group which issued a report on *Cooperative Enterprise in Europe.* See that title.)

Buck, S. J.: *The Granger Movement.* (A very interesting history of the Grange, or Patrons of Husbandry.)

Campbell, Wallace J.: *The Consumers' Cooperative Movement: A Factual Survey.* (Published by the League for Industrial Democracy in a booklet containing also *Consumers' Cooperation: A Social Interpretation,* by Harry W. Laidler.)

Cooperative Enterprise in Europe—1937. Report of the group appointed by President Roosevelt to make an inquiry on this subject in Europe. (This report can be obtained from the Superintendent of Documents, Washington, D. C., for 65 cents. It contains fourteen chapters describing a wide range of cooperative activities, individual reports by each of the six members of the group—including comparative comments on cooperative activities and prospects in America—and a good deal of supplementary detail.)

Cooperative League Year Book—1936. (Includes a history of the Cooperative League of the U.S.A. by Dr. J. P. Warbasse, résumés of the three regional Leagues, and

descriptive reports by the cooperative organizations
which are affiliated with the national League.)

"Consumers' Cooperation: An examination of its principles, social relationships, achievements and present
status"; *Annals of the American Academy of Political
and Social Science*, May, 1937. (Twenty articles about
consumers' cooperation in America, three on the cooperative movements in Great Britain, the Scandinavian countries and other parts of Europe, and two criticisms of
consumers' cooperation.)

Elsworth, R. H.: "Statistics of Farmers' Cooperative Business Organizations, 1920-1935." (*Bul. No. 6*, May, 1936,
Cooperative Division, Farm Credit Administration.)

—"Statistics of Farmers' Marketing and Purchasing Associations, 1935-36 Marketing Season." (*Misc. Report No.
12*, February, 1937, Cooperative Division, Farm Credit
Administration.)

Fetrow, Ward W.: "Cooperative Marketing of Agricultural
Products." (*Bul. No. 3*, February, 1936, Cooperative Division, Farm Credit Administration.)

Fowler, Bertram B.: *Consumers' Cooperation in America:
Democracy's Way Out.*

Knapp, Joseph G., and Lister, John H.: "Cooperative Purchasing of Farm Supplies." (*Bul. No. 1*, September, 1935,
Cooperative Division, Farm Credit Administration.)

Valgren, Victor N.: *Farmers' Mutual Fire Insurance in the
United States.* (The only complete historical account,
description, and discussion of the accomplishments and
possibilities of these local cooperative insurance groups.)

Warbasse, J. P.: *Cooperative Democracy.* (Comprehensive
history, principles and practice of consumers' cooperation in Europe, America and other parts of the world.)

INDEX